Praise for *CHILE, CLOVE,*

"Celebrated ethnobotanist Gary Paul Nabhan makes a bold argument for why arid lands produce the world's most aromatic foodstuffs we humans crave and trade. Cookbook author extraordinaire Beth Dooley's irresistible recipes prove each of his succulent points. By showing how fragrant and delectable life on a warming world can be, this book fills your mind and belly and lifts your heart."

— **Alan Weisman**, author of *The World Without Us* and *Gaviotas*

"In *Chile, Clove, and Cardamom*, Beth Dooley and Gary Paul Nabhan offer an exploration of culinary traditions from some of the world's most arid regions. As someone presently delving into the unique flavors and techniques of these diverse cuisines, I find this work to be an invaluable resource. It beautifully captures the essence of these regions, providing both valuable inspiration and deep appreciation for their culinary heritage—a cookbook I will cherish."

— **Barbara Massaad**, chef and TV host; author of *Soup for Syria*

"If you've ever traveled in desert lands, you know that the foods take on an almost hypnotic intensity. *Chile, Clove, and Cardamom* explains why and shows you how to bring that intensity into your own kitchen. By celebrating the commonalities and innovations of the planet's arid cuisines in these gorgeous recipes, Dooley and Nabhan have given us a manual for living well in a sun-kissed world."

— **Rowan Jacobsen**, author of *Wild Chocolate*

"Drought-tolerant? Try drought-embracing, drought-loving, drought-grateful. Thank you, sumac and chipotles, turmeric and cloves. Thank you, camels and caravans. And thank you, Beth Dooley and Gary Paul Nabhan, for this spicy, fragrant, mind-expanding book that reveals what we all owe to migrants from the hot and dry places of this world."

— **Lawrence Downes**, writer; former member of the *New York Times* editorial board

"Follow the new spice roads as climate change forces some of the world's most pungent and floral spices and herbs into new latitudes. This sumptuous, optimistic journey reveals how to combine and cook with ancient flavors in both time-honored and entirely new, delicious recipes."

— **Janos Wilder**, James Beard Award–winning chef

"As a somewhat smell-blind person, holy *mole*, I'm grateful for this book! It's widened my ability to enjoy the many wondrous aromas and tastes of desert cuisines. Looking beyond my own nose, I can see that, though disguised as a cookbook, this book really offers a broader recipe for eating and living well as our planet becomes hotter and drier. By sharing sensuous pleasures of food from across Earth's more arid reaches, our inimitable guides 'Brother Coyote' Gary Paul Nabhan and Beth Dooley invite us to join in their delicious mission: Let's savor the flavors and partners involved in the meaning-making meals that root us in our places and bridge us into global community."

— **Keefe Keeley**, coeditor, *The Driftless Reader*; executive director, the Savanna Institute

"When two of my all-time favorite food writers find common ground, I know I am going to be both thrilled and surprised. Beth Dooley and Gary Paul Nabhan did more—they have created a whole new perspective on how we face the hotter, drier future we're creating on this planet. This remarkable new book *Chile, Clove, and Cardamom* takes you inside the world of intense flavors and aromas you cannot imagine while bringing you foursquare into considering how our food sources must and will shift as we adapt and reinvent."

— **Mark Ritchie**, chair, Minnesota USA Expo 2031 Steering Committee

"This book is an important culmination of culinary and ethnographic research that tells a story of desert regions through the spices and plants that define regional cuisines. *Chile, Clove, and Cardamom* is a guidebook for the future as our climate gets hotter and drier."

— **Elizabeth Johnson**, chef and owner, Pharm Table

"In this book, the authors are your personal sommeliers of fragrances, flavors, and terroirs of desert cuisines shaped by heat and aridity. Dooley and Nabhan, both recipients of James Beard Awards for their food writing, are also eloquent guides for a gastronomic tour of what they call Planet Desert. Along the way, they explain the science of why foods become more interesting and intense when they struggle in hot, dry climates. They also describe the shared patterns of desert food traditions and trace the routes of dishes that historically moved from their homelands to other desert regions. The thoughtfully selected recipes shared in the second half of the book will inspire home cooks to take their own culinary journeys with a new appreciation for cuisines already adapted to climate change. Use this book to taste the future!"

— **Jonathan Mabry**, director of community engagement, College of Social and Behavioral Studies, University of Arizona

Chile, Clove, and Cardamom

Also by Beth Dooley

The Perennial Kitchen: Simple Recipes for a Healthy Future

Minnesota's Bounty: The Farmers Market Cookbook

The Northern Heartland Kitchen

With Loretta Barrett Oden:
Corn Dance: Inspired First American Cuisine

With Sean Sherman:
The Sioux Chef's Indigenous Kitchen

With Mette Nielson:
Savory Sweet: Simple Preserves from the Northern Kitchen

Sweet Nature: A Cook's Guide to Using Honey and Maple Syrup

With Lucia Watson:
Savoring the Seasons of the Northern Heartland

Also by Gary Paul Nabhan

The Desert Smells Like Rain

Gathering the Desert

Enduring Seeds

Renewing America's Food Traditions

Coming Home to Eat

Growing Food in a Hotter, Drier Land

Where Our Food Comes From

Cumin, Camels, and Caravans: A Spice Odyssey

Desert Terroir

The Nature of Desert Nature

With David Suro Piñera:
Agave Spirits: The Past, Present, and Future of Mezcals

With Kraig Kraft and Kurt Michael Freise:
Chasing Chiles: Hot Spots along the Pepper Trail

Chile, Clove, and Cardamom

A Gastronomic Journey Into the Fragrances and Flavors of Desert Cuisines

Beth Dooley and Gary Paul Nabhan

Chelsea Green Publishing
White River Junction, Vermont
London, UK

Copyright © 2024 by Beth Dooley and Gary Paul Nabhan.
All rights reserved.

Unless otherwise noted, all photographs copyright © 2024 by Ashley Moyna Schwickert.
Photographs on pages x, 2, 9, 12, 16, 20, and 25 by Gary Paul Nabhan. Photograph on page 28 by iStock.com/mariusz_prusaczyk. Photographs on pages 69 and 75 by iStock.com/Nungning20. Photograph on page 79 by iStock.com/igorr1. Photograph on page 103 by iStock.com/Creative-Family. Photograph on page 122 by iStock.com/fcafotodigital. Photograph on page 165 by iStock.com/photohampster. Photograph on page 170 by iStock.com/bhofack2.

No part of this book may be transmitted or reproduced in any form by any means without permission in writing from the publisher.

Developmental Editor: Matthew Derr
Copy Editor: Diane Durrett
Proofreader: Rachel Markowitz
Indexer: Elizabeth Parson
Designer: Melissa Jacobson
Page Layout: Abrah Griggs

Printed in the United States of America.
First printing October 2024.
10 9 8 7 6 5 4 3 2 1   24 25 26 27 28

Our Commitment to Green Publishing
Chelsea Green sees publishing as a tool for cultural change and ecological stewardship. We strive to align our book manufacturing practices with our editorial mission and to reduce the impact of our business enterprise in the environment. We print our books using vegetable-based inks whenever possible. This book may cost slightly more because it was printed on paper from responsibly managed forests, and we hope you'll agree that it's worth it. *Chile, Clove, and Cardamom* was printed on paper supplied by Versa that is certified by the Forest Stewardship Council.®

Library of Congress Cataloging-in-Publication Data
Names: Dooley, Beth, author. | Nabhan, Gary Paul, author.
Title: Chile, clove, and cardamom : a gastronomic journey into the fragrances and flavors of desert cuisines / Beth Dooley and Gary Paul Nabhan.
Description: White River Junction, Vermont ; London, UK : Chelsea Green Publishing, [2024] | Includes bibliographical references and index.
Identifiers: LCCN 2024031227 (print) | LCCN 2024031228 (ebook) | ISBN 9781645022459 (paperback) | ISBN 9781645022466 (ebook)
Subjects: LCSH: Cooking. | LCGFT: Cookbooks.
Classification: LCC TX714 .D666 2024 (print) | LCC TX714 (ebook) | DDC 641.5—dc23/eng/20240801
LC record available at https://lccn.loc.gov/2024031227
LC ebook record available at https://lccn.loc.gov/2024031228

Chelsea Green Publishing
White River Junction, Vermont USA
London, UK
www.chelseagreen.com

For the many Indigenous, Peasant, and Agrarian cooks, farmers, gatherers, and herders whose traditional knowledge of aromatic desert foods can demonstrate to the rest of the world place-based ways to adapt to climate change.

What will happen to smells, and smelling, in the future? Will human activities continue to change our environment so dramatically that we will see profound changes? Or will the interactions shaped by evolution remain functional and intact? Will our use of smells develop into new, maybe unexpected directions?

—**Bill S. Hansson**, *Smelling to Survive*, 2022

CONTENTS

Introduction   xi

Part I
The Refreshing Fragrances and Sun-Drenched Flavors of Desert Cuisines

1: The Braised New World and How Much Its Aromatics Matter   3
2: Why Are Arid-Land Aromatics So Potent When Eaten, Imbibed, or Inhaled?   7
3: Rethinking the Ways We Perceive and Use Aromatics   11
4: Cuisines Shaped by Heat and Water Scarcity   15
5: Building Your Own Desert Pantry   20
6: Celebrating the Spice Odyssey That Bridges Many Cuisines   23
7: Spice Blends and the World We Taste   27

Part II
The Recipes

8: Dips and Sauces   35
9: Light Fare, Small Plates   53
10: Main Dishes   77
11: Soups and Stews   113
12: Salads   129
13: Breads   143
14: Drinks and Desserts   151
15: Spice Blends   163

Acknowledgments   171
Appendix I: The Desert Pantry: An Introduction   173
Appendix II: Online Sources of Desert Ingredients   183
Further Reading   185
Index   187

Frankincense tree on incense trail in Raysut, Oman.

Introduction

Opening Up to the Fragrances and Flavors of Desert Cuisines

We invite you to journey with us into a world that is best explored with your nose, lips, tongue, and throat, more than your eyes and your ears. The fragrances and flavors in our favorite foods are so deeply memorable even though we often lack the vocabulary to describe them; nevertheless, they become embedded in our identities, and even in our dreams.

Like other creatures on this planet, we are sentient beings of scent who choose our dinners and our partners, and recognize our mothers, fathers, lovers, daughters, and sons, by their soothing aromas and entrancing perfumes. Most humans are born with the innate capacity to discern as many as a trillion different smells from one another, thanks to some six to ten million odor receptor cells hidden in our nasal cavities.

Of course, much of what we call the flavors of foods are in fact these aromas. They are inhaled and mapped in the olfactory bulbs of our brains milliseconds before they hit our lips and our tongues. These aromas are freely gifted to any of us who wish to enjoy and celebrate with friends the food biodiversity of this earthly household.

Now, whether we fully use these capacities to sniff and smell what is hardwired into us with 3 percent of our genes is another issue. Because of aerial contaminants, injuries, and diseases such as Alzheimer's, Covid, and Parkinson's, some of us are hardly able to recognize many of the odors—pleasant or putrid—of the hundred million different volatile chemical compounds swirling around us at any moment. And of course, our capacity to take pleasure in fragrances atrophies through time if we don't frequently "wake up and smell the roses."

Many people living in modern industrial cities suffer from olfactory dysfunctions that limit their pleasure in eating fragrant and flavorful foods; moreover, their capacity to celebrate the delights of the diverse fragrances in the natural world also has been diminished, mostly by factors beyond their control. Compared to many Indigenous farming, foraging, or fishing cultures in Africa, Asia, or Latin America, Western societies lack a lexicon to describe the panoply of aromas encountered in their daily lives.

Yes, some of us suffer from the olfactory equivalent of being tone-deaf and mute in our capacity to describe precisely and descriptively many flavors and fragrances. Happily, a diminished capacity to smell is largely reversible for many. Preparing, eating, and drinking aromatic foods and beverages can become the means to restore and even broaden the range of fragrances and flavors you can recognize and relish. More frequently partaking of the planet's highly aromatic desert cuisines can lead you back toward more enjoyable, sensual, and healthful interactions with the "osmocosm" in which we are all immersed. Master cook and food chemist Harold McGee defines the osmocosm as the aromas, odors, and other chemical signals in the air that sweep and swirl around us every moment of the day, even when we are not conscious of them. Many plant ecologists now believe that fragrance may be the primary means whereby plants "signal" or communicate with other plants, microbes, and animals, including the spoon-and-fork–carrying species we call *Homo sapiens*.

Desert cuisines have taken advantage of the many deliciously fragrant plants that grow within arid and semiarid landscapes. These plants are rich in volatile oils, which are full of aromatic compounds that function as antioxidants. These oils can buffer both plant tissues and the tissues of our own bodies from the damaging stresses of high temperature, toxins, radiation, and dehydration. Since many leafy vegetables must spend energy to repel browsing insects and grazing wildlife or livestock, it should come as no surprise, then, that they are decidedly pungent.

Many, if not most, of the aromatic oils in desert herbs and spices can positively contribute to a feast or family repast if well integrated in the proper proportions. They have underpinned many of the greatest culinary traditions on our planet. They are celebrated as part of our "intangible cultural heritage" in many of the UNESCO-recognized Cities of Gastronomy—Tucson, San Antonio, Ensenada, Buraidah (Saudi Arabia), Kermanshah (Iran), and Gaziantep (Turkey)—cities that happen to be situated in hot, dry climes.

One of us (Beth) came to this "project" after decades as a food writer, scholar, and cook who has delved into the lessons that can be learned from regional and Indigenous cuisines about human well-being and sustainability in the face of climate change. The other (Gary Paul, or "Brother Coyote") grew up with aromatic Lebanese foods, and soon began to study their desert origins as an ethnobotanist. Only after he suffered from accidents that impaired his vision and speech—but that, miraculously, broke open his capacity to smell—did he begin his research on the fragrances in gardens and kitchens.

We both love foraging, gardening, and cooking with one another and our families, but we are also dedicated to making the future more delicious and resilient in the face of climate change. Our collaboration is a way to "give back" to the home cooks, regional chefs, farmers, fishers, and plant gatherers from the many cultures who have taken us in and broken bread with us over the last half-century. It is also meant to be a gift to you, dear readers—and to your noses!

PART I

The Refreshing Fragrances and Sun-Drenched Flavors of Desert Cuisines

Souk in Paradise Valley, High Atlas Mountains, Morocco.

Chapter 1

The Braised New World and How Much Its Aromatics Matter

The fragrances and flavors of the most memorable foods from our personal histories tell us *where they*—and perhaps *where we*—have come from.

As much of the planet's terrain becomes hotter and drier with climate change, the fragrant aromatics embedded in the cuisines from desert cultures all around the world might also hint to us *where we may be going*. They may be signaling to us that parts of the world are becoming more desiccated, more parched, and more erratic in their capacity to produce. In the Sun Belt of the United States, for example, such changes will affect many of the conventional water-intensive crops that have nourished Americans over the last century.

By 2080 in North America, the climate of any foodshed will have shifted to resemble the climates in places at least 500 miles to the south of them. The grape varieties and vegetables now optimally grown in the climate of Napa Valley, California, will have a tough time reaching harvest there in 2080, but will be more easily grown near the Willamette Valley and Portland, Oregon. The truck farms outside of Washington, DC, and Baltimore, Maryland, will need to shift their crop mix to those that currently do well between Little Rock, Arkansas, and Jackson, Mississippi. The citrus trees, olive varieties, and herbs best grown between Mexicali and Tecate in Baja California, Mexico, will have an easier time being cultivated between Los Angeles and the Ojai Valley near Santa Barbara, California. Of course, if farmers shift what crops they grow, they will need consumers, cooks, and chefs to adapt what they are willing to prepare and eat in the "new normal." While climate change has many severe impacts on our food systems, these shifts are among the few that may lead to fresh gastronomic innovation and pleasure.

Curiously, many herbs and shrubs become more pungent, and many fruits become more potent in their flavors, when heat and drought team up on them. To resist the stresses that come with searing sun, heat waves, and lack of rainwater, many plants of hot, dry lands exude more aromatic oils onto their leaves as a means of self-protection. Indeed, the herbs and spices of desert climes are often priced higher than those from temperate climes, not merely because of higher irrigation and production costs, but because of the high regard for their heightened aromas. More of those deeply fragrant and flavorful foods are likely to end up on our plates and in our bodies in the coming years, giving us a modicum of both enhanced protection and pleasure in an otherwise uncertain future.

Many of us have strong olfactory memories of the foods that either enthralled or repulsed us during our childhoods: Gramma's bitter herbs; Uncle Tonoose's bloody grilling of game or offal on a skewer; or Aunt Emmie's stinky cheeses and sour pickles. If we have been blessed with the chance to travel as adventurous adults, we can recognize (even years later) the aromas and colors of curries from India; the salted bacalaos from North Atlantic coastlines; African-influenced gumbos from the Low Country of the American South; or *manchamantel* (tablecloth-staining) moles from the Mesoamerican highlands stretching from Oaxaca to Mexico City.

The discerning enthusiast of Mediterranean cuisines might be able to identify—even while blindfolded—some of the subtle variations in scents of similar seafood-and-rice dishes from Cairo, Istanbul, Palermo, or Valencia. They might likewise distinguish those from another set of cities along the northern Pacific Rim: Petropavlovsk-Kamchatsky, Sapporo, Shanghai, Seoul, Taipei, or Tokyo.

And yet, far fewer of us can decipher the culinary distinctions coming to us from the hottest and driest hearths and roasting pits on this Earth. Desert travelers may cherish sensory memories of foods unique to the Chihuahuan Desert of northern Mexico, the Peruvian coast, the Canary Islands, the Sahara, the Empty Quarter of the Arabian Peninsula, the Thar Desert of the Indian subcontinent, or the Gobi and Taklimakan Deserts of Central Asia, but for most of us, distinctions among these places may be blurred, caricatured, or altogether absent.

It is from these desert margins on four continents that much of the earliest innovations in cooking, pickling, fermenting, farming, livestock-raising, and orchard-keeping originated. They may be the true cradles of our cuisines.

Anciently, the "deceptive barrenness" of arid landscapes emboldened the culinary imaginations of hardy, resourceful women and men who found ways to feast where the unacquainted inevitably feared the risk of famine and thirst. These gastronomic wizards mastered the art of desert peasant cookery, despite the prevailing aridity, heat, and water scarcity in austere stretches of lava, sand, and slickrock that surrounded them. They gratefully took what the land seasonally offered up—a hare here, a sprig of herbs there, some land snails, snakes, shoots, or rough-barked roots hidden in the sands—and ran for their lives with them. Over the long haul, they ingeniously conjured up remarkable repasts from the aromatic foliage, the hygroscopic seeds, the deeply buried tubers, and the thorny creatures of those arid landscapes.

The seldom-seen treasures of desert terrain palpably protected desert nomads from all manner of stresses—heatstroke, drought, dehydration, muscle wasting, and hunger—but also enriched their lives with aromas and flavor notes so potent and pleasurable that they have graced their stories, such as from *One Thousand and One Arabian Nights*.

What ancient gastronomic innovators in traditional cultures found in the desert and its austere coastlines were some of the most aromatic and erotic edibles that humankind has ever tasted. This includes dozens of powerfully fragrant culinary herbs, salad greens, and flowers; pungent spices, gums, and fruits; bitingly sharp seeds, tender shoots, and bittersweet roots; breeds of sheep, goats, squabs, and snails whose gamy flesh embodied terroirs so distinctive and divine that they have remained treasured three millennia later by the greatest chefs of our own times.

The most sophisticated culinary artists from desert climes both blended and bumped up the characteristic scents, textures, and tastes particular to arid habitats, forming gastronomic traditions more sensorily satisfying than most of the innocuous drivel we eat today. We can liken the culinary artisans of desert regions to shamans who used plants to nourish, to heal, and to enchant. They foraged for solutions that could restore vigor to the body, enliven all the senses, and ignite the imagination. Remarkably, they did so with what was immediately and seasonally at hand in their austere environs. They learned exactly when they had to gather the resinous herbs, redolent roots, sour fruits, oily nuts, succulent stalks, and delicately scented flowers to retain their potency.

The wind-beaten, sometimes gnarly food plants from which these masters of aridity drew upon collectively comprise one of the most fragrant and flavorful floras on what we call Planet Desert. Their suffering and surviving so many challenges has distilled this flora down to its essence. By employing certain culinary techniques that have barely persisted to this day, they transformed a curious mélange of raw materials into some of the most provocative cuisines humans have ever crafted.

And now, we are, all of us, crossing a threshold into that Planet Desert, or Braised New World. Rather than staying in denial, sliding blindly into that new reality, we should embrace its new possibilities with our arms, hearts, minds, and senses. It will be one in which global temperatures are likely to rise 2.7°F (1.5°C) over the next two decades, prompting rivers, springs, and wells to go dry, and species to become scarce. During what we think of as the growing season for vegetables and fruits, summer daytime temperatures will surpass 120°F to 131°F (49°C to 55°C) over two-fifths of North America alone. Most tomatoes can't think straight—let alone flower and fruit—in such heat!

We can either change our attitudes, or our latitudes, but either way, what we eat and drink will surely shift. As a Tamazight (Siwan Berber) friend once confessed to us on a 115-degree (46-degree) day, as we glanced over at 600-foot-tall (182 m) sand dunes of the Sahara slowly moving toward his back door in the Siwa Oasis in Egypt, "It takes a special kind of consciousness to learn how to be cool, chill out, and lay low under such conditions."

Most of us now living on this new Planet Desert will need to learn how to chill appropriately or face a degree of duress that we did not imagine, let alone acclimate to, during our childhoods.

We need not hop into the frying pan or the roasting pit to feel the wrath of Mama Earth over how we have mistreated and degraded her gifts! If Mama loses her cool, *ain't nobody gonna chill* until we appropriately shift our consciousness, our addiction to growth and fossil fuel, and our eating habits!

Now, that's about all the preachiness you're going to get out of us; for the rest of this book, we'll be a bit more laid-back. *All we are saying is to give desert life a chance*, to proactively adapt our ways of cooking and eating to those better suited to hotter, drier climes.

For many of us, it becomes a wildly imaginative adventure *to think like a desert*, that is, to find ways to adapt to the desert as much as its native flora and fauna do. Deciding what we choose to eat (or not) is one of the most direct interactions we have with our surroundings. Not only that, but knowing the habitats that our foods and beverages come from can add to the *delight* we are gifted by them.

So come with us on this journey across the driest reaches of Planet Desert to see how we have something to gain—not merely to lose—by recalibrating our gardening, gathering, curing, cooking, fermenting, and eating to solar-powered, pungent cuisine. You, too, may find yourself grateful for the cacti, capers, century plants, chia, and chickpeas that offer sufficient sensuous pleasures to assure us our lives need not be impoverished as the planet's climates change.

Chapter 2

Why Are Arid-Land Aromatics So Potent When Eaten, Imbibed, or Inhaled?

Some of the most fragrant cuisines in the world have emerged from arid climes, places such as Samarkand, Baghdad, Jaipur, Gaziantep, Damascus, Aleppo, Zahle, Amman, Jerusalem, Alexandria, Fez, Marrakech, Alicante, Cádiz, Lanzarote, Saltillo, Puebla, Guaymas, Ensenada, Tecate, Sedona, Santa Fe, and Tucson.

When you wander through a desert just after a drenching rain, the aromas of the volatile oils of the glistening herbs and shrubs can propel you into a synesthetic trance, moving you toward the verge of elation if not ecstasy. You are entering what scientist and author Harold McGee calls the osmocosm of arid lands—the Land of Olfactory Delights—an invisible but intricate reality that only your nose may lead you to know.

The Sonoran Desert region alone features 68 different kinds of aromatic herbs, shrubs, trees, vines, and cacti. Together they release more than 120 tantalizing fragrances into the air, especially during an all-too-brief monsoon season. Many of them are more than marginally edible; they are delectable.

More precisely, over 250 species of Sonoran Desert plants are edible, and at least four dozen of them are deliciously so. Because much of what we think we taste is really what we smell before a food or beverage ever enters our mouth, these four dozen wild edibles are luring us with their aromas long before they cross our lips and land on our tongues with flavor.

To claim that desert floras exceed those of other regions in their number of potent aromatic herbs is neither hyperbole nor happenstance. The very aromas and flavors of these desert foods arose out of adaptations to arid conditions that have always allowed arid-land floras and faunas to survive and even thrive during punishing heat waves, lingering droughts, dust devils, sandstorms, and brutal bouts of damaging solar radiation.

Let's examine that last assertion. The desert's various and sundry herbs, shrubs, thorny succulents, and trees have elegantly adapted themselves to their austere environs through various chemical, morphological, and physiological means. Their production of volatile oils, gums, an okra-like mucilage, and inulins (a storage carbohydrate that allows them to function as a "slow release" hypoglycemic food) represent evolutionary strategies for slowing down water loss, reducing UV radiation damage, and repelling the myriad pests, plagues, and predators on Planet Desert. We as humans are the *incidental beneficiaries* of hundreds of thousands of years of plant and animal co-evolution in arid landscapes.

In other words, evolutionary processes in desert regions have coincidentally gifted us with some of the most healthful, aromatic, and flavorful food plants known to gastronomy and to science.

As cacti and critters learned to take root in and emerge from dry, stony, sandy, or salty soils, they took on the crisp minerality and bitter or brutal reality of their existence. Those terroirs later landed in our cups and bowls and lightly spilled onto our plates. At their best, desert terroirs capture and softly echo a sense of taste and struggle distilled from a dauntingly arid place.

We have recently discovered a provocative gastro-geographic pattern. The regions with the most distinctive terroirs are where high densities and diversities of plants rich in aromatic volatile oils occur. They occur there because the more stressed the climate and stony soils, the richer they are in aromatics. Given this pattern, it is not surprising that food plants from desert regions offer experiences of sensory intensity and complexity that those of better-watered (but more dilute or drowned-out) regions hardly ever equal.

The same pattern may hold for the flesh of livestock breeds and game. The Churro sheep foraging in the Painted Desert and Chuska Mountains on the Navajo Nation in Arizona are sharply sagebrush-fed rather than mildly grass-fed. In Syria's Anti-Lebanon Mountains in the summer, fat-tailed sheep mutton tastes like za'atar (Syrian thyme). No need to rub spices onto their legs of lamb; the spiciness is already embedded in the meat.

And yet, desert *nature* is not the only gift-giver to terroir; desert *cultures* have added their own culinary presence to the mix. The home cooks and culinary artisans of arid lands have carefully elaborated juices, sauces, syrups, pastes, and oils pressed from local plants to soothe parched lips and furrowed tongues. And they have sun-dried their fruits—from apricots and figs to okra and winter squash—to intensify their flavors and to rehydrate for later use upon demand.

West of the Mississippi in North America, no fewer than five dozen wild herbs can help us and our neighbors to psychologically and physically adapt

Colorful ground herbs and spices.

to the daunting hyperarid conditions of hot and dry that we will shortly be facing. They include a number of wild sages, true mints, bushmints, oreganos, wormwoods, desert lavenders, Texas rangers, beebalms, tarragons, and cinchweeds that are good as potherbs, salad toppings, teas, and infusions.

Psychologically, desert herbalists, wild foragers, and cooks who use these "adaptogens" may do so through a phenomenon that has subtly emerged in the best of these culinary traditions. Whether the desert food artists, present or past, were home cooks or the celebrated chefs who presided over village feasts, they found a way to bring their families or communities into a feeling of elation by using the right amounts of fresh herbs at the onset of a particularly intense season.

How? The desert foods and drinks they offered were filled with the anticipation of rain—rain that allowed the world to be renewed and its hidden abundance revealed. Just how they did so was no cheap trick or culinary sleight of hand. It was a magic inherent in the desert flora itself.

After building up a luminous, resinous coating of oils on their leaves over weeks of harsh, hot weather, these chemo-protective volatiles are suddenly released in the air in copious quantities whenever a downpour occurs. Desert dwellers subconsciously begin to associate these heady aromas with hope, opportunity, and even wonder.

Whether released by the oily tissues of creosote bush, by the tiny leaves of Mexican oregano, by the flowers and stems of desert lavender, or by the peeling bark and gums of the elephant tree (akin to frankincense), these aromas became equated with a sudden windfall of abundant food and drink for many deserter dwellers. And so, desert cuisines, by their very nature, can claim a volatile potency, pungency, or penetrating flavor profile that has been embedded within them over deep time. As one of our chile-eating friends said to us over lunch one day, "These foods bite you even before you bite into them. And you sweat so profusely after eating them that you get to enjoy evaporative cooling!"

That's right: Desert foods may bite, sting, stick, singe, stun, or spring upon you with a sudden blast of fragrance and flavor that seems to come out of nowhere. A good chef knows how to let place-based ingredients loose with a potency appropriate for the event. Like a musical blast from a bugle or trumpet, they announce the presence of something altogether reassuring about the past and present, but also the hopeful possibility of a brighter, tastier, more fragrant future. Journalist Juan Estevan Arellano once called that "rooted" feeling *querencia*: "that which gives us a sense of place, that which anchors us to the land, that which makes us a unique people, for it implies a deeply rooted knowledge of place."

Chapter 3

Rethinking the Ways We Perceive and Use Aromatics

If you read older cookbooks or look online for recipes now and then, undoubtedly you have seen write-ups that instruct, "First, grab a saucepan and sauté the aromatics." Whether preparing a meat dish, stew, soup, casserole, or grilled vegetables, you may have been surprised to learn that these recipes refer to just five ingredients: carrots, celery, garlic, ginger, and onions.

Should such recipes also call for a broader realm of spices and herbs, they may direct you to obtain the dried herbs and inviable seed spices that may be slowly decomposing into dust in a can or bottle on a home or store shelf, harvested from who knows where or when, perhaps originally gathered many eons ago.

The herbs and spices we both grew up with in the 1950s and '60s did have some aroma left to them: the stuffy scent of a rusty, oxidized tin, dented aluminum can, or hard plastic bottle!

And as for most of those innocuous spice blends that pretend to be aromatics suited for rubs, dips, and bastes? Well, you have probably seen them sold in national chains of kitchenware stores and spice warehouses: sad sacks of poorly harvested, interminably stored bouquet garni and sachet d'épices that have seen better days and should be shuffled off to a retirement home.

Whoever came up with these poor substitutes for aromatics should win a Nobel Prize for reductionism, for they somehow forgot that everything which makes food memorable tends to be fresh, entrancingly complex, and aromatic!

While you can indeed place a few herbs or spices in cheesecloth so as to retrieve them more easily from a stew pot or Dutch oven, do not confuse the finger with where it is pointing. The ways you can make your homemade food more aromatic and memorable may take a thousand other forms, starting with the freshest ingredients.

Aromatic herbs in Moroccan market.

While it is true that some herbs, when properly dried, retain some of their fragrances for months, don't push the river! Unless kept in a cool, dark place, most "go under" in a matter of months, losing their volatile oils one by one. It is advisable to cull them from your cabinet every few months rather than let your guests at the table ingest the marginally aromatic fragrances of fine, dry dust. But ultimately, it is best to grow your own.

To do this, start with your own values and aspirations: What do you wish to evoke within yourself and among your fellow eaters? Herbs and spices are like color palettes of oil paints. With the right combination of just a few selections, you can set a tone, strike a mood, or build a stage upon which others can play.

But a stage needs good lighting, structure to its spacing, or colors and textures to emotionally situate a story. Yes, most recipes do have a protein source, a carb, a fat or oil, and some fiber, but that skeleton is not enough to make them dance and sing. Aromatics must underlie and link them, rather than being window dressings or quick-fix bandages for a bleeding bunch of undercooked meats or mushy beets.

We like to think of aromatic herbs and spices as dream weavers, matchmakers, and midwives that *dar a luz* ("give birth") to a body of sumptuous aromas, tastes, and textures greater than the sum of the parts. For us, it is easiest to come to know them in "triads"—*mélanges à trois*—whose members complement rather compete or crash into one another.

Aromatic Triads

Here is a starting set of aromatic triads derived from desert cultures that have coveted these combinations as if they were holy trinities. Some, such as licorice, anise, and fennel, or cilantro, culantro, and papalo, are kindred spirits that can virtually replace one another. Other triads are complementary when balanced but induce creative tensions when one takes the lead over the others: cinnamon, coriander, and cumin; or damiana, lavender, and rose. In the right measures, the synergistic effects of their mutually reinforcing fragrances can be greater than the sum of the parts.

As a disclaimer, most Peasant cooks and seasoned chefs seldom limit themselves to a triad, but these threesomes set the stage for other invitees. Once you learn how to play the basic chords with such triads, you can graduate to blending multiple herbs, seeds, and spices into the orchestral symphonies that we all know by name even when we can't remember all their constituents.

Of course, these lists of ingredients in spice triads will inevitably vary with the cook, the family, the village, the valley, the province, the nation, or the region. Much to a purist's dismay, a given spice trader might make different versions of a blend on two consecutive days! And so, these traditional cuisines come from mutable, adaptive scripts, not from rigid laws handed down by the likes of Moses, Jesus, Allah, Siddhartha Gautama Buddha, Mayahuel, or even Diana Kennedy, Claudia Roden, or Paula Wolfert.

Even for gastronomically timid Americans and Europeans who have never heard of—let alone experienced—some of marvelously elegant spice and herb triads, we can offer them the opportunity to be initiated into the micro-universes of scent called osmocosms.

Many osmocosms have been just beyond the sniffing distance of mainstream America, hidden in tiny ethnic delis and import groceries in bigger cities, patiently waiting to come out of the cupboard and leap up from the dusty tin.

The Triads

Achiote • Bitter Orange Juice or Zest • Sweet Chiles (including paprika)
Agarwood • Ambergris • Orange Blossom Water
Ajwain • Coriander • Fennel Seed
Allspice • Cacao • Mexican Tarragon
Allspice • Cloves • Nutmeg
Almond Oil • Chervil • Fennel
Anise • Florence Fennel • Mexican Tarragon
Arugula (rocket cress) • Sorrel • Watercress
Asafetida • Fennel Seed • Mustard Seed
Basil • Greek Oregano • Lemon Balm
Bay Laurel • Geranium • Hibiscus Flower (Jamaica)
Bergamot • Seville Orange • Sorrel
Cacao • Chile Ancho • Vanilla
Cardamom (black) • Clove • Ginger
Cardamom (green) • Cinnamon • Ginger
Cardamom (white) • Cinnamon • Mahleb Cherry Seed
Cassia Cinnamon • Kaffir Lime Leaf • Lemon Zest
Chiltepin (green) • Desert Lavender • Oregano Indio
Chives • Dill • French Tarragon
Cilantro • Culantro • Papalo
Coriander • Cumin • Turmeric
Damiana • Lavender • Rose
Epazote • Garlic • Lime
Frankincense • Orange Zest • Peppermint
Ginger • Star Anise • Turmeric
Lavender • Rosebuds • Violet-Flavored Orris Root
Lime Juice or Zest • Mexican Tarragon • Peppermint
Parsley • Sage • Rosemary
Saffron • Black Pepper • Cardamom (green)
Sesame Seed • Sumac • Syrian Thyme (za'atar)

Chapter 4

Cuisines Shaped by Heat and Water Scarcity

As humans have traveled, foods and their seedy propagules have traveled, too. Seeds travel by land, by air, and by sea. Pollen can travel on the beaks of hummingbirds and on the raging frontal winds of thunderstorms, cyclones, or hurricanes. But most food plants have moved from culture to culture and continent to continent in the hands of women or an occasional man. Pilgrims and refugees hid them in muslin or rawhide bags around their necks, sewed them into the seams of smocks and socks, or taped them to the inner side of hatbands.

We should not be surprised that many food crops are grown in several different arid regions around the world, for human cultures have had thousands of years to carry them great distances by camel, canoe, rickshaw, horse-drawn wagon, or passenger pigeon. On the edges of the Gobi and Taklimakan Deserts, both of us have seen sailing ships that were used not to navigate lakes or oceans but to bring spices and teas across vast seas of shifting sands.

Nevertheless, we have both been surprised when eating in a distant land to encounter the spitting image and familiar scent of an emblematic food that we associate with the deserts along the border that separates the United States and Mexico. One evening, not at all far from the Lebanon-Syria border, we ordered a baked eggplant dish at an Armenian restaurant, anticipating that something akin to moussaka would be delivered to our table. But when the young Armenian waiter presented us with a dish that looked identical to chiles en nogada—Mexican stuffed peppers in a creamy walnut sauce—we quietly requested that he take it back and bring the eggplant we had ordered.

Smirking, he whispered that it *was* the eggplant we had ordered. The *only* dissimilarity between what lay before me and what lay in my memory from harvesttime meals in northern Mexico was the use of Old World

Farmer planting in water-harvesting field, Canary Islands.

eggplant in place of New World chile pepper. The script was the same.

We should not be surprised that many food crops are grown in several different arid regions around the world, for human cultures have had thousands of years to switch out the likes of Old World eggplant for New World chile. There is something wondrous about these patterns of hidden culinary connections. They offer us the flexibility to riff on an ancient food processing script that set up hundreds of kindred recipes that have, in turn, diffused from one desert culture to another, all around the world.

To be sure, some of these recipes were carried well beyond deserts and found homes in more temperate and tropical zones, as people born and raised in these zones became refugees, voluntary immigrants, or itinerant traders far from their original homelands. Just like the oasis-like fragrance gardens that first took shape in Baghdad and Damascus, and which later made it all the way to Cádiz, Fez, Marrakech, Málaga, Granada, Saltillo, Santa Fe, San Antonio, Tucson, Puebla, and Oaxaca City, these recipes form a chain through space and time that help us reconstruct a deeply adaptive attentiveness to fragrance.

We want to discuss how and why those links in the spice chain hang together. But before we do that, let us remind you what the rewards might be for an amateur cook or professional chef who learns to focus on an entire gastronomic chain of recipes rather than on a single link in the chain. If you metaphorically move toward seeing the gastronomic "forest" rather than the "trees" embedded in each desert cuisine, you can imagine the whole rainbow of interchangeable ingredients that can enhance the fragrances, flavors, and textures of any desert-derived food you choose to prepare.

What's more, you can gain additional insights by seeing each version of the same basic recipe as a fragment or snapshot within the entire script as it moved through space and time. This imaginative exercise may then allow you to "reverse engineer" the recipe back toward its roots or toward the pinnacle of its expression.

By taking hints from all the various versions, you might create something even more delectable and memorable. You can show your respect to the creator of the original recipe by grasping their initial intentions, then taking them to a higher level rather than freezing the creative process.

Do you get where we are going? We are not asking you to join us on some esoteric historic, gastronomic, or anthropological sleuthing along the trail of any single desert food or beverage merely for its own sake. Instead, we are inviting you to imagine how to bring the fullest array of pleasing aromas, tastes, and healthful qualities into your own rendition.

In essence, you are encouraged to use the recipe script in a way that allows you to reassemble the pieces from various places and times and bring them together into a fresh culinary feast fitted to the current conditions in our Braised New World.

To offer you a tangible example of what we may regain by culinary reverse-engineering, let us explore the roots and various offshoots of an ancient recipe for a lamb and chickpea stew. How ancient? Well, it appears that sheep were among the first livestock to be domesticated 11,000 to 13,000 years ago, in arid mountain ranges surrounding the Tigris-Euphrates delta in Mesopotamia. Chickpeas (or garbanzos) were domesticated just west of the delta—in what we now call Syria and Turkey. The sheep were naturally inclined to graze on wild perennial herbs that grew prolifically under mountainous desert conditions, namely thyme, marjoram, hyssop, and oregano. It is no wonder that the mutton and lamb of the region carry their herbal flavors in the shish kebabs and kefta prepared there.

Where sheep take shelter beneath the remaining sacred cedars of Lebanon in the high mountains that rise above the Syrian plains, wild chickpeas grow alongside wild lentils and fava beans, amidst pastures dominated by wild barleys, wheats, and oats. If you are looking for how humanity might persist under dry, uncertain conditions, these wild relatives of our staple foods are the gold-medal winners, surviving ten millennia of climatic changes along the desert's edges.

Nevertheless, flavors and textures of these chickpea seeds and sheep breeds were just too good to stay restricted to their cradle of origin for very long. They left home and diverged into distinctive ethnic renditions of lamb and chickpea stews that now go by many different names in the drier reaches of this planet: *shurpa* in Uzbek and other dialects of Central Asian deserts; *abgoosht* and *dizi* in the Persian Farsi of Iran; *qeema* in Iraq; *piti* in Azerbaijan; *nohut* in Turkey; *shawraba* in Lebanon; *qidreh* in Palestine; *sharba* in Libya; *chorba frik* in Tunisia; *al-harira* in the Arabic of Algeria;

askkif in the Berber dialects of Algeria and eastern Morocco; and *carne de cordero en la olla* in the Castilian of Spain.

Curiously, there is a very similar stew in the Canary Islands, the Caribbean, and Latin America. It is one among several that are known as *ropa vieja*, "old clothes." That is not a pejorative. It refers to the multicolored shreds of meat and vegetables in the dish, which resemble colorful strips of rags, as sometimes used in a crazy quilt.

A crazy quilt this itinerant stew may be. Nearly everywhere it traveled, common threads were carried across its many regions and nations: black peppercorns, coriander seed and leaves (that is, cilantro), cumin seed, garlic, and onion. A dozen and a half other spices and herbs occasionally join these five in the dozen desert countries where we trace this stew. Gum mastic, lime, parsley, and bay laurel from the Old World, and red pepper originating in the New World, show up frequently as a second tier of aromatics now found in more than one region.

Now here is the most curious part of this entire saga. Some of our favorite food history scholars—including Paul Buell and Eugene Anderson—have pointed us toward two different snapshots of lamb and chickpea stews from Asia 700 to 800 years ago, and another remarkably similar one from northern New Mexico a little over 80 years ago. All attest to the tenacity and perspicacity of the guild of spices associated with meat and legume stews. Although we can speculate on a common origin of these three recipes, one went far to the east into the deserts of Mongolia, one went west across the ocean with the conquest of Mexico and its frontier province of New Mexico, and one stayed close to home, around Aleppo, Syria.

The one that stayed home was recorded as a lamb, chickpea, and carrot stew of medieval Syrian Arabs, named *dinariyya* for the carrot discs cut the size and thickness of dinar coins of that era. It was spiced with garlic, black peppercorn, coriander, cassia cinnamon, and caraway, but oddly, no onions were recorded in the recipes.

The recipe for the East Asian version was written just two generations after the reign of Kublai Khan. It is credited to Hu Szu-hui, a court physician who trained in the Persian and Arab world. The dish was recommended by the doctor to keep his sponsor, Mongol Emperor (Qan) Tutemur, healthy and invigorated. It includes the garlic, black pepper, coriander, and cumin common to most Asian renditions, as well as mastic, which appears in fewer Asian versions.

Mastic is a gum derived from the wounded bark of a wild pistachio tree whose range rims the Mediterranean but reaches eastward only to the Tigris and Euphrates. Here is the surprise part of this story: the Hispanic version of lamb and chickpea stew from the Rio Arriba of New Mexico lacks only one ingredient—gum mastic—found in Hu Szu-hui's "Soup for the Qan" in Mongolia. That rendition—recorded by Hispanic folklorist Cleofas Jaramillo in 1939 in a little collection first called *Potajes Sabrosas* (that is, *Tasty Stews*)—hails from the high and dry mountain villages that crypto-Jews and crypto-Muslims fled to from Spain and the Canaries during the Spanish Inquisition three centuries earlier!

What we are proposing is that these lamb and chickpea stews did not arise as independent inventions but are desert-adapted vestiges of cultural diffusion routes that can be traced at least halfway around the world, from Mongolia to New Mexico. Surely some itinerant spice traders were directly involved in these peregrinations, carrying with them to the far corners of the earth rucksacks full of seeds, herbs, spices, and *recipes for resilience*.

What these analogous dishes might suggest to us is that if we wish to survive in a hotter, drier world, we might want to pay attention to the very foods that have helped some people in many desert cultures survive with pleasure and good health!

Now, if you presume that this parable of lamb, chickpeas, coriander, cumin, and cinnamon is an anomaly, think again. Over the last 20 years of roaming along the spice trails of four continents, we've found that there are several other recipes—replete with associated cultural scripts—that have spread out from the deserts of Central Asia, the Indian subcontinent, and the Middle East, over North Africa's camel caravan routes that cross the Sahara and coastal waterways that edge the shores of the Maghreb, all the way to Iberia, the Canaries, the Caribbean, Mexico, and the US Desert Southwest.

The recipes in this book are certainly not all the foods that have traveled from one arid region to another, but they are the easiest ones to linguistically trace without deterministically attempting to reduce every one of them to an adaptation to arid conditions. Later, we will try to answer why these foods filled such important niches among desert cultures—especially in those with Jewish, Christian, and Muslim rituals and seasonal meals. But for now, let us move into setting up the sensory enjoyment of these desert foods, for that may be the strongest reason for picking up this book.

Chapter 5
Building Your Own Desert Pantry

Just as an herbalist, a *curandera* (medicine woman), or a midwife always keeps her remedies and tool kit at hand, a good desert cook watches the weather to gauge when to harvest, collect, or capture each seasonal resource that arrives in abundance when the rains come. These windfalls are sometimes made rare by droughts or other disruptions in the annual cycle, so they are both prized and carefully conserved in a pantry or *dispensa* that shields them from excessive heat, glaring light, insect pests, or rodents.

Of course, it will be best to make some spice or nut blends, floral infusions, or scented vinegars on your own, so tools such a *molcajete* grindstone and pestle from Mexico, three sizes of colanders, cheesecloth bags, an infusion bottle, screens, and funnels will be essential. You may want to gift yourself a small *alambique* distillation apparatus, a stainless steel corer for zucchinis and eggplants, a good paella pan, and tagine pots, as well. But for starters, keep some core ingredients on hand for elaborating typical dishes in desert cuisines.

Dispensa pantry, Oaxaca, Mexico.

Cereal Grains and Flours and Legume Flours

Bulgur; durum wheat; couscous (balls of durum wheat mixed with semolina, or barley, corn, or millet); green, fire-charred freekeh wheat; Sonora white bread and pastry flour; bomba "paella" rice; basmati rice; pearl millet; bird-tongue orzo; popped amaranth seeds; amaranth flour; chickpea flour; mesquite pod flour (or carob pod flour); barley-maize gofio meal; toasted flint corn pinole; corn atole; blue, yellow, and white nixtamalized maize (corn); pear millet; sorghum seed; agave inulin powder; powdered *kishk* wheat with kefir yogurt.

Whole Dry Legumes or Pulses
Yellow-brown and white tepary beans; Anasazi and pinto beans; yellow (split) mung beans; red and yellow lentils; yellow peas; fava beans; yard-long beans; crowder peas / black-eyed peas; carob and mesquite bean pods.

Nuts and Crunchy Seeds, Toasted or Raw
Ajwain; amaranth; bellota acorns; celery seed; chia; coriander seed; cumin seed; pinyon (snobar) pine nuts; hazelnuts; pecans; nonbitter acorns; poppy seeds; hulled pumpkin seeds; black or white sesame seeds; nigella seeds.

Infusions and Syrups of Flower Blossoms
Rose water; rosewater syrup; mint syrup; hibiscus (Jamaica) water; elderflower blossom water; orange blossom water and other citrus blossom waters.

Oils and Pastes
Achiote (annatto) paste; argan oil; Moroccan harissa paste; olive oil; pistachio oil; sesame oil; tahini; hazelnut, pecan, or walnut oil.

Culinary Ashes
Saltbush/chamisa (Atriplex); sage (Artemisia or Salvia); Aleppo pepper or chile de arbol; corn cob; lime (cal).

Pickled Leaves for Rolling and Stuffing
Fig leaves; grape leaves; hoja santa leaves.

Spice Blends
Adobos; baharat; berbere; chermoula; curries; garam masala; harissa; kamouneh (for kibbeh); karouia; mojo picón; mole negro; ras el hanout; Yucatecan recaudos, tzatzikis, green za'atar; brown za'atar.

Dried Culinary Herbs
Arabian mint; bay laurel; bergamot; damiana; Greek oregano; kaffir lime leaf; lavender; lemon verbena; marjoram; Mexican oregano;

Mexican tarragon (yerba anís); oregano indio (Poliomintha); sages; spearmint; thymes.

Syrups of Pods and Fruits
Sour pomegranate molasses; sweet pomegranate syrup (or grenadine); carob pod syrup.

Pickled Vegetables
Artichoke hearts; beets with turnips; black olives; capers; caper shoots; carrots; chiltepín wild chiles; cholla cactus flower buds; garlic; green olives; fermented lime or lemon strips in salt and asafetida; watermelon-cucumbers (mikti); red onions; walnut-stuffed eggplants in vinegar or oil.

Dried Ground Spices
Asafetida; Aleppo pepper; allspice; anise seed; black peppercorn; cardamom; cassia cinnamon; cloves; coriander; cumin; gum mastic; malagueta pepper; mace; mahlab pepper; nutmeg; saffron; star anise.

Aromatic Roots
Orris (iris) roots; galangal; ginger; turmeric.

Vinegars and Sour Juices
Balsamic vinegar; concentrated bitter orange juice; lemon juice; lime juice; pomegranate vinegar; verjuice; sherry vinegar; white or red wine vinegar.

All of these—and more—will not only make your taste buds and olfactory receptors tingle; they will also brighten your life.

Chapter 6
Celebrating the Spice Odyssey That Bridges Many Cuisines

We live in a world of great political, economic, and social divides. The inequities between and among different peoples and nations not only diminish the lives of the poorest of the poor on this planet but impoverish us all spiritually. And yet, sometimes it is worth remembering and celebrating all that bridges rather than divides us, to acknowledge our debt to other cultures that have often been villainized or disparaged.

When we find that we cannot travel for financial, familial, medical, or political reasons, we may instead find that the fragrances in our spice cabinet and the recipes in which they are employed can do the mind-and-heart traveling for us.

Open any spice cabinet, and then trace the origins of the barks, berries, buds, corms, flowers, fruits, pistils, rhizomes, roots, seeds, and tubers within them. They will offer you a lesson in gastronomic geography and world history, tracing the elaborate ancient trade routes, the rise and fall of empires, the emergence of cookbooks and herbals, and the dispersal of refugees and their most beloved plant partners that they still cling to.

We grew up in North American landscapes where a variety of sumac bushes, trees, and vines grew, some with toxic leaves, others with delightfully sour berries. Why then did our neighbors and relatives seek out sumac berries and their burgundy-colored powders that had to be imported from halfway around the world?

The answer may be that our families have for so long participated in global spice trade routes that herbs from our ancestral country of origin are more likely to show up on our kitchen table than the ones found just beyond our back doors, in the woods, deserts, or marshlands, or out beyond the fence!

That may be because the cuisines that are often part of our family identities rely on recipes and ingredients that have traveled down certain well-worn paths for millennia: the Silk Road, the Frankincense Trail, the Camel Path across the Sahara from Tripoli to Timbuktu, and the Chichimecan Corridor from present-day Mexico City to Santa Fe.

At the earliest moments of long-distance navigation, spice traders were also navigating shipping routes around the Mediterranean from Alexandria to Salonica, and across the Indian Ocean from Persia and Oman to India and the Spice Islands.

But one desert-dominated set of pathways for aromatic oils, herbs, spices, and gums carried traders and chefs back and forth between western China and Persia, between Baghdad, Damascus, Petra, and Cairo, down the Nile, and on across the Maghreb of North Africa. In some cases, they then went on from the central Moroccan coast near Chichaoua and Agadir to the Canary Islands, as the Indigenous peoples, the Guanches, did thousands of years ago, or to Al-Andalus on the Iberian Peninsula. After the voyages of Columbus, they used the Canary Islands as a crossroads for bringing recipes, cooking techniques, and spice blends from the Levant and Maghreb to the Caribbean, Mexico, and the Desert Southwest of the United States.

The spice traders who accomplished these gastronomic dispersals were often Muslims and Jews working together, often with Buddhist, Zoroastrian, Hindu, Christian, Druze, and Indigenous counterparts of many cultures and nations. They created a sense of *convivencia* (creative, cross-cultural collaboration) with one another across great distances and time periods, through many generations of the same clans and families. In the face of ugly competition, occasional conflict, and cultural appropriation, these spice traders generated this collaboration, which we could learn from today.

Of course, the exotic spices, fruits, and vegetables from Latin America and North Africa quickly made it back to the Mediterranean, not so much through Spain and Portugal, but through shipping routes that rimmed the southern coasts of the Mediterranean and the seas of Eastern Europe.

By that time, it was common knowledge that certain plants—ones that survived and even thrived in the desert heat—were richer in aromatic oils, barks, and gums than those which grew in more temperate or tropical climes. And so, desert aromatics were enthusiastically welcomed and rapidly integrated into many other cuisines.

As we reflect on this pattern of splendid culinary diffusion when visiting the terminus of these migration corridors, we are reminded of our visit to the Baja California peninsula in the Guadalupe Valley between Ensenada and Tecate. There, we were struck by the stunning presence of date palms, Mission olives, Mission grapes, and Mission figs, all brought by Jesuit missionaries from the southern Mediterranean via the Canary Islands more than three centuries ago.

Recently one of us witnessed trees and vines genetically identical to those in Baja California and Alta California around the ancient port city of Agadir, Morocco. They may have had different names—such as Picholine for the heirloom olives—but they are cousins to four of the mainstays in the two Californias: dates, grapes, figs, and olives.

These horticultural travelers are but signposts to deeper connections among desert cuisines and cultures that have been generated over centuries of human migration: Phoenicians colonizing ports on the Iberian Peninsula more than three thousand years ago, and even reaching the Canaries in prehistoric eras; the Guanches of coastal Morocco becoming the first inhabitants of the Canaries; Arabs from Damascus fleeing Greater Syria to settle in Al-Andalus, bringing the renowned chef and entertainer Ziryab along with them; and Sephardic Jews and Morisco Muslims being evicted from Spain, only to use the Canaries as a way station to the deserts of the Americas.

Whether refugees, outcasts, or intentional migrants, these itinerants brought along their gastronomic sensibilities, culinary utensils, methods, spices, and scripts to infuse the fare in their newly found homes. But what is most remarkable is how many aromatic recipes—carried along in oral histories rather than cookbooks—now span the reach of so many desert cuisines in a relatively unchanged manner.

The almond paste confections called *alhasuú* in Arabic and Amazigh (Imazighen or Berber) dialects became known as *alajú* in historic Al-Andalus, and *alfajor* in the Canaries and in much of Latin America, as well.

The tiny hazelnut-sized meatballs known as *al-bunduq* or *al-bundiqa* in Arabic became *al-bóndiga* in Al-Andalus, *albóndigas en salsa* in the Canaries, and *albóndigas* in the deserts of Mexico and the US Southwest.

The tripe and chickpea stew of the Middle East known as *qalyas*

Plaza of the Spices, Marrakech, Morocco.

Celebrating the Spice Odyssey ▪ 25

became *qaliyas* or *qallos* in Al-Andalus, *callos* in the Canaries, and *menudo* in Mexico and the US Desert Southwest.

The seafoods cooked in citrus juice, known as *sikbaj* in the Middle East, became *e-sicbaj* in Al-Andalus, *escabeche* in the Canaries, and *ceviche* in Mexico, coastal Peru, and the US Desert Southwest.

The sweet fritters drizzled with honey or orange syrup called *zalabia* in the Middle East became *zlebia* or *zulubia* in Al-Andalus, *zulabia* in the Canaries, and *sopapilla* in the Desert Southwest and Mexico.

Similar travels for nearly identical aromatic recipes have included gazpacho soups, stews, paella-like casseroles, savory salsas and *pan de semita* breads, *capirotada* bread puddings, and powdered almond paste wedding cookies in the shape of gazelle's horns.

Most important, the carriers and traders of aromatic herbs and dry spices memorized "scripts," or orally transmitted sets of principles, for blending and using diverse aromatics in cooking. If the immigrants could not find nutmeg and mace in their newly found home, they might substitute allspice. If there was no turmeric to brighten a dish, they might feature the color of achiote or marigolds instead. If Mediterranean oreganos could not be had, they might turn to oregano indio, beebalm, or Mexican oregano for similar effects. Particular ingredients were interchangeable, so long as the overall structure of the spice blend was kept.

Often a new plant with leaves glistening with thymol and carvacrol could be found for harvesting to produce much of the same aromas as Greek oreganos offer.

In this way, Mexico and the US Desert Southwest came to share patterns of spicing soups, stews, casseroles, and flatbreads that had long been employed in northern Africa, southern Europe, the Middle East, and Central Asia.

Today, we are lucky enough to be able to use that ancient "pattern language" of spice wherever we live, garden, and cook. And it offers us a chance to show our deep respect for and solidarity with the many cultures around the world that may now be in harm's way, marginalized rather than honored for their intangible contributions to the ways we may need to produce food and eat during the drier, warmer days that are coming to Planet Desert.

Chapter 7

Spice Blends and the World We Taste

It takes most of us a while to move past our affection for particular spices and herbs in order to consider why anyone might blend 7, 10, 17, 101, or 313 herbs and spices into something they place on or integrate into their foods. Our weakness is obvious: unlike elephants, dogs, or raccoons, we can hardly differentiate—let alone integrate—so many aromas that are all around us.

But members of some cultures on this planet, by both tradition and personal practice, have been able to hold in their "palettes" many flavors and fragrances all at once, like an olfactory orchestra playing a symphonic composition of grandeur and elegance.

So it is with the *ras el hanouts* of Morocco among the Amazight peoples; the *baharats* among Turks; the *garam masalas* among the Gujaratis of India; the *chermoulas* among Venezuelans; the *mojos picónes* among Canarians; the *adobos* for Filipinos; the *berberes* for Ethiopians; the *souvlakis* for Greeks; the *recaudos* among Yucatecan Mayas in Mexico; and the *moles* among Zapotecos in Puebla, Mexico. The composite effect of many herbs and spices delicately balanced is always greater than the sum of the parts, both in the pleasures they offer and the health benefits they confer in the face of climate change.

What we have recently learned about the worlds of fragrance or osmocosms we live in is this: *There is something very tangible gained when the spices in the foods on a plate sing together as a chorus.*

Hidden in those pleasurable harmonies are health benefits—reduced levels of cortisol stress hormones, increased capacities for tranquility or endurance, stronger immune responses, and enhanced dimensions of tolerating searing heat, blistering sun, or lip-chafing dehydration that our bodies and minds might otherwise accrue if we were simply swallowing one capsule of a single herbal antioxidant each morning.

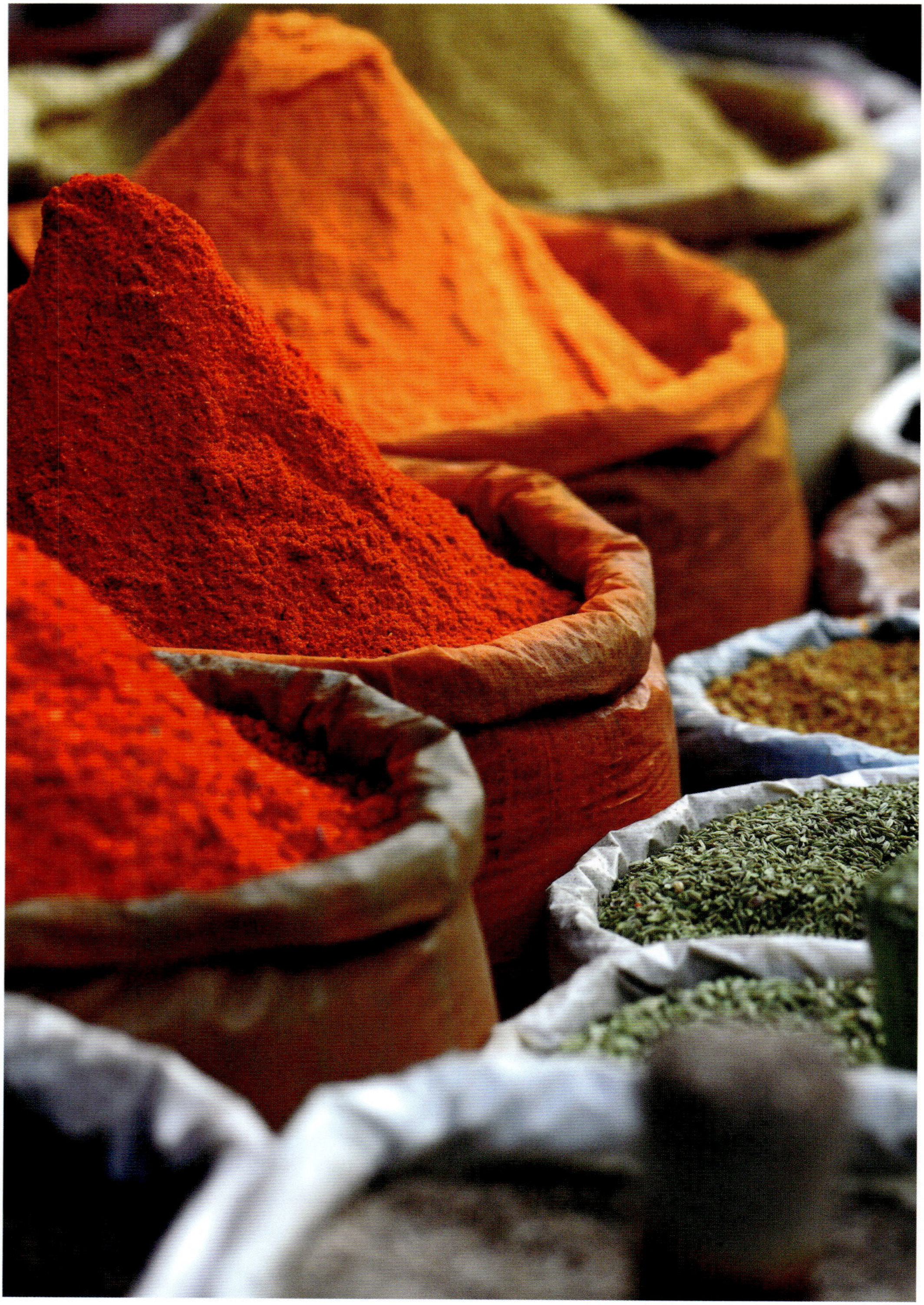

The synergistic benefits of spice blends can be bestowed upon anyone, no matter where they live, but are perhaps most evident and appreciated among those who live in hot, seasonally dry climes, where the abiotic stresses of sun, wind, and water scarcity can be grueling, and where the biotic challenges of keeping meat and fish from spoiling can also be daunting.

Let's face it, Scandinavians and Siberians have never needed the antioxidants of savory spice blends as much as the Somalians, Sudanese, Saudis, Syrians, or Sonorans have needed them. Before the advent of swamp coolers and mini splits for cooling in the summer, the most common kind of "air-conditioning" used by desert dwellers was a "good sweat" afforded by eating pungent peppers that cooled down the body through old-fashioned evaporative cooling!

It is no wonder that the most intensive use of spice blends around the planet is in the deserts and seasonally dry subtropics, where meat can rot, fish can putrefy, and cooked vegetables can spoil in the sun merely on a moment's notice. The antioxidants in herbs and spices do more than help preserve or "defend" certain foods against deleterious microbes. They also buffer farmworkers and fishermen from the exhaustion and the wear and tear they endure from working all day in the blazing sun.

The higher the density of herbal antioxidants there is in the diets of dwellers of deserts and monsoonal subtropical coasts, the more likely they are to be buffered from heat exhaustion, heatstroke, muscle wasting, and dehydration. Such buffering capacity will become ever more important as the planet becomes increasingly hotter and (at least seasonally) drier.

Frequent culinary use of spice blends can surely help build this buffering capacity to resist all matter of stresses, but alas!—there is no silver-bullet spice mix or one-size-fits-all miracle blend to do the job in all settings for all sorts of people.

To make matters even more complex, each of the most famous spice blends, ras el hanout for starters, is not just one fixed mix of the same spices. There is no culinary, cultural, or religious orthodoxy about the blend's composition, even within or between desert cultures. Even the four to six diagnostic spices that form the featured core of a particular spice blend may vary from one souk shopkeeper to another, between shops, or among cultures in the same arid region.

That may be in part because of the personal preferences and genetic capacities of spice keepers for receiving and enjoying various compounds in herbs and spices, but it is also because their clients request different things from them.

What blend might be easy on my husband's stomach ulcers, or help my pregnant sister gain more weight during her last trimester before giving birth to her baby?

What spice blend might reduce inflammation or ease congestion during the time of high winds, pollen counts, and allergic reactions?

Which ras el hanout fits well with grilled fish as opposed to a prune, almond, and pigeon tagine?

Which blend will be best as a marinade for meats, or as a dust or rub for grilled vegetables?

While visiting souks in Marrakech, Morocco, we realized that the most revered spice keepers had a remarkable capacity to think of their blends as communities—ones destined to be used for specific purposes.

Just off the main square, called Jamaa el-Fna, is the Place des Épices, where botanist Mohamed El Laoudi took us to meet a particular master of blending spices, Mr. Erraoudi. A hardworking, agile man with an unshaven face, Erraoudi offered us several different ras el hanout blends, each with either 12, 15, or 17 different herbs and spices curated into ground or raw blends. Mohamed—a tall, balding Muslim scientist with an enormous knowledge of botanicals—explained why Erraoudi's culinary and medicinal herbs were so highly regarded:

"*Ras el hanout* means 'top of the shop,' meaning the spice trader's best selection. If he wants his ras el hanout to fit the needs of his clients, he knows that it has to work like a team, to capture its synergies for both the pleasurable power of its pungency and for its underlying health benefits. For him, there is no dichotomy between food and medicine here—he knows that the mothers will feed his blends to sick babies in milk, or elders will take them in olive or argan oil."

Mohamed paused for a minute to ask Erraoudi a question, which he thoughtfully answered. Mohamed then translated the response for us:

"So, to deliver its efficacies, he must curate it like a coach would select a soccer team, with fast players as well as slower steady ones that can work as a solid defense. He might select four or five bold, savory spices to form the core of the blend that you instantly notice, that entrance you. But he also must include two or three 'catalysts' who can keep the team integrated, cohesive, and functioning at a high level. He knows what else to add to those core and catalyst spices to cure a cold, purge a toxin, or settle an upset stomach, so he selects ones that are antibiotics, anti-inflammatory, expectorants, or purgatives. His customers might come back to ask what healed them so quickly, but he cannot simply refer to one miracle cure. It's the synergistic effects of a good team, not the accomplishment of one superstar!"

It had been a week in which Morocco's national soccer team had been in an all-Africa tournament, so soccer had been on everyone's mind. But a finely curated herb and spice blend might be likened to a great symphony orchestra, a jazz band, a rowing crew, a women's quilting circle, or a squad of paramedics who do emergency medical rescues.

Whether it is a *mole oaxaqueño* from Zapotecs, a Kashmiri *curry*, an Ankaran *baharat*, or a Spanish *adobo* from Cádiz, there are properties hidden in the mixture that our noses can sense before our minds can logically articulate why it is so perfectly potent, so stale, or so out of balance. Of course, these qualities may shift with the preparation and subsequent care of the spice blend—whether it is finely ground or kept as seeds and stems; whether it is stored in the sun or concealed in a cool, dark place; and whether it is tossed out after six months or kept around year after year until dermestid beetles and desiccation degrade its value.

The duration of optimal potency for a spice blend is to some extent determined by its weakest parts. Mints and rosebuds can lose their aromas relatively quickly, but the fragrance of some gums, such as frankincense; musk, such as those from the glands of Tibetan or Mongolian deer; and underground corms of orris irises can last for years. It is claimed that centuries ago, some incenses and musks were mixed into the mortars of mosques, synagogues, and cathedrals in Turkey, and they still emit their aromas each time there is a soaking rain!

We should not be surprised that mixes of incenses, aromatic herbs, and spices are associated with the sacred in so many cultures around the world and presented as "burnt offerings" to the spirit world. Their aromas remind us that we can be touched by things we cannot see, or smell aromas that are just as "palpable" as what we can see. They communicate messages to us from plants, fungi, microbes, and animals that are beyond words.

The volatile airborne, waterborne, and soilborne signals that reach us from other beings—signals often hidden from sight—are the primary means by which most organisms on Earth communicate with one another. Simply by inhaling the fragrances of volatile oils in herbs, aromas in spices, and heady odors in gums, we may become aware of our tangible connections to other lives on Planet Desert, and to the "spirits" that may guide us into a healthier world.

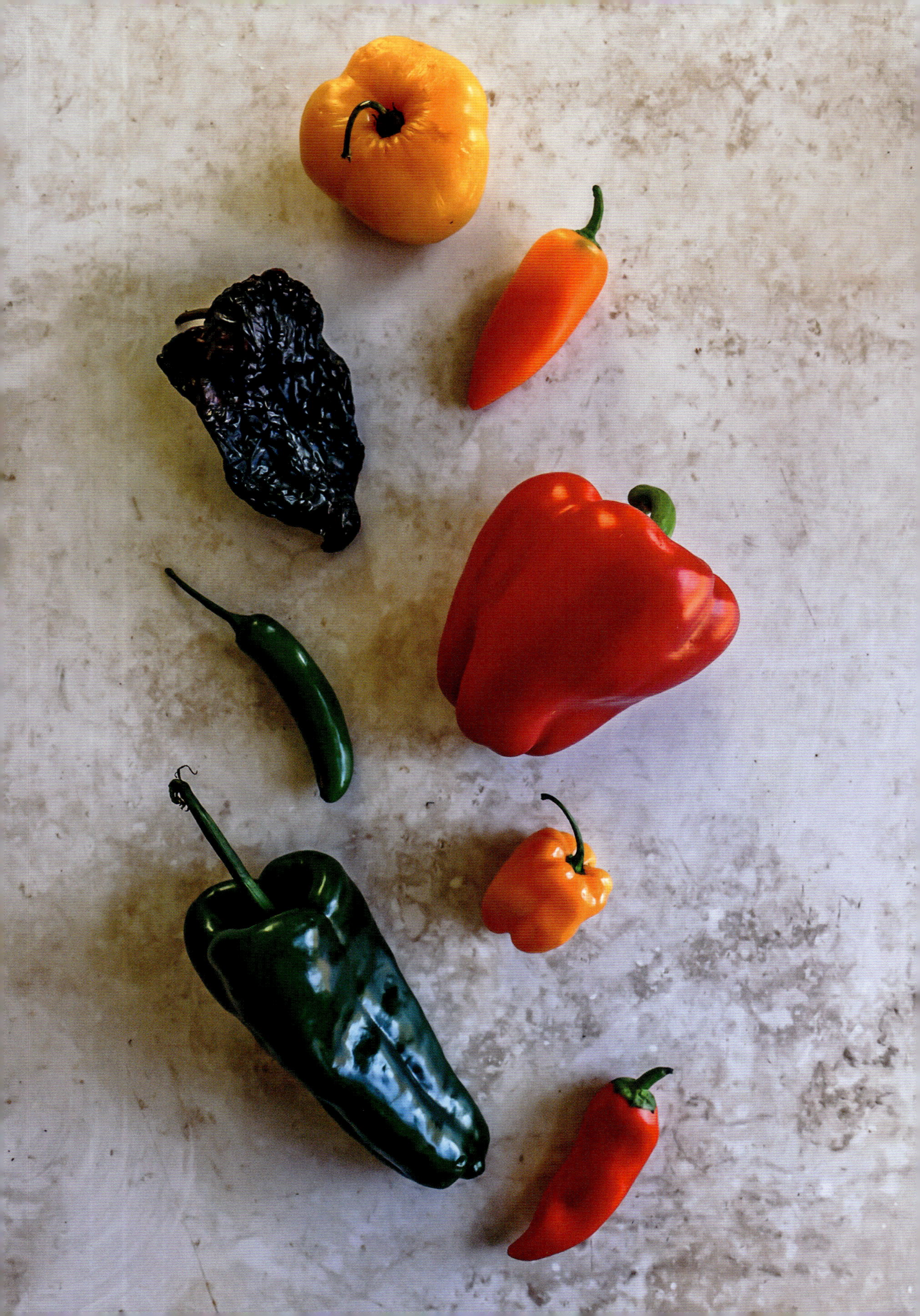

PART II
The Recipes

The spices and flavors in these recipes may be new to those of us living in the Northern Hemisphere. Lucky are we that Gary's stories and recipes make them delightfully accessible. Here are insights into the cultures of countries many of us may never travel to on our own. In developing and testing these recipes, I've come to appreciate how ras el hanout can lift a simple soup to a new level and have discovered the distinctive qualities of Mexican oregano.

We hope that as you explore these dishes drawn from the Old and New Worlds, you'll make them your own, adjusting the recipes to suit the season and your own tastes. We've taken some liberties with some of the traditional dishes, reducing the number of ingredients and shortening steps in an effort to streamline the process. If you're interested in further exploring the individual cuisines, you'll find a list of our favorite cookbooks in Further Reading (page 185). Happy cooking!

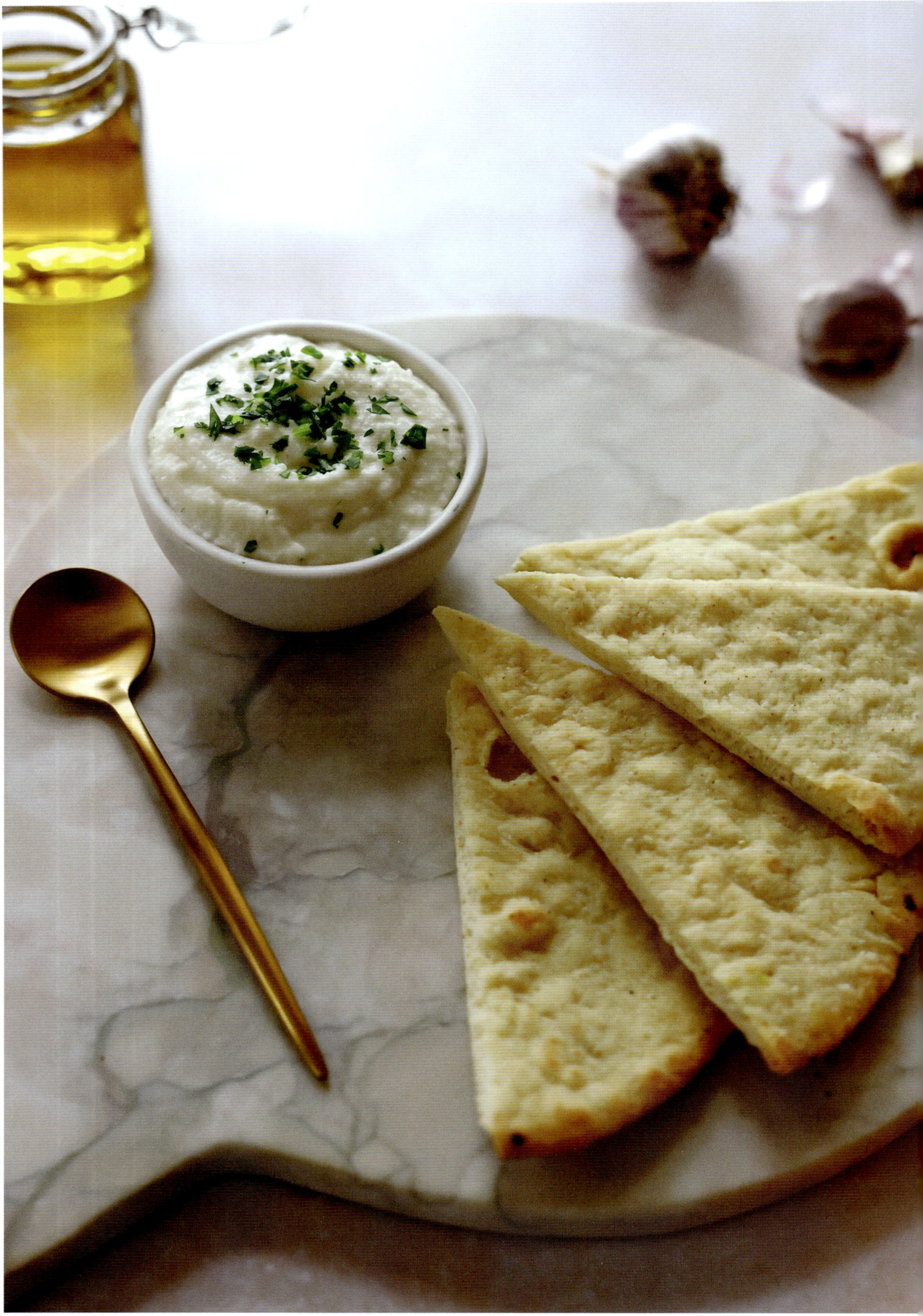

Chapter 8
Dips and Sauces

Try these dips and sauces as appetizers and condiments. They can be prepared ahead and be at the ready for last-minute guests or to dress vegetables and roasts. Keep them on hand and use them with abandon.

Cucumber, Fennel, and Garlic Dip	36
Aromatic Chickpea Dip	38
Sonoran Tepary Dip	39
Almond Potato Dip	41
Red Pepper and Walnut Dip	42
Black Chickpeas, Black Sesame, and Black Garlic Dip	43
Fire-Roasted Eggplant Dip	44
Cilantro-Pistachio Pesto	45
Tomatillo with Prickly Pear Sauce	46
Aromatic Red Pepper Sauce	47
Green Chile Dipping Sauce	48
Cilantro, Ginger, and Date Chutney	49
Fig and Pomegranate Jam	50
Preserved Lemons	51

Cucumber, Fennel, and Garlic Dip
(Tzatziki Me Máratho, Cacik, Mikti bi Labneh)

Crete, Greece, Lebanon, Syria, and Turkey

Makes about 3¼ cups

This classic yogurt and cucumber sauce is just right with lamb shawarma, and it makes a wonderful dip for toasted pita bread. Food writer Aglaia Kremezi shared her recipe using fennel and mint along with cucumber and garlic. Ours calls for wild cucumbers, aka *mikti*, from Lebanon. When shredded, their green skins add color and a pleasing delicate texture to the sauce.

- 2 small wild (mikti) or Persian cucumbers
- 1 medium fennel bulb, finely grated (about ⅔ cup [230 g])
- ½ cup fennel fronds, lightly chopped
- ½ teaspoon orange zest
- 2 to 3 garlic cloves, minced
- Generous pinch white pepper
- 2 to 3 teaspoons fresh lemon juice
- 2 tablespoons extra-virgin olive oil or argan oil
- 2 cups (480 ml) kefir, preferably sheep or goat
- 1 tablespoon finely chopped fresh spearmint for garnish

Grate the cucumbers into a strainer set over a bowl. Press to remove as much liquid as possible.

Transfer the cucumbers to a medium bowl and stir in the fennel, fennel fronds, orange zest, garlic, pepper, lemon juice, oil, and kefir. Cover and refrigerate until cold. Serve garnished with the spearmint.

Kitchen Notes

Kefir and yogurt are both cultured dairy products, but kefir is fermented for a longer period of time so it contains more probiotics. Sheep and goat kefirs are creamier than cow's milk kefir because they contain more of the rich, healthy fats and flavor.

Cucumbers are infused with electrolytes for natural rehydration. Desert cultures use them with abandon for flavor and nutrients. Persian cucumbers contain fewer seeds, are extra crisp, and are slightly sweeter than conventional varieties. If unavailable, use regular cucumbers, peeling and seeding them before shredding.

Argan oil is pressed from the fruit of the argan tree, indigenous to Morocco. Because the fruit's kernels are roasted before pressing, the oil has a rich, nutty flavor, similar to hazelnut or walnut oil. Find it online and in specialty shops.

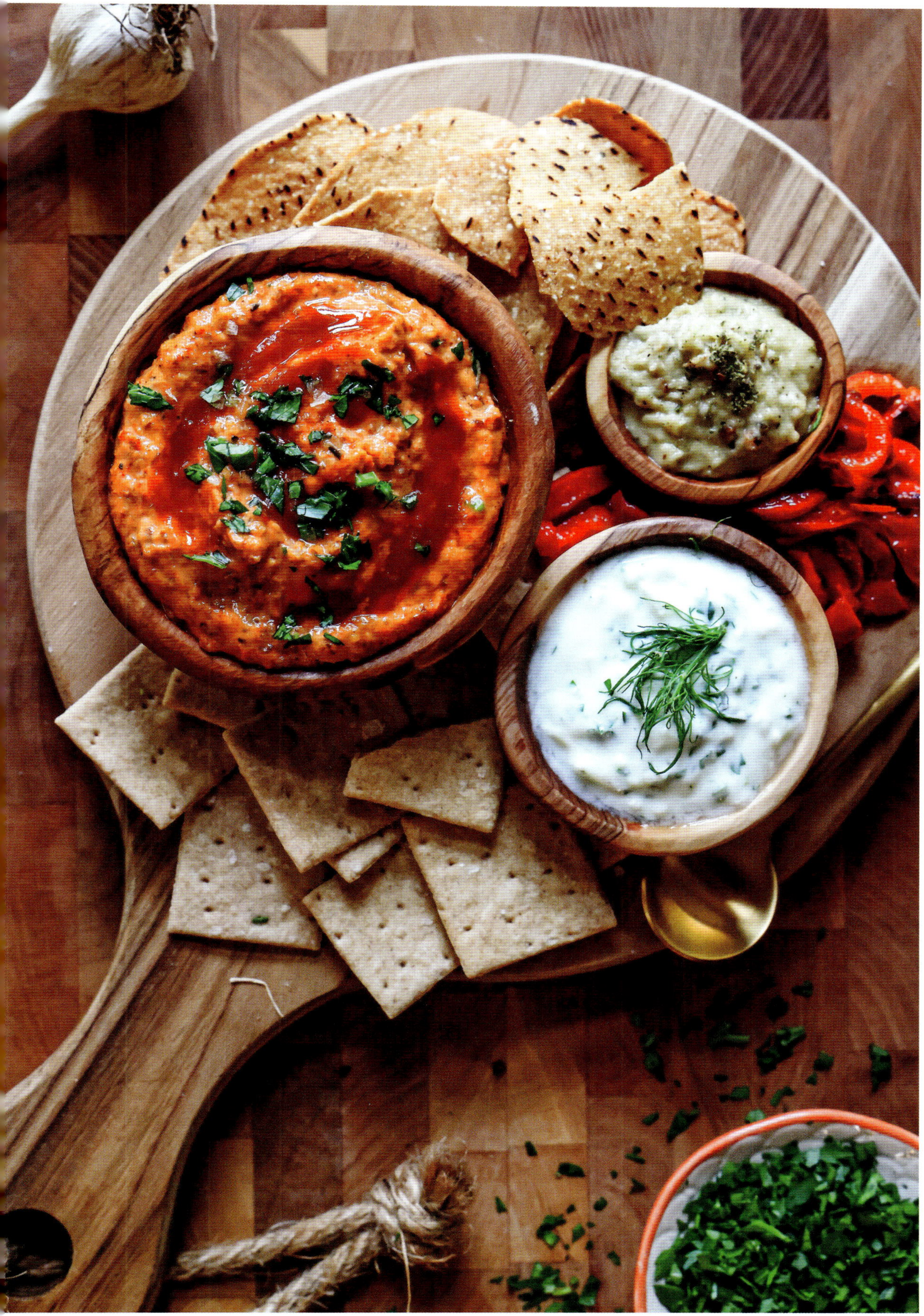

Aromatic Chickpea Dip

(Serrouda)

Lebanon, Morocco, Palestine, Syria, and Turkey

Makes 3 to 3½ cups

Serroudas are often compared to hummus, but because they don't contain tahini, they are lighter and brighter and said to be the most aromatic, the highest compliment a dip can receive.

1½ cups (340 g) dried chickpeas
1 teaspoon baking soda
1 teaspoon sea salt, plus more as needed
Generous pinch crumbled saffron threads
Generous pinch ground turmeric, plus more for garnish
Freshly ground black pepper
¼ cup (60 ml) olive oil or argan oil for serving
Pinch sweet paprika for garnish
2 small red tomatoes, finely diced
1 small onion, finely chopped
Pinch ground cumin for garnish
1 to 2 pita breads, toasted, for serving

Put the chickpeas into a large pot with the baking soda and enough cold water to cover by 4 inches (10 cm). Soak for 8 to 12 hours. Drain through a colander. Pinch the skins off with your fingers.

Place the chickpeas into a 3-quart (3 L) pot and add enough water to cover by 2 inches (5 cm). Set over high heat; bring to a boil for 15 minutes. Reduce the heat and simmer until the chickpeas become tender, about 1½ more hours, adding the salt, saffron, and turmeric the last 30 minutes of simmering. The chickpeas should be very soft and tender.

Transfer the chickpeas with their cooking liquid to a blender or food processor and puree, adding more water if necessary. The texture should resemble a thick soup. Season with salt and pepper and transfer to a serving dish.

Garnish with oil, paprika, tomatoes, onion, turmeric, and cumin. Serve with pita bread.

Sonoran Tepary Dip
(O'am Bawi, Tstatai Mori, Salsa de Tépari)

Mexico and US Desert Southwest

Makes about 2½ cups

Tiny tepary beans, native to the Sonoran Desert, are thought to have been first domesticated from wild plants in northwest Mexico. Cultivated by desert-dwelling Indigenous peoples in this region for 4,000 years, they're now planted in deserts throughout the world.

Culturally important to the Tohono O'odham and Pima peoples of southern and central Arizona, these beans are woven through legends and are a key to traditional recipes. The white tepary beans are relatively mild, close in flavor to navy and cannellini beans, while the brown tepary beans have an earthier, more robust taste. Both are wonderful in this dip recipe (or use a mix of white and brown).

2 cups (360 g) cooked tepary beans (see Note)
¼ cup (60 ml) water
2 garlic cloves, chopped
1 small jalapeño or Anaheim pepper, seeded and diced
¼ cup (60 ml) fresh lime juice
1 teaspoon ground cumin
¼ teaspoon chile powder
Coarse salt
Freshly ground black pepper
1 small onion, chopped
1 cup (16 g) cilantro leaves, chopped
2 to 3 tablespoons extra-virgin olive oil
Pine nuts for garnish

In a large bowl, stir together the beans, water, garlic, jalapeño, lime juice, cumin, chile powder, and salt and black pepper to taste. Using a potato masher or the back of a fork, smash the ingredients until you have a rough paste. Stir in the onion and cilantro. Transfer to a serving bowl and serve garnished with the oil and pine nuts. Store in the refrigerator in a covered container for up to 3 days.

Kitchen Note
Tepary beans take longer to cook than most dried beans. If cooking dried tepary beans, it's best to soak them in a pot with enough water to cover by about 3 inches (7.5 cm) for at least 12 hours and up to 24 hours. Drain, rinse, return to the pot, and add enough water to cover the beans by 4 inches (10 cm). Set over high heat, bring to a boil, reduce the heat, cover, and simmer until tender, 2 to 4 hours (or longer).

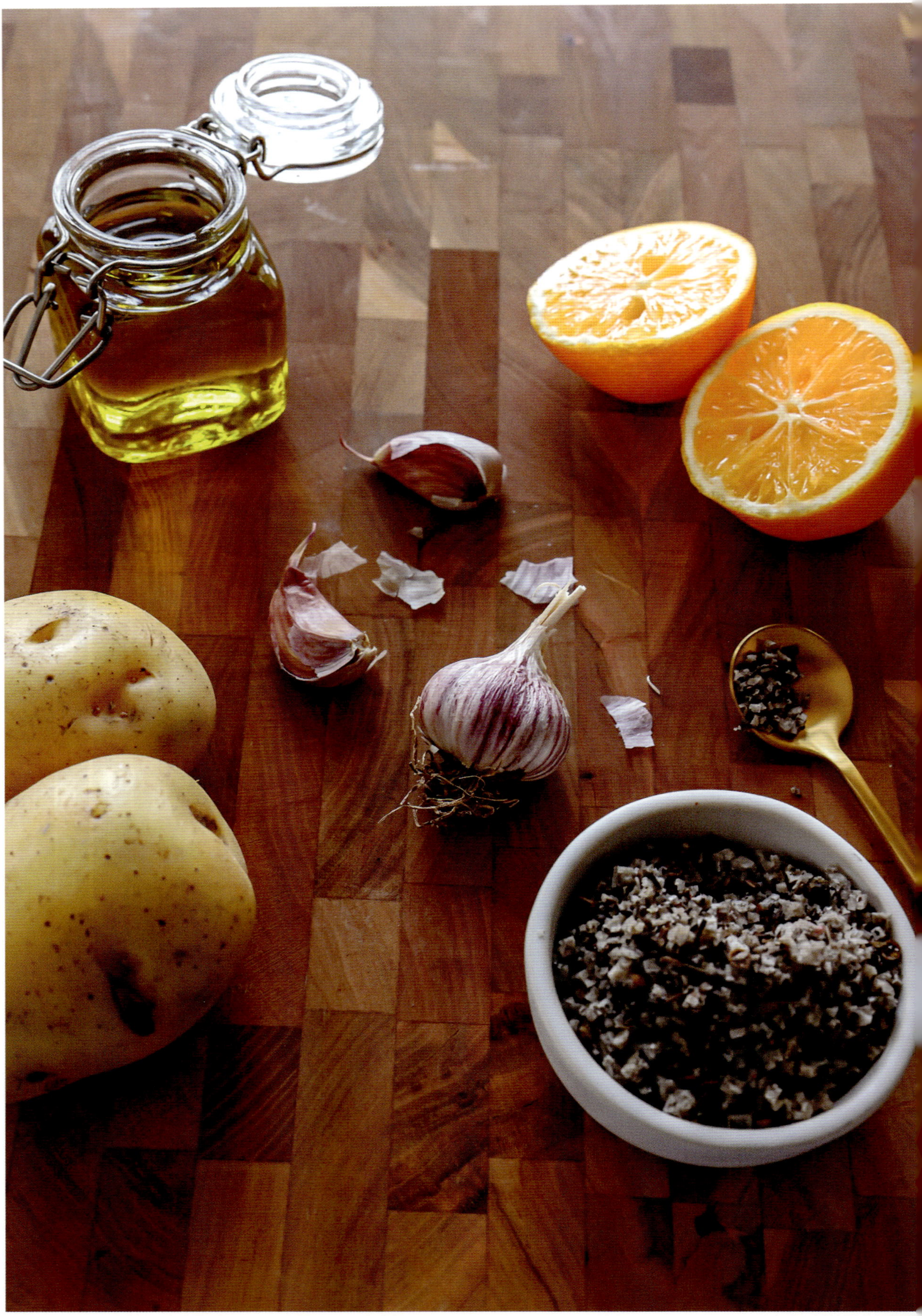

Almond Potato Dip

(Skordalia, Skorthalia, or Tarator)

Cyprus, Greece, and Turkey

Makes 3 cups

Skordalia is the classic spread of nuts and oils, bread and vinegar. It's derivative of the bread soups favored by the ancient prophets and philosophers. Nuts—almonds or walnuts—give the spread its depth. More recent versions replace bread with potatoes to make the spread especially smooth and glossy.

Serve it with toasted pita bread, veggies, and as a side dish to roast meat. It's very assertive and rich, and a little goes a long way.

2 russet potatoes, peeled and cut into 1-inch (2.5 cm) cubes
Coarse salt
½ cup (85 g) whole blanched almonds
6 garlic cloves
2 tablespoons cold water, plus more as needed
⅓ cup (80 ml) white wine vinegar
⅔ cup (160 ml) extra-virgin olive oil
Minced fresh flat-leaf parsley for garnish
Warm pita bread for serving

Preheat the oven to 350°F (180°C). Line a baking sheet with parchment paper.

Rinse the potatoes in a colander under cold running water. Transfer to a medium pot and add enough water to cover the potatoes by 2 inches (5 cm) along with a generous pinch of salt.

Set the pot over high heat, bring to a boil, reduce the heat to medium-low, and simmer until a knife slides easily through the potatoes without resistance, about 15 minutes. Drain in the colander, then rinse with hot water.

In a food processor, pulse together the almonds, garlic, cold water, and vinegar until the garlic and almonds become a paste. Season with salt.

Spread the potatoes out on the prepared baking sheet and bake until any excess moisture has evaporated and the surface of the potatoes is dry and chalky, about 6 minutes.

Transfer the potatoes to a bowl and mash. Stir in the oil and almond-garlic mixture. If the mixture does not emulsify, stir in more water, 1 tablespoon at a time, beating well until smooth. Season with salt and garnish with the parsley. Serve with the pita bread.

Red Pepper and Walnut Dip
(Acuka, Muhammara)

Jordan, Lebanon, Palestine, Syria, and Turkey

Makes about 2 cups

This robust puree of roasted red bell peppers, chiles, cumin, rose water, and nuts makes a terrific dip, and it is also wonderful drizzled over scrambled eggs and roast meats.

- 2 pounds (1 kg) red bell peppers or pimentos, halved and seeded
- 2 cups (226 g) lightly toasted walnuts or hazelnuts, plus more for garnish
- 1 teaspoon ground cumin
- 1½ cups (168 g) toasted breadcrumbs or cracker crumbs
- 1 tablespoon smoked Aleppo pepper paste or powder
- Juice of 2 lemons
- 2 teaspoons tahini
- 1 teaspoon honey, preferably dark
- 2 tablespoons pomegranate molasses
- 2 tablespoons rose water
- 1 cup (240 ml) extra-virgin olive oil
- 1½ teaspoons fine sea salt, or more to taste
- Chopped fresh spearmint

Preheat the broiler to high. Line a baking sheet with aluminum foil.

Set the peppers cut side down on the prepared baking sheet and broil until the skins are well charred, 5 to 8 minutes. Transfer the peppers to a large bowl, cover, and cool to room temperature. Holding the peppers over the bowl, peel away the charred skin of the peppers, capturing their juices in the bowl.

Transfer the peppers with their juices to a food processor and add the walnuts, cumin, breadcrumbs, pepper paste, lemon juice, tahini, honey, pomegranate molasses, rose water, oil, and salt. Pulse the ingredients together, scraping down the sides of the bowl as needed, then process to a rough puree. Transfer to a serving bowl and garnish with the mint. Store extra in a covered container in the refrigerator for up to 2 weeks.

Kitchen Note
Chock-full of antioxidants and nutrients, rose water has long been prized for its medicinal and therapeutic benefits, as well as its lovely flavor. It's a breeze to make. Place 3 cups of clean, fresh rose petals in a large pot and add enough water to cover the petals by about 5 inches (12.5 cm). Place the pot over low heat, cover, and simmer until the petals lose their flavor, 30 to 35 minutes. Remove from the heat and allow the liquid to come to room temperature. Strain into a covered container, discarding the petals, and store in the refrigerator up to 2 weeks.

Black Chickpea, Black Sesame, and Black Garlic Dip
(Hummus bi Tahini Al-Sawda)

Israel, Jordan, Lebanon, Palestine, and Syria

Makes about 3 cups

The black chickpeas and black sesame seeds of the Arab world make a stunning hummus. Charring the garlic over a flame or under the broiler helps to temper its bite. Finish the hummus with a drizzle of black nigella oil and a sprinkle of red sumac for a glorious presentation. No more ho-hum hummus!

1½ cups (340 g) dried black chickpeas, sorted
1 tablespoon baking soda
⅔ cup (95 g) black sesame seeds, ground
2 tablespoons lemon zest
⅓ cup (80 ml) fresh lemon juice
2 charred garlic cloves (see Notes)
⅓ cup (80 ml) extra-virgin olive oil, plus more for garnish (optional)
1½ teaspoons honey, preferably mesquite honey or any light, flowery honey
1 teaspoon ground cumin
1 teaspoon ground coriander
1 teaspoon coarse salt or kosher salt, plus more as needed
Black nigella oil for garnish
2 tablespoons sumac for garnish
1 handful pomegranate seeds for garnish

Put the chickpeas in a large bowl or pot and add enough water to cover by about 4 inches (10 cm). Stir in the baking soda and allow to stand 8 to 10 hours. Drain in a colander and run under cold water. Return to a large pot and add enough water to cover by 4 inches (10 cm). Set over high heat and bring to a boil. Reduce the heat and simmer until the chickpeas are very tender, 45 minutes to 1 hour. Drain.

Transfer the chickpeas to a food processor or blender and add the sesame seeds, lemon zest and juice, and garlic. Pulse the ingredients together. With the motor running, slowly drizzle in the olive oil and process until smooth. Taste and pulse in the honey, cumin, coriander, and salt.

Transfer the hummus to a serving bowl, drizzle with a swirl of nigella oil or olive oil, and serve garnished with the sumac and pomegranate seeds.

Kitchen Notes
To char the garlic, using tongs, hold the unpeeled garlic cloves over a flame, turning until nicely charred, 1 to 2 minutes. Remove the peels. Alternatively, lay the unpeeled garlic cloves on a sheet pan and broil until charred, 3 to 5 minutes, turning occasionally, then remove the peels.

Find black chickpeas, black sesame seeds, and black nigella oil in specialty shops, natural foods stores, or online.

Fire-Roasted Eggplant Dip
(Baba Ghanoush)

Jordan, Lebanon, Palestine, and Syria

Makes about 2½ cups

Baba ghanoush is a baba's (aka Lebanese grandfather's) favorite dip. It is often mistakenly compared to mutabbal. Both rely on roasted eggplant as the primary ingredient, but the difference is that mutabbal contains tahini, whereas baba ghanoush does not.

1 large eggplant or 2 smaller eggplants
½ to 1 teaspoon sea salt
2 garlic cloves, smashed
Juice of 1 medium lemon
2 tablespoons extra-virgin olive oil
Generous pinch ground cumin
Pinch Aleppo pepper
1½ to 2 tablespoons pomegranate molasses
Pomegranate seeds for garnish

Prepare a charcoal or wood-fired grill or preheat the broiler. Pierce the eggplant all over with the point of a sharp knife. Place the eggplant 2 or 3 inches (5 or 7.5 cm) from the heat and roast, allowing the skin to char and turning with tongs until the entire surface is blackened and the eggplant is very tender and has collapsed, about 20 minutes. Set aside to cool.

To remove the eggplant skin, slice the eggplant in half lengthwise and lay, skin side down, on a cutting board. Using a spoon, scrape away the flesh and transfer to a colander. Discard the burned skin (it's okay if a little of the skin remains on the eggplant flesh). Lightly salt the eggplant and leave to drip for about 10 minutes, then squeeze out the remaining juice by pressing with a large spoon.

Transfer the eggplant to a large bowl and, using a large spoon or whisk, beat in the garlic, lemon juice, oil, cumin, Aleppo pepper, and molasses. Season to taste and serve garnished with the pomegranate seeds.

Cilantro-Pistachio Pesto
(Pesto de Pistache y Cilantro)

Italy and Mexico

Makes about 1½ cups

The term *pesto* comes from the Genovese dialect of Italian and means "to crush, pulverize, or pound." It is the Mediterranean equivalent of Mexican moles made by pounding seeds or oils, greens, and spices into a thick creamy sauce. Here we use pistachios, a major crop in the Middle East, grown in the area between the Sonoran and Chihuahuan Deserts, near Gary's home. Cilantro grows nearby throughout the year. These two key ingredients bridge the Old World and New World deserts.

Try this with our Chickpea Flour Crepes (page 60). Store in a covered container in the refrigerator for up to a week.

Zest of 1 large lemon
½ cup (8 g) packed cilantro leaves
½ cup (8 g) packed parsley leaves, plus more for garnish
½ cup (120 ml) extra-virgin olive oil
½ cup (60 g) shelled raw pistachios
2 garlic cloves, smashed
½ teaspoon coarse salt, or more to taste
Generous pinch freshly ground black pepper

Put the lemon zest, cilantro, parsley, oil, pistachios, garlic, salt, and pepper into a food processor. Pulse until well combined. Season to taste.

Tomatillo with Prickly Pear Sauce
(Salsa Verde con Nopalitos)

Mexico and US Desert Southwest

Makes 2 cups

This salsa, or mojo verde, is amazingly versatile. Keep a batch in the fridge for dunking chips and drizzling over grilled chicken and lamb. Nopalitos, or prickly pears, are not just cultivated in Mexico, they are major crops in the Canaries, Morocco, and islands of the Mediterranean. Serve hot on the Sonoran Blue Corn Enchiladas (page 56) or serve chilled as a dip.

1 pound (454 g) tomatillos (about 8), husked and rinsed
4 large garlic cloves, unpeeled
1 serrano chile
1 small onion, cut into 1-inch (2.5 cm) chunks
Pinch sea salt
1 cup (240 ml) chicken broth
1 cup (113 g) diced nopalitos

Line a rimmed baking sheet with aluminum foil and preheat the broiler to high.

Spread out the tomatillos, garlic, serrano, and onions on the prepared baking sheet. Slide under the broiler 1 to 2 inches (2.5 to 5 cm) from the flame. When everything is blotchy-black and softening, turn the vegetables and roast on the other side until everything is charred, soft, and cooked through, 3 to 5 minutes. Remove and allow to cool.

Slip the skins off the garlic and pull the stem from the chile. Put them, along with the tomatillos and juices, into a blender. Season with salt and puree.

Transfer the puree to a saucepan and add the broth and nopalitos. Bring to a boil, reduce the heat, and simmer until the nopalitos are tender and the sauce has reduced by half. (It should resemble a very thick spaghetti sauce.)

Aromatic Red Pepper Sauce
(Harissa, Harissa Arbi, Berbere)

Algeria, Israel, Libya, Morocco, and Tunisia

Makes 1½ to 2 cups

This bold piquant sauce is served throughout Marrakech, Essaouira, and elsewhere in Morocco. It's similar to the mojo picón sauces of Lanzarote and the other Canary Islands, and it is close to the adobos, recaudos, and moles of Mexico.

The name *harissa* is derived from the Arabic term meaning "to crush, grind, mash into a puree." Just a dab will punch up soups, sauces, and marinades. Thin it with a little oil and drizzle over grilled meat and vegetables. Store it in a covered container in the refrigerator for up to a month.

2 ounces (57 g) dried red chile (ancho or nora), stemmed and seeded
1 red bell pepper or pimento pepper
1 tablespoon tomato paste
2 teaspoons fresh lime juice, or more to taste
Coarse salt
1 cup (240 ml) extra-virgin olive oil, plus more as needed
2 teaspoons ground coriander
2 teaspoons ground cumin
1 teaspoon ground fennel
½ teaspoon ground caraway
3 garlic cloves, smashed
1 tablespoon rose water
Cayenne pepper

Preheat the oven to 350°F (180°C). Spread the dried chiles out on a rimmed baking sheet and toast until they begin to curl at the edges, 3 to 5 minutes. Transfer to a medium bowl and add enough water to cover the chiles by about 1 inch (2.5 cm). Rehydrate for 20 minutes.

Turn the oven to broil. Line a rimmed baking sheet with parchment paper. Roast the bell pepper on the prepared pan, shaking occasionally, until all sides are blistered, 10 to 15 minutes. Transfer to a paper bag to steam for about 20 minutes. Scrape the charred skin from the pepper and remove and discard the seeds and stem.

Drain the chiles and transfer to a blender along with the roasted bell pepper, tomato paste, lime juice, a generous pinch of salt, and ½ cup (120 ml) of the oil. Pulse together then add the coriander, cumin, fennel, caraway, garlic, rose water, and a little more of the oil, about 1 teaspoon at a time, to make a creamy sauce. Add the cayenne to taste and adjust the seasoning. Transfer to a glass jar with a lid and cover with the remaining oil. Store in the refrigerator up to 2 weeks.

Green Chile Dipping Sauce
(Mojo or Molho Verde)
Canary Islands, Latin America, and Portugal

Makes 2½ to 3 cups

The Spanish mojo or Portuguese molho originated in the Canary Islands during the Columbian Exchange (1492 to 1640) and spread rapidly to the Caribbean and Latin America. Mojo verde (green) and mojo rojo (red) or mojo picón (spicy) sauces are a fragrant blend of garlic, fresh herbs, and chiles with a snap of vinegar.

This versatile Canary Island version of mojo verde sauce is quite different from the mojos in Cuba and Puerto Rico. On Lanzarote in the Canary Islands, it's served in the seaside cafés in Puerto del Carmen as well as on the lovely and quieter Costa Teguise side of this volcanic island. Mojo verdes made with Canarian-grown ingredients exposed to high midday heat and salty soils are especially sharp and bright. This sauce is a taste of the desert seacoasts—briny with wave after wave of fragrances. The balanced blend of cilantro, garlic, chiles, vinegar, and salt lifts up everything on a plate, from scrambled eggs to wrinkled potatoes.

2 cups (120 g) green pimento peppers, seeded and roughly chopped

4 to 6 green tomatillos, minced, or Cape gooseberries (aka golden berries)

½ cup (30 g) finely minced cilantro, plus more for garnish

3 charred garlic cloves, (see page 43), minced

1⅓ teaspoons sea salt

½ teaspoon ground cumin

1 tablespoon sweet paprika

5 tablespoons sherry vinegar or sour (Seville) orange juice

3 tablespoons extra-virgin olive oil or argan oil

½ cup (56 g) toasted breadcrumbs

2 to 4 tablespoons water

In a food processor or large mortar, combine the peppers, tomatillos, cilantro, and garlic. Pulse or mash in the salt, cumin, and paprika. Work in the vinegar and oil, then work in the breadcrumbs and water, pulsing or mashing to create a blended rough sauce. Refrigerate, covered, for at least 30 minutes before serving.

Cilantro, Ginger, and Date Chutney
(Dhania Chutney)

Egypt and India

Makes about 1 cup

This vivid green chutney combines plenty of cilantro with fresh ginger, cumin, and jalapeño, along with sweet dates and tangy lime. Inspired by the sauces of medieval Persia, it's delightful with roast lamb, goat, and chicken, and brightens rice, fish, and vegetable dishes. Swirl it into yogurt for a dipping sauce.

3 cups (180 g) chopped cilantro
5 dates, pitted
2 tablespoons chopped basil
1 jalapeño pepper, seeded and diced
2 large garlic cloves, smashed
1 tablespoon fresh lime juice, or more to taste
2 teaspoons freshly grated ginger
1 teaspoon ground cumin
Generous pinch sea salt, plus more as needed

Put all the ingredients into a food processor and pulse until finely chopped. Season with more lime juice or salt as needed. Transfer to a bowl, cover, and refrigerate for about 30 minutes so the flavors marry before serving. Store in a covered container for up to 2 days.

Fig and Pomegranate Jam
(M'rabbah al Teen)

Lebanon and US Desert Southwest

Makes 1 cup

When Catholic priests from southern Europe, North Africa, and the Canaries arrived in the US Southwest, they brought with them cuttings of pomegranates and figs that the desert peoples of Arizona quickly adopted. The Tohono O'odham Indianized their Mozarabic names, so that pomegranate became known as *galniyu* (from the Spanish term *granada*), and figs became known as *suuna*, which was derived from the term for olive in Spanish (*aceituna*) and in Arabic (*zaytun*). Along with date palms, these two tree crops (pomegranates and figs) are the most heat- and salt-tolerant crops of desert coastal and oasis areas.

7 ounces (198 g) figs, stemmed and sliced
½ cup (120 ml) unsweetened pomegranate juice
1 tablespoon fresh lemon juice
1 tablespoon pomegranate molasses, or more to taste
1 small jalapeño pepper, seeded and diced
Pinch coarse salt
Pinch red pepper flakes

Put the figs into a medium bowl and cover with boiling water. Allow to stand until plump, about 15 minutes. Drain the figs and transfer to a food processor along with the pomegranate juice, lemon juice, pomegranate molasses, jalapeño, salt, and red pepper flakes. Process into a thick puree, scraping down the sides of the bowl as necessary.

Transfer the fig mixture to a 10-inch (25 cm) skillet and set over high heat. Bring to a boil, reduce the heat, and simmer, stirring often to reduce the jam, until a rubber spatula leaves a trail when dragged across the bottom of the skillet, 3 to 5 minutes. Allow to cool to room temperature before using. Store in the refrigerator for up to 2 weeks.

Preserved Lemons
(Achar, Leems, Limoo Omani, Oorga)

India, Iran, Morocco, and Oman

Makes a 24-ounce jar

Preserved lemons and limes are key ingredients for cooks in the cultures of North Africa and Asia. The method preserves the abundant citrus harvest while providing a fabulous condiment, especially for tagines. These lemons are as bright as they are versatile, perking up fish, potatoes, salads, soups, and vinaigrettes.

6 lemons
1 cup (128 g) coarse salt
1 cinnamon stick
3 bay leaves
1 teaspoon cardamom pods
1 teaspoon whole peppercorns

Have ready a clean 24-ounce mason jar and lid. Wash and cut the lemons into 6 to 8 wedges each. Place the lemons and the rest of the ingredients in a large bowl and mix well. Pack into the mason jar, pushing the ingredients down to be sure they reach the bottom of the jar.

Put the lid on the jar and place in the refrigerator. Allow the lemons to marinate for 2 weeks before using. Store in the refrigerator for up to 3 months.

Dips and Sauces

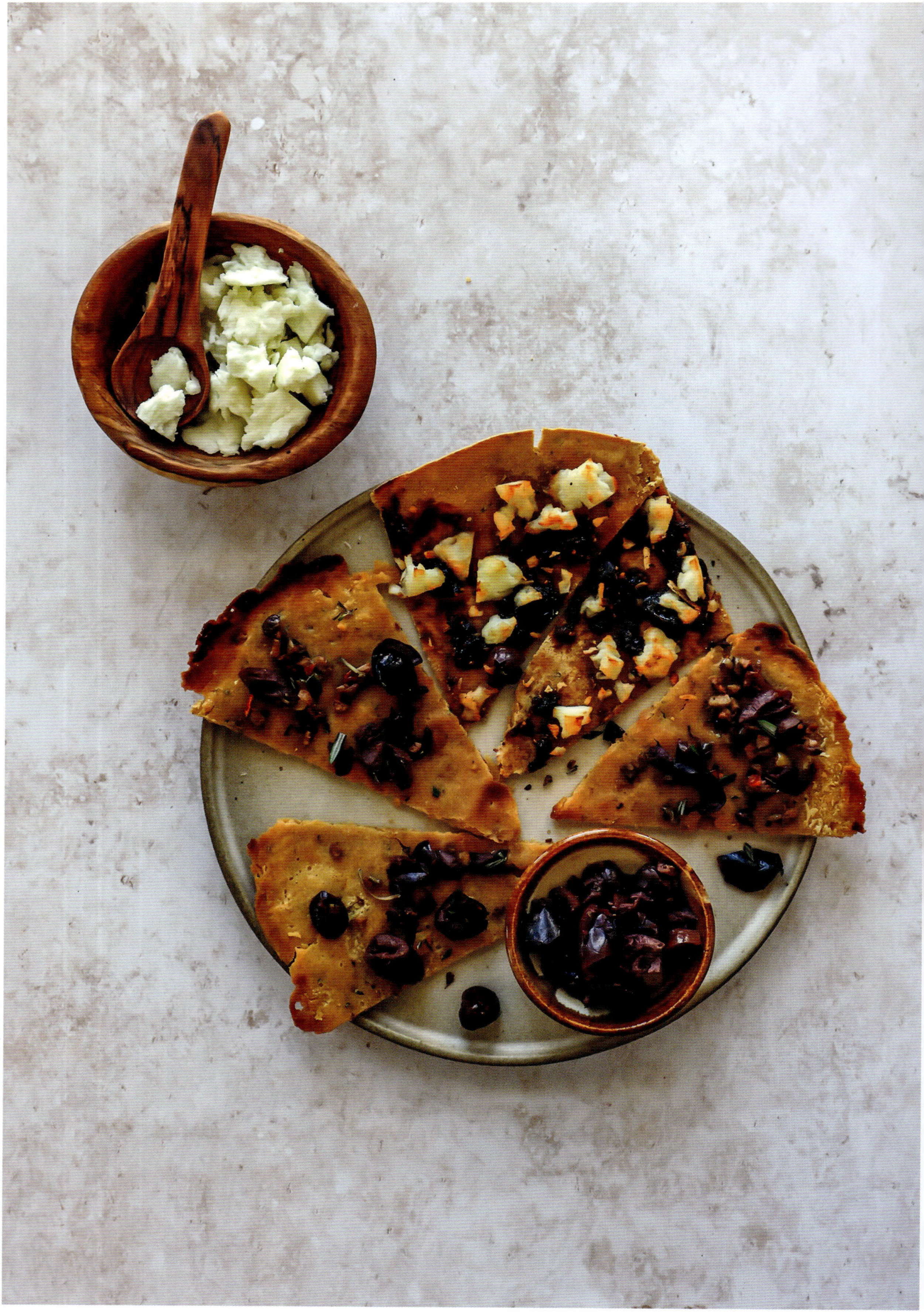

Chapter 9
Light Fare, Small Plates

Appetizers, meze, tapas . . . whatever the name, these small plates symbolize hospitality. Every culture has a unique collection of dishes to share. Here are our favorite savory bites to enjoy before a meal. Serve three or four together for a vibrant lunch or dinner.

Sweet, Salty, Spicy Nuts, Fruit, and Seeds	54
Blistered Padrón Peppers	55
Sonoran Flat Enchiladas	56
Citrus-Marinated White Fish	57
Chicken-Stuffed Figs in Tamarind Sauce	58
Chickpea Flour Crepes	60
Stuffed Grape Leaves with Lemon Sauce	62
Eggplant Fries with Desert Syrup	65
Sweet Potato Fries	67
Pan-Fried Okra and Calamari	68
Quince with Aromatic Turkey Stuffing	70
Stuffed Squash Blossoms	71
Savory Pies of Wild Greens and Feta	72
Sun-Dried Desert Squash, Tomato, Pepper, and Apricot Sauté	74

Sweet, Salty, Spicy Nuts, Fruit, and Seeds
(Bzourat, Bzoorat Makhlouta)

Lebanon and Syria

Makes 2 cups

Mixed fruit and nuts are served with cocktails from Damascus to Istanbul, and across the Chihuahuan and Sonoran Deserts. Years ago, they nourished crypto-Jews and crypto-Muslim spice traders during the Spanish Inquisition. Later, they were a staple food for the Syrian and Lebanese refugees who landed in the ports of Veracruz and Yucatán in Mexico before moving north to drier lands that felt more familiar.

2 teaspoons cumin seeds
2 teaspoons coriander seeds
2 tablespoons extra-virgin olive oil
2 tablespoons honey
2 tablespoons water
1 teaspoon Aleppo pepper or other chile flakes
½ teaspoon ground turmeric
1 cup (142 g) raw almonds
1 cup (113 g) raw cashews
¼ cup (32 g) raw pumpkin seeds
¼ cup (35 g) raw sunflower seeds
1 teaspoon flaky salt

Preheat the oven to 320°F (160°C). Line a baking sheet with parchment paper.

Set a heavy small nonstick skillet over medium heat and add the cumin and coriander seeds. Toast, stirring, until the seeds are fragrant, about 30 seconds.

Whisk in the oil, honey and water, then add the Aleppo pepper and turmeric. Cook until the mixture bubbles and thickens, about 3 minutes. Add the nuts and seeds and mix well. Remove from the heat and spread the mixture over the prepared baking sheet. Sprinkle with the salt.

Bake until golden, 12 to 15 minutes. Allow to cool, then break up into clusters and store in a covered container until ready to serve.

Blistered Padrón Peppers
(Pimientos de Padrón Asados, Chiles Toreados)

Mexico and US Desert Southwest

Serves 4 to 6

Known as pimientos de Padrón, these small green peppers—native to Galicia, Spain—are mild and tangy, and are a hit on the tapas circuit. Similar to the shishito ("lion") peppers of Japan, these are fabulous when charred and sprinkled with flaky salt. You might also dust them with smoked paprika or sumac or grated cheese. Be warned that sometimes a hot pepper will sneak into a handful of tame peppers, as they look identical.

10 ounces (284 g) padrón or shishito peppers
1 tablespoon vegetable oil
Flaky salt

In a large bowl, toss the peppers with the oil. Heat a large heavy skillet over high heat until very hot. (A drop of water will dance on the surface.) Add the peppers in a single layer without touching and cook until blistered on all sides, 4 to 5 minutes, shaking the pan and turning the peppers occasionally. Season with the flaky salt and serve right away.

Sonoran Flat Enchiladas
(Enchiladas Chatas Sonorenses)

Mexico and US Desert Southwest

Makes about 18 (6 to 8 servings)

The hand-formed corn patties in Sonoran flat enchiladas are thicker than machine-pressed tortillas, and they do not stack or roll. These are made of nixtamalized corn and are closer to the cheese-filled gorditas of Michoacan in central Mexico and the arepas of Venezuela. The chubby patties are traditionally grilled on a comal, but a heavy cast-iron skillet works equally well. Serve with your favorite sauce.

2 pounds (907 g) fresh blue corn masa
1 teaspoon baking powder
2 teaspoons sea salt
2 tablespoons soft lard or olive oil
1 cup (114 g) grated queso fresco
Vegetable oil for frying

Line a baking sheet with parchment paper and preheat the oven to 250°F (120°C).

In a deep bowl, stir together the masa, baking powder, and salt, then work in the lard and the cheese. Knead the dough for a few minutes until fully combined. Using a tablespoon, scoop up the dough and shape into patties about ½ inch (1.25 cm) thick by about 3 inches (7.5 cm) around.

Pour about 2 inches (5 cm) of vegetable oil into a large skillet and set over high heat. When the oil reaches 350°F (180°C), slip a few patties into the pan, being careful not to crowd them. Fry until just brown on one side, 3 to 5 minutes, and then flip and continue frying on the second side until browned, another 3 to 5 minutes. Transfer to the prepared baking sheet and hold in the oven while continuing to fry the remaining enchiladas.

Kitchen Note
Blue cornmeal has a slightly sweeter, nuttier, and cornier flavor than the more familiar yellow or white cornmeal. It's ground from a heritage variety of Tarahumara blue corn, and it's higher in protein and nutrients.

Citrus-Marinated White Fish
(Asukkabag Ceviche, Escabeche, Iskebech, Sakbai, Sekba)

Chile, Colombia, Costa Rica, Ecuador, El Salvador, Guatemala, Honduras, Iran, Iraq, Mexico, Nicaragua, Panama, Peru, and US Desert Southwest

Serves 4 to 6

Sour oranges, aka Seville oranges, give this marinade a puckery kick. Sour oranges have thick, wrinkled skins and are the best choice for making orange marmalade. These oranges are available in Cuban and Caribbean specialty markets and some stores. Their sour juice can be replicated by mixing one part fresh orange juice with one part lime juice.

Ceviche is the technique of using acid—sour citrus juice or white wine vinegar—to "cook" raw fish and some meats. It was introduced to the West by Persian and Arab cooks. Preparing food without heat or smoke evolved throughout desert and tropical regions and is well suited to our fuel-short world.

1 pound (454 g) firm white-flesh fish (snapper, halibut, flounder, whitefish)
Coarse salt
½ cup (120 ml) sour orange juice or ¼ cup (60 ml) fresh lime juice mixed with ¼ cup (60 ml) fresh orange juice
Butter lettuce leaves
¼ cup (36 g) diced red onion
Lime wedges for garnish
½ to 1 small jalapeño pepper, seeded and finely diced, for garnish
Tortilla chips for serving

Cut the fish into 1-inch (2.5 cm) cubes and place in a large ceramic or glass bowl. Sprinkle with just a little salt, then toss with the sour orange juice. Cover with plastic wrap and press down so the fish is submerged. Refrigerate for 30 minutes.

Drain the fish in a colander and serve on lettuce leaves garnished with red onion, lime wedges, and jalapeño peppers. Serve with chips on the side.

> **Kitchen Notes**
> *Be sure to use a nonreactive (aka nonmetal) bowl. When acidic preparations, such as ceviche, are placed in a reactive bowl, the food can change color and take on a metallic taste after it's been sitting for a while. Ceramic or glass is best.*
>
> *In this recipe, you can also use albacore or sole.*
>
> *Be sure to remove the skin, bones, and bloodline from the fish before cutting.*

Chicken-Stuffed Figs in Tamarind Sauce
(Higo Relleno, Incir Tatlisi, Tarifi)

Israel, Jordan, Palestine, and Turkey

Makes 18 stuffed figs

Here, spiced chicken sausage is stuffed into figs and finished with tart-sweet tamarind sauce for a stunning first course or light meal. We have simplified this traditional recipe for the home cook. You can also try using either frankincense or myrrh in the stuffing. Both are dried resins noted for their fragrance and woodsy, slightly licorice notes. They're available in specialty shops and online (see Appendix II on page 183). Fresh figs, especially the big Smyrna variety, are ideal for stuffing, but dried and rehydrated figs will also work well.

18 large figs, fresh or dried
Extra-virgin olive oil
1 onion, finely chopped
1 pound (454 g) chicken sausage (preferably dark meat)
¼ teaspoon ground cardamom
⅛ teaspoon ground nutmeg
⅛ teaspoon freshly ground black pepper
Pinch ground cloves
Coarse salt
¼ cup (60 g) tamarind paste
3 tablespoons brown sugar
1 tablespoon fresh lemon juice
2 dried figs, diced
2 cups (480 ml) water
Pomegranate seeds for garnish

If using dried figs, rehydrate in boiling water (about 5 to 10 minutes), drain, and set aside. Split the figs down the center and open. With a small spoon, scoop out most of the flesh from each fig, leaving a thick shell for stuffing. Set aside the removed flesh and the fig shells.

Film a medium skillet with oil and sauté the onion and sausage, breaking up the sausage so that it crumbles and cooks through, 5 to 7 minutes. Season with the cardamom, nutmeg, pepper, cloves, and salt to taste.

In a small bowl, stir together the tamarind paste, brown sugar, lemon juice, reserved fig flesh, diced figs, and ½ cup (120 ml) of the water. Transfer to a large pot and set over medium-low heat, adding about 1 cup (240 ml) and stirring to make a sauce thick enough to lightly coat the back of a spoon. Keep warm while you stuff the figs.

Fill each of the fig shells with the sausage mixture and close the slit over the stuffing so that the sausage doesn't show. Use a toothpick to secure the figs closed. Place the figs in the pot with the sauce, cover, and simmer until the sauce has thickened and the figs appear glazed and shiny, 15 to 20 minutes. Serve garnished with pomegranate seeds.

> **Kitchen Note**
> *Tamarind is a subtropical legume tree that yields a sticky, sweet fruit. Its name is derived from the Arabic **tamr hindi**, meaning "date of India."*

Chickpea Flour Crepes

(Cade, Cecina, Farinata di Ceci, Socca, Torta di Ceci)

Argentina, France, Italy, Turkey, and Uruguay

Serves 4 to 8

These big crepes with crisped edges and fluffy interiors originated in Genoa, Italy, where they're served as a snack with midmorning coffee. In villages across the Mediterranean, they're baked on a copper skillet in a wood-fired oven and then cut into triangles, rolled, and presented in a paper cone. They make wonderful appetizers and can be paired with a crisp sparkling wine, sherry, sangria, or an arak cocktail (see page 154). No copper or wood fire? No problem. These are easily made in a heavy skillet baked off in a hot oven. Try them with Cilantro-Pistachio Pesto (page 45), or serve with any of our dipping sauces (see Dips and Sauces, starting on page 35).

1 cup (85 g) chickpea flour
1 teaspoon sea salt
1 teaspoon freshly ground black pepper
1 cup (240 ml) lukewarm water
¼ cup (60 ml) extra-virgin olive oil, plus more for brushing
2 teaspoons finely chopped fresh rosemary

Place the chickpea flour, salt, and pepper into a medium bowl and whisk together. Slowly add the lukewarm water, whisking briskly to eliminate any lumps. Whisk in 2 tablespoons of the oil and the rosemary. Cover and let the batter rest for at least an hour or overnight (8 to 10 hours). (It will taste richer if it rests longer.) It should resemble heavy cream.

Preheat the oven to 450°F (230°C) and place a large heavy skillet in the oven to heat up. When the pan is hot, remove it from the oven and pour in the remaining 2 tablespoons oil; swirl it around to coat the pan. Immediately pour the batter into the pan and bake for 3 to 6 minutes until firm.

Set the oven to broil. Brush the pancake with a little oil and place under the broiler until the pancake has browned in several spots, 3 to 5 minutes. Remove and cut into wedges.

> **Kitchen Note**
> *Chickpeas, or garbanzos, are among the most drought-tolerant nitrogen-fixing legumes, and are sure to play an important role in the future of agriculture in desert regions. In Lebanon, chickpeas grow with wild wheat, oats, and barley not far from the birthplace of the poet Kahlil Gibran. Chickpea flour was brought into the Mediterranean countries of Europe by the Turkic-speaking Saracens. The light and frothy batter is quite like the injera bread made from Ethiopian millets.*

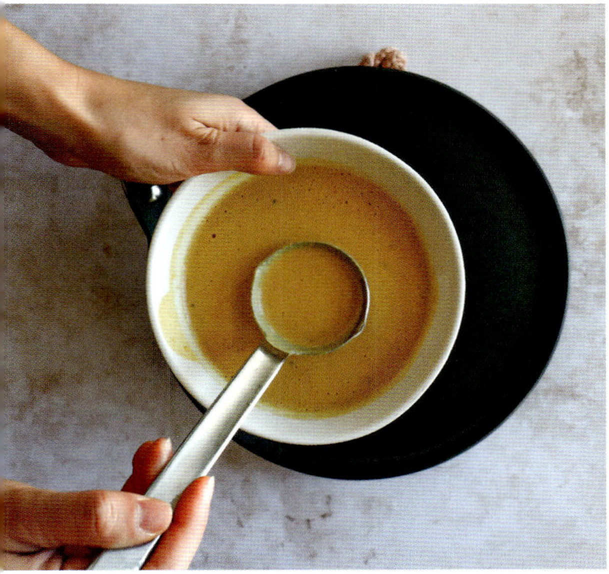
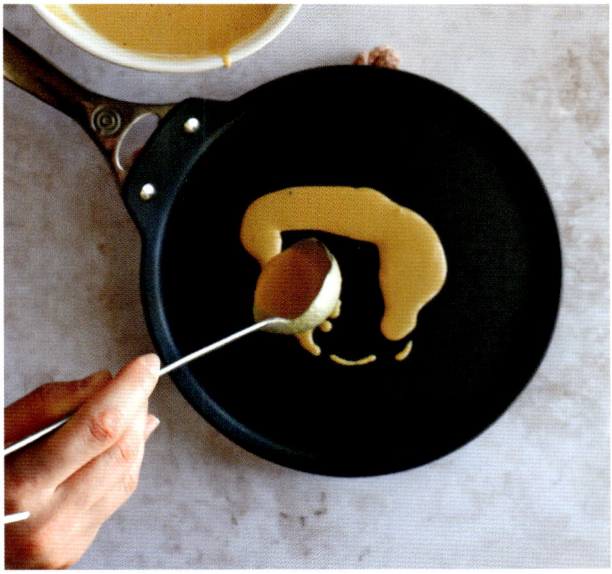
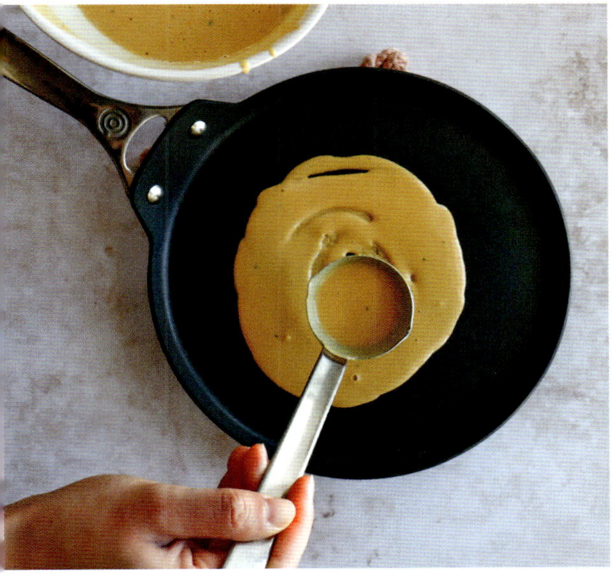
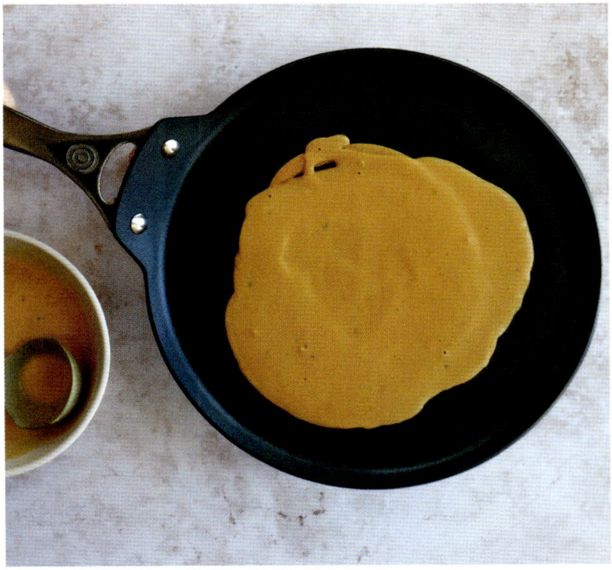
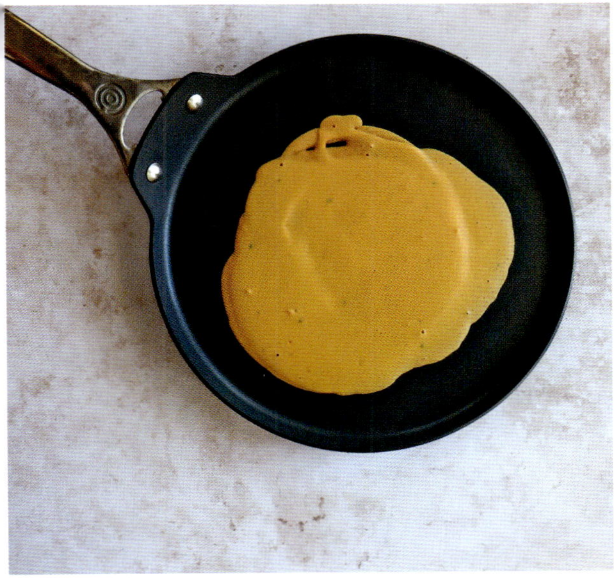
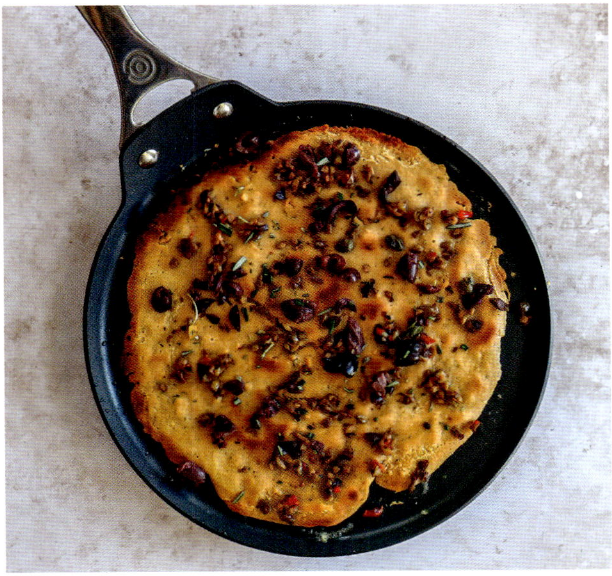

Stuffed Grape Leaves with Lemon Sauce
(Dolmadakia Avgolemono, Dolmas, Dolmades, Warak Enab, Yalanci Dolma)

Greece, Lebanon, Syria, and Turkey

Makes about 45 stuffed leaves

Gary recalls foraging with his grandfather Ferhat Nabhan and an Armenian friend, Mike, on the Indiana dunes, where wild grapes sprawled over the sand. Gary's Papa Ferhat looked for the "voluptuous" female grape leaves that were optimal for stuffing as *dolmades* (Greek) or *warak enab* (Arabic). They'd harvest over a thousand grape leaves for the Orthodox Church's women's auxiliary.

There are as many different recipes for stuffed grape leaves as there are good home cooks. Feel free to vary the seasonings. We like to serve these with avgolemono, which is a traditional lemony sauce. But if you're short on time, a thick Greek-style whole-milk yogurt also works well.

1 jar grape leaves in brine, or 45 fresh grape leaves, brined
Extra-virgin olive oil
1 small onion, chopped
1 garlic clove, smashed
½ teaspoon ground cumin
⅓ cup (66 g) long-grain rice
3 cups (720 ml) lamb, chicken, or vegetable stock
8 ounces (227 g) ground lamb
¼ cup (15 g) chopped fresh parsley
¼ cup (15 g) chopped fresh cilantro
1 tablespoon chopped fresh mint
1½ teaspoons coarse salt
Freshly ground black pepper
½ cup (85 g) raisins, plumped in warm water
¼ cup (36 g) pine nuts

Drain the grape leaves from the brine and rinse under cold running water. Set aside to dry.

Film a large Dutch oven or deep pot with oil and set over medium-high heat. Add the onion, garlic, and cumin and cook, stirring, until the onion is translucent, about 3 minutes. Stir in the rice and 1½ cups (360 ml) of the stock. Cover and continue cooking until the rice has absorbed the liquid, about 15 minutes. Stir in the lamb, parsley, cilantro, mint, salt, pepper to taste, and the raisins with their soaking water. Cook, stirring, for another 5 minutes. Transfer the mixture to a medium bowl and stir in the pine nuts. Wipe the pot clean.

Place 1 grape leaf with the rough side down on a work surface. Remove the stem with a small, sharp knife. Place 1 heaping tablespoon of the filling in the center of the leaf. Fold the sides to the center and then roll up. Place seam side down in the Dutch oven or deep pot. Repeat with the remaining rice mixture and leaves and stack the rolls on top of each other. Pour the remaining stock over the grape rolls, adding enough to cover the tops. Place a plate on top of the grape leaves to keep them from floating above the level of the liquid. Set the pot over high heat and bring the liquid to a boil. Cover, reduce the heat, and simmer for about 45 minutes until very tender.

To serve, use a slotted spoon to transfer the stuffed leaves to a serving bowl and drizzle with the Avgolemono Sauce (recipe follows).

Kitchen Note
To brine grape leaves, pack 45 leaves into a clean quart-sized jar with a lid. Dissolve 1 tablespoon kosher salt into 1 cup (240 ml) boiling water and pour over the leaves. Add more water as necessary to fully cover the leaves. Allow to come to room temperature. Cover and store in the refrigerator for at least 2 weeks before using and up to one year.

Avgolemono Sauce

Makes about 1½ cups (375 g)

This is the traditional sauce for stuffed grape leaves. Store any extra sauce in a covered container in the refrigerator for up to 3 days.

2 tablespoons fresh lemon juice
½ teaspoon all-purpose flour
2 large eggs, separated
Coarse salt
1 cup (240 ml) simmering chicken stock
Freshly ground black pepper

Fill the bottom of a double boiler one-third full of water and set over medium-high heat. Bring to a boil; reduce the heat to a slow simmer.

In a small bowl, whisk the lemon juice and flour until smooth, then whisk in the egg yolks until thoroughly combined. Set aside.

Using a steel whisk, whip the egg whites and a pinch of salt in the top of the double boiler until fluffy. Slowly drizzle the yolk mixture into the whipped egg whites, whisking constantly to maintain the volume. Place this over the simmering water and cook, whisking constantly, until the mixture is light, fluffy, and begins to thicken, about 4 minutes. Very slowly, whisk in the hot stock. Continue cooking and whisking for another 2 minutes to thicken. Taste and season with salt and pepper.

Eggplant Fries with Desert Syrup
(Berenjenas de la Abuela or Berenjenas Fritas con Miel del Datil)

Canary Islands, Morocco, and Spain

Serves 4

Inspired by the popular Spanish tapas, we oven-roast the eggplant to serve with honey or date syrup. These are ready in no time and must be served super hot!

Use the youngest, most tender eggplant in any of its many varieties—purple, reddish, yellow, or white. These were the primary nightshade fruits of desert regions; Spanish *berenjenas*, from the Arabic *batenjen*, came through the Mozarabic-speaking Morisco communities of southern Spain and traveled west to the New World, just as tomatoes and potatoes headed east to the Old World.

If you cannot find date palm syrup, drizzle these fries with prickly pear syrup or mesquite honey. You might also dip strips of zucchini and jicama in the same batter to fry and serve alongside.

It's a good idea to lightly salt the eggplant and drain before beginning. This removes much of the eggplant's moisture and bitterness.

---

2 eggplants, about 1/2 to 1 pound (227 to 454 g) each (the smaller the better)
1 tablespoon sea salt
2 cups (480 ml) sparkling water or beer
½ cup (43 g) chickpea or all-purpose flour
Date palm syrup or honey for drizzling
Coarse salt for finishing

Cut the eggplant into matchstick-thin slices. Sprinkle with the sea salt and set aside in a colander to drain, about 15 minutes.

Transfer the eggplant to a large bowl, add the sparkling water, and soak, covered, for about 30 minutes.

Drain the eggplant. Pat dry. Lightly coat with the flour, shaking off any excess.

Preheat the oven to 400°F (200°C). Line a baking sheet with parchment paper. Transfer the floured eggplant to the prepared baking sheet and roast, turning occasionally, until nicely browned and crisp, 20 to 30 minutes.

Serve immediately, drizzled with date syrup and sprinkled with coarse salt.

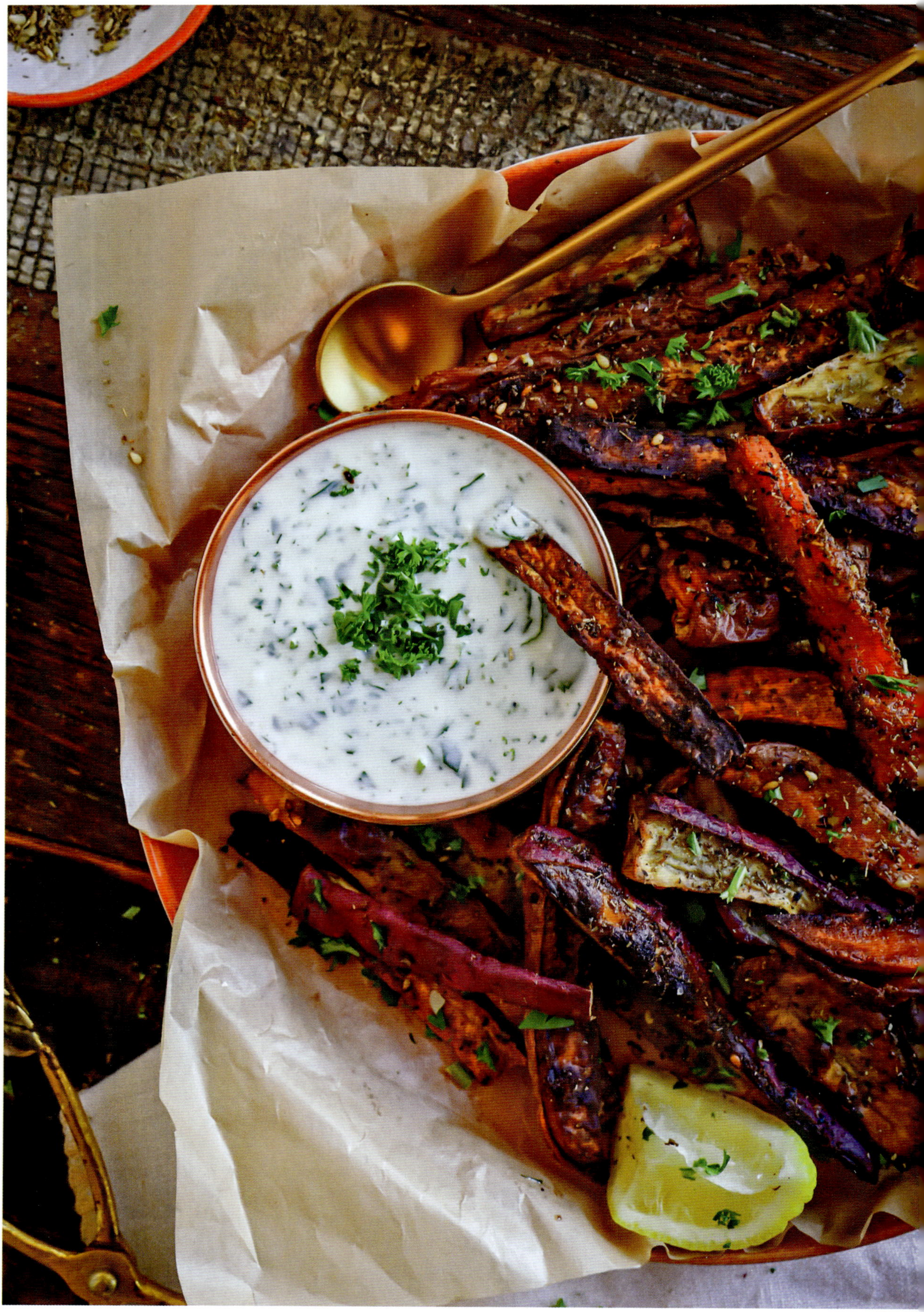

Sweet Potato Fries

(Batatas Fritas, Batata Harra)

Lebanon, Mexico, and Morocco

Serves 4

These oven-roasted sweet potato fries are coated in spices and garlic and finished with lime juice. They make a terrific snack or appetizer, and an excellent vegetarian filling for tacos and fajitas. Serve them with any of our dipping sauces (see page 35).

2 teaspoons ground cumin
2 teaspoons smoked paprika
1 teaspoon chile powder
Generous pinch coarse salt
2 garlic cloves, grated
3 tablespoons extra-virgin olive oil
Juice of 1 lime
1 large sweet potato, cut into ½-inch (1.25 cm) fingers

Preheat the oven to 425°F (220°C). Line a baking sheet with parchment paper.

In a large bowl, stir together the cumin, paprika, chile powder, salt, garlic, oil, and lime juice. Toss in the sweet potato fingers and, using your hands, stir to coat thoroughly.

Spread the sweet potatoes out on the prepared baking sheet making sure they do not touch. Roast until nicely browned and crisped, shaking the pan several times, about 20 minutes. Serve hot.

Light Fare, Small Plates

Pan-Fried Okra and Calamari
(Calamar Quimbombo Frito or Kurkuri Bhindi)
India and Mexico

Serves 6 to 8

Cooks who live along the desert coasts know a thing or two about transforming the humblest local ingredients into irresistible dishes. In these two short recipes, we dispense with heavy cornmeal batters and instead dust the ingredients with corn or mesquite flour to allow the beauty and taste of the key ingredients to shine through. Serve with Tzatziki (page 36), Tomatillo Sauce (page 46), or just a drizzle of fresh lemon juice.

Okra

1 cup (100 g) okra
Coarse salt
1 cup (120 g) corn flour, corn pinole, or corn mesquite flour
2 cups (480 ml) vegetable oil

Rinse the okra and set aside while still damp. Cut the okra crosswise into ½-inch (1.25 cm) pieces, season with salt, and transfer to a bowl. Pour the flour over the okra and toss to completely cover the pieces; they should be evenly and lightly coated.

Preheat the oven to 200°F (95°C) and place a baking sheet in the oven.

Pour the oil into a large skillet and set over medium-high heat until it shimmers. Drop a pinch of flour into the oil; when it's hot enough, it will sizzle.

Working in batches so as not to crowd the pan, carefully drop the okra into the oil. Cook, stirring occasionally, until golden and crisp, about 5 minutes. Using a slotted spoon, remove the okra to a paper towel–lined plate and repeat with the remaining okra. Transfer to the pan in the oven to keep warm until ready to serve.

Calamari

½ pound (227 g) calamari, rinsed and patted dry
1 lemon
½ cup (60 g) corn flour, corn pinole, or mesquite flour
Coarse salt
Freshly ground black pepper
1 cup (240 ml) vegetable oil, plus more as needed

Cut the calamari tentacles in half and the bodies into ¼-inch (.6 cm) rings. Slice the lemon lengthwise into quarters and then slice each quarter crosswise, discarding the seeds. In a wide, shallow bowl, whisk together the flour and the salt and pepper to taste. Dredge the calamari in the flour mixture.

Preheat the oven to 200°F (95°C) and place a baking sheet in the oven.

Pour the oil into a large, deep skillet and set over medium-high heat until it shimmers. Drop a pinch of flour into the oil; when it's hot enough, it will sizzle.

Working in batches so as not to crowd the pan, carefully drop the calamari pieces into the oil and cook, stirring occasionally, until golden and crisp, about 1 minute. Using a slotted spoon, remove the calamari to a paper towel–lined plate and repeat with the remaining calamari. Transfer to the pan in the oven to keep warm until ready to serve.

Light Fare, Small Plates

Quince with Aromatic Turkey Stuffing
(Dolmeh-'Ye Beh)

Iran, Iraq, and Turkey

Serves 4 to 6

This recipe for baked quince is inspired by the ancient Persian dish *dolmeh-'ye beh*. If quince is not available, substitute tart apples or semi-ripe pears. The dish may be assembled ahead, held in the refrigerator, and then baked off before serving.

4 medium quinces, halved
2 tablespoons olive oil
1 pound (454 g) ground turkey
2 small onions, chopped
2 garlic cloves, chopped
2 to 3 teaspoons Turkish Baharat (page 164)
Generous pinch red pepper flakes
Generous pinch coarse salt
Generous pinch freshly ground black pepper

Place the quinces in a medium pot and add enough water to cover by 1 inch (2.5 cm). Set over high heat, bring to a boil, reduce the heat, and simmer for 20 minutes. Drain and set aside to cool.

Film a large skillet with the oil, set over medium-high heat, and add the turkey, onion, garlic, and baharat, breaking up the turkey with a wooden spoon. Cook until the turkey is no longer pink, about 5 minutes.

Preheat the oven to 350°F (180°C). Cut the quinces in half lengthwise. Use a melon baller or small spoon to remove and discard the seeds and hollow out the quince halves so that you are left with a ⅔-inch (1.5 cm) shell. Set the scooped-out flesh in a medium bowl. Add the turkey mixture to the bowl and mix to combine. Season with the red pepper flakes, salt, and black pepper. Stuff each quince with the turkey mixture and place in a baking dish. Cover and bake for 15 to 20 minutes until very hot and tender.

Stuffed Squash Blossoms
(Flor de Calabazas en Frituras Rellenas)

Mexico

Serves 4 to 6

Desert dwellers in nearly every arid landscape use the big, bright flowers of squash and yucca in salads and sautés. When stuffed and then roasted, they make a wonderful appetizer or side dish. In this recipe, squash blossoms are filled with tangy goat cheese and creamy burrata. Serve the olive tapenade alongside.

1 cup (142 g) mixed black olives, chopped
3 anchovy fillets, chopped
1 large garlic clove, minced
1 teaspoon chopped fresh rosemary
1 teaspoon grated lemon zest
3 tablespoons extra-virgin olive oil, plus more for drizzling
12 squash or yucca blossoms
12 ounces (340 g) burrata or mozzarella, cut into 12 pieces
12 tablespoons chèvre
Coarse salt to finish

Preheat the oven to 350°F (180°C). Line a baking sheet with parchment paper.

Put the olives, anchovies, garlic, rosemary, and lemon zest into a food processor and pulse until coarsely chopped. Continue to pulse, while adding the oil, until you have a coarse puree.

Cut a slit into each squash blossom and spoon in 1 piece of the burrata, 1 tablespoon of the chèvre, and 1 teaspoon of the tapenade. Pinch the blossoms closed and arrange on the prepared baking sheet. Drizzle a little oil over the blossoms and roast until the cheese is melted (it may ooze a little), 10 to 15 minutes. Drizzle the blossoms with a little more oil and sprinkle with salt. Serve warm.

Savory Pie of Wild Greens and Feta
(Hortopita)
Crete, Cyprus, and Greece

Serves 4 to 6

In the spring all throughout Greece and its surrounding islands, villages and towns host festivals to celebrate local wild greens. The greens are baked into phyllo pies, called *hortopita*, which are different from the more familiar spanakopita made with cultivated spinach. The vibrant green, peppery filling is a fine match to salty, creamy feta. Nearly every desert culture enjoys hand pies of wild greens, whether baked in a flaky phyllo crust or a leavened dough of wheat, maize, or barley.

If you are lucky enough to forage wild amaranth, lambsquarters, nettles, purslane, or watercress, please toss these into the pie. But arugula, bergamot, dandelion greens, dill, fennel bulbs and fronds, summer savory, and radicchio work just as well.

Sea salt
1 pound (454 g) de-stemmed fresh wild greens such as amaranth, lambsquarters, nettles, purslane, or watercress
3 large eggs
4 ounces (113 g) chèvre
4 ounces (113 g) feta cheese
½ cup (120 ml) whole-milk Greek-style yogurt
2 garlic cloves, minced
½ cup (30 g) chopped fresh herbs such as bee balm, bergamot, dandelion greens, dill, fennel fronds and bulbs, or summer savory
Freshly ground black pepper
3 tablespoons extra-virgin olive oil, plus more as needed
10 sheets frozen phyllo dough, thawed

Bring a large pot of lightly salted water to a boil and blanch the greens for 30 seconds. Drain in a colander and press to squeeze out the excess water. Remove and chop fine; you should have about 1 cup.

Preheat the oven to 350°F (180°C). In a medium bowl, mix together the eggs and cheeses, then work in the yogurt and garlic. Stir in the greens, herbs, and salt and pepper to taste.

Brush a 9- or 10-inch (22 to 25 cm) tart pan with some of the oil and place on a baking sheet. Lay a sheet of the phyllo in the prepared pan, tucking it into the seam, with the edges overhanging the rim. Brush it with oil, then place another sheet on top so that the edges overlap another section of the pan's rim. Continue layering the remaining sheets, brushing each with oil both on the edges and seams and staggering them so that the overhang on the rim of the pan is distributed evenly and covers the whole pan.

Transfer the filling to the phyllo-lined pan. Fold the overhanging phyllo over the filling and brush again with oil. Bake until the phyllo is puffed and golden and the filling is bubbling beneath, 20 to 25 minutes. Remove and allow to sit for about 5 minutes before serving.

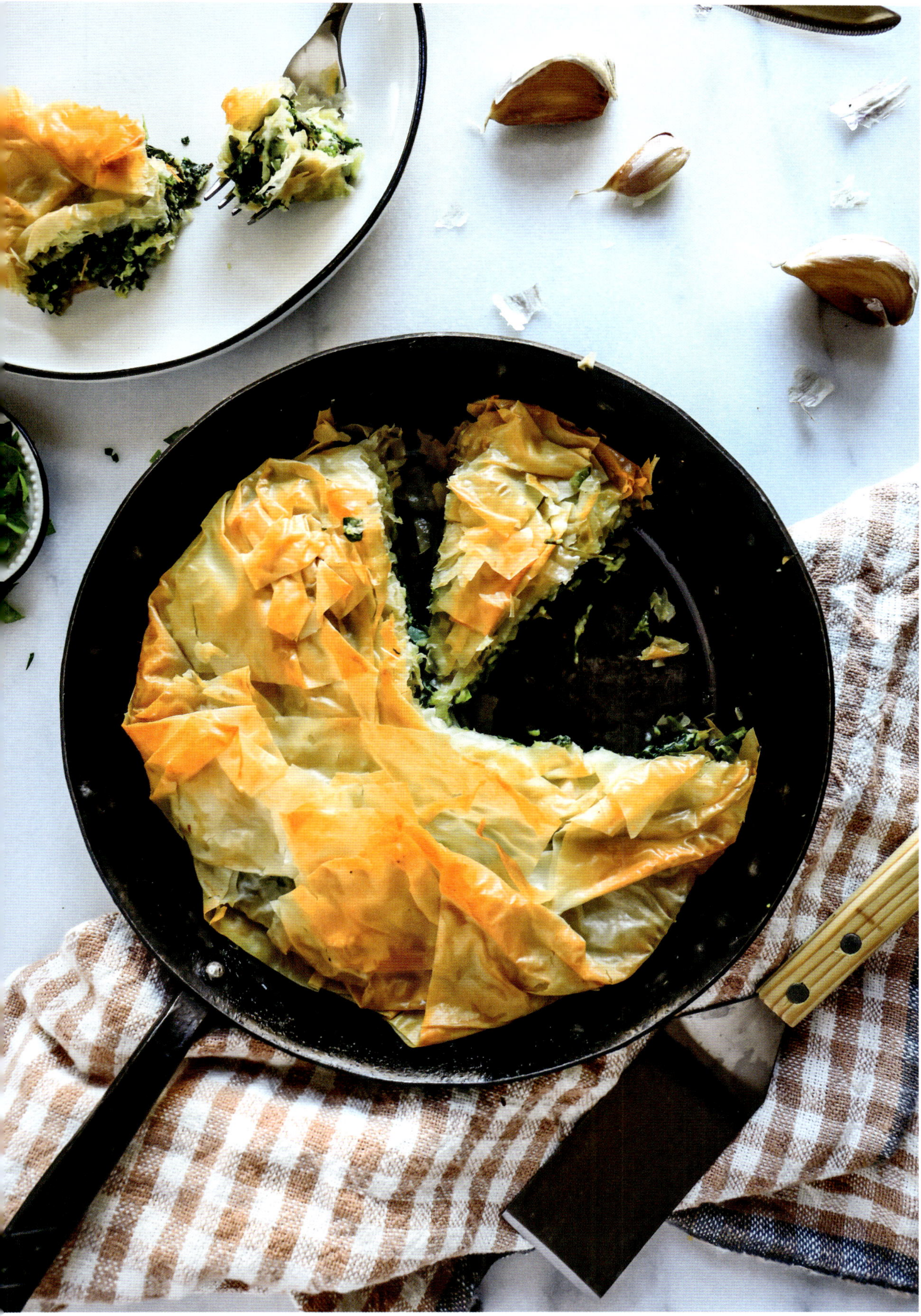

Sun-Dried Desert Squash, Tomato, Pepper, and Apricot Sauté
(Bichicoris)

Mexico and US Desert Southwest

Serves 4 to 6

This hearty sauté is popular throughout the desert areas of northern Mexico, especially the Sonoran Desert. We've adapted the original recipe that calls for sun-dried squash and tomatoes using fresh squash and a bounty of herbs and seasonings to reflect the intense flavors of the dried vegetables. We like to serve this dusted with salty cotija cheese for a hearty side dish, or as a satisfying entrée with a side of Blue Corn Bread (page 146).

1 cup (110 g) sun-dried tomatoes
1 cup (130 g) dried apricots
2 tablespoons extra-virgin olive oil
1 medium butternut or cushaw squash, peeled and seeded
1 small onion, diced
2 garlic cloves, smashed
1 red bell pepper, seeded and diced
1 teaspoon Mexican oregano, plus more as needed
Sea salt
Freshly ground black pepper
½ cup (64 g) crumbled semi-dry cotija cheese

Put the tomatoes and apricots in a large pot with enough water to cover by 1 inch (2.5 cm). Set over high heat, bring to a boil, reduce the heat, and simmer until the tomatoes and apricots become plump, about 10 minutes. Set aside.

Film a large skillet with the oil and set over medium heat. Add the squash, onion, garlic, and bell pepper and toss to coat with the oil. Cover, lower the heat, and cook until the vegetables release their juices and the squash begins to become tender, 5 to 8 minutes.

Remove the lid and add the apricots and tomatoes with their cooking liquid, the oregano, and salt and black pepper to taste. Simmer until the squash is tender all the way through, 10 to 15 minutes longer. Taste and adjust the seasonings. Sprinkle with the cheese and serve.

Kitchen Notes

Desert climes are ideal for sun-drying fruits and vegetables, preserving and intensifying their flavors and making them ready for transport and future dinners. In the Sonoran Desert and Sierra Madre regions, there is a long tradition of sun-drying squash, tomatoes, and peppers, among other fruits and vegetables. The Indigenous people of the region cut long, thin loops of squash to dry on a clothesline, called **bichicoris**, *a term that originated in the Yaqui or Cahitan language.* **Bichi** *refers to a thing stripped down, skinned, skinny, or naked.* **Cori** *refers to a chile or to the spiral string of sun-dried vegetables.*

While it may sound odd to hang fruits and vegetables on a clothesline to dry in the sun, the taste is unforgettable, as the vegetables become more of their flavorful selves. Give this a try, though your neighbors may give you a few strange looks.

The best squash for this dish are butternut or the green-striped cushaw. Cut loops of the squash and hang them over the clothesline in the sun on a hot day until they dry out. Depending on the level of humidity and the temperatures, this may take 10 to 15 hours. If using a dehydrator, peel and cut the squash into thin slices then arrange on the dehydrating racks and dry for 8 to 10 hours. When ready, the squash should feel dry and leathery to the touch. Store in an airtight container in a cool, dry place.

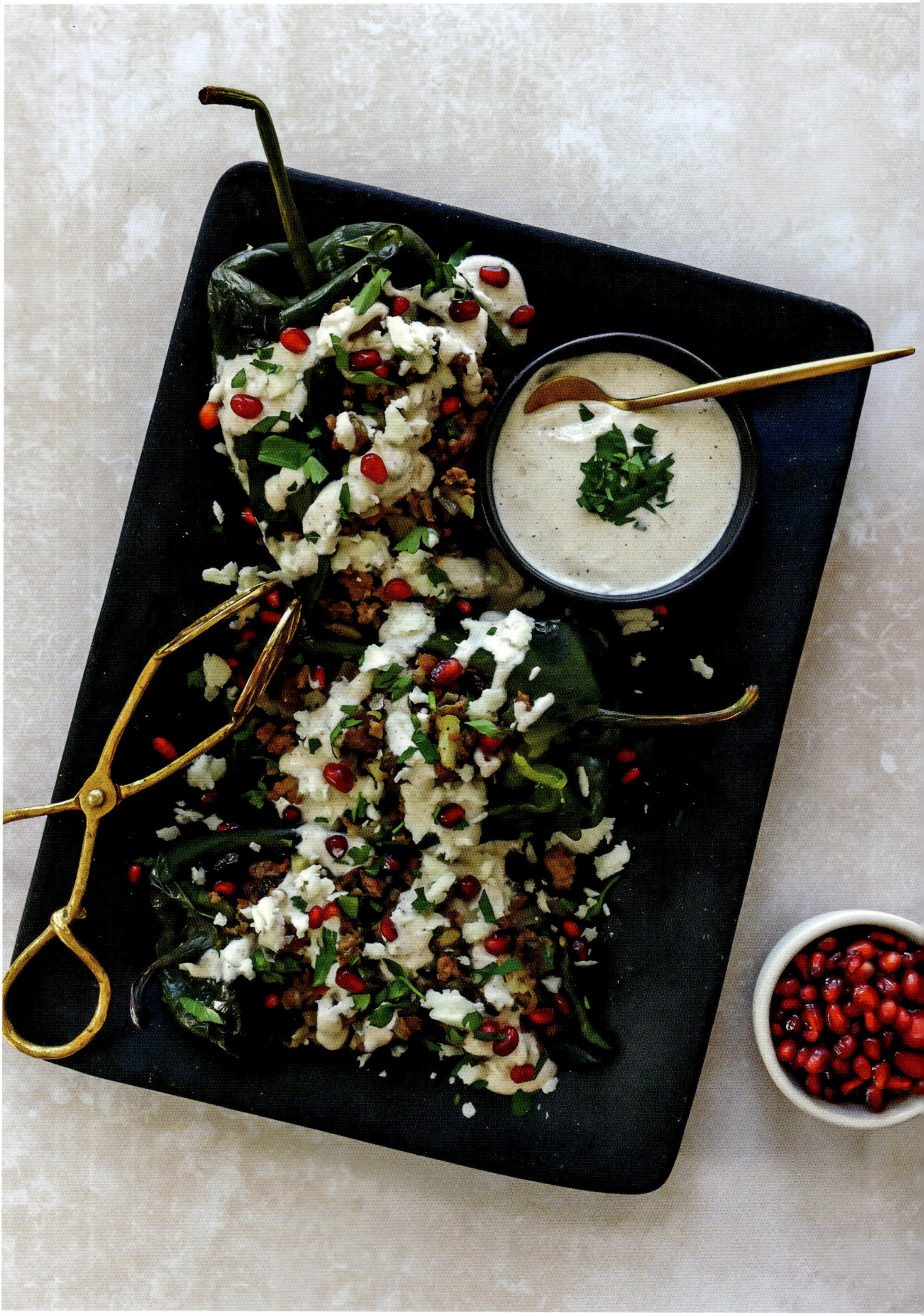

Chapter 10

Main Dishes

In desert countries, a main course is satisfying without being overwhelming, comforting yet not so rich as to weigh you down. It embraces all the bounty Mother Nature offers—lots of vegetables, local seafood, grass-fed meat, and wild game.

Tiny Lamb Meatballs in Hazelnut Sauce	78
Aromatic Lamb and Bulgur	80
Sheet Pan Chicken in a Spiced Nut Crust	81
Goat Tagine with Apricots, Pineapple, and Warm Spices	82
Sticky Lamb Ribs	84
Lamb Kebabs with Moroccan Spices and Pomegranate Molasses Glaze	86
Persian Duck in Tart Fruit Sauce	87
Upside-Down Rice, Vegetable, and Chicken Casserole	88
Spiced Orange Chicken	90
Roast Chicken with Tarragon and Capers	93
Stuffed Mexican Peppers in Yogurt Walnut Sauce	94
Tajín Grilled Chicken	96
Turkey in Pumpkin Seed Sauce	97
Turkey Tacos	98
Sea Scallops in Tamarind Glaze	100
Shrimp with Wild Sea Greens and Potatoes	101
Grilled Fisherman's Catch with Chermoula	102
Pan-Roasted Fish with Olive-Caper Relish	104
Borderland Ranch-Style Beans	105
Millet Polenta with Blistered Tomatoes	107
Spiced Red Lentils	108
Poached Eggs in Spicy Tomatoes	110

Tiny Lamb Meatballs in Hazelnut Sauce
(Al-Bunduq or Albondigas)

Jordan, Lebanon, Mexico, Spain, and US Desert Southwest

Serves 4 to 6

These tiny lamb meatballs are named for their resemblance to hazelnuts. The recipe celebrates the Middle Eastern origins of this dish and relies on a blend of fennel, coriander, and za'atar—desert seasonings that work beautifully with lamb. The meatballs are finished with a rich hazelnut sauce.

MEATBALLS

- 1 day-old white roll, about 3 inches (7.5 cm) round
- 1 cup (240 ml) whole milk
- 3 to 4 tablespoons clarified butter
- 1 shallot, finely chopped
- 1 large egg
- 1 pound (454 g) ground leg of lamb
- 2 tablespoons finely chopped fresh parsley
- 2 tablespoons green za'atar spice blend or Kamouneh (page 165)
- ½ tablespoon coarse sea salt
- 1 tablespoon ground coriander
- 1 teaspoon finely chopped fresh fennel fronds or ½ teaspoon fennel seeds
- Generous pinch freshly ground black pepper
- Panko breadcrumbs or dried ground pita breadcrumbs, if needed

To make the meatballs: In a medium bowl, soak the roll in the milk. Squeeze the roll to remove all the excess liquid. Discard the milk. Return the soaked roll to the bowl.

Film a large skillet with 1 tablespoon of the clarified butter and set over medium-low heat. Add the shallots and cook until translucent, 3 to 5 minutes.

Transfer the shallots to the bowl with the roll and add the egg, ground meat, parsley, za'atar, salt, coriander, fennel, and pepper. Stir to combine. If the mixture is too soft, add panko to reach the desired texture.

Using wet hands, shape the meatballs into small balls the size of hazelnuts. Add the remaining 2 to 3 tablespoons clarified butter to the skillet and set over medium heat. Fry the meatballs until nicely browned on the outside and no longer pink within, 4 to 6 minutes. You may need to work in batches so as not to crowd the pan. Set the cooked meatballs aside while making the sauce.

HAZELNUT SAUCE

1 cup (89 g) hazelnuts
2 slices white bread, crusts removed
¼ cup (58 g) tomato paste
2 tablespoons fresh lemon juice
¼ cup (60 ml) extra-virgin olive oil
1 cup (248 g) crème fraîche, Oaxacan crema, Jocoque, or Lebanese whole-milk yogurt
1 teaspoon mahlab cherry pit powder
2 garlic cloves
Up to 1 cup (240 ml) water

To make the hazelnut sauce: Put the hazelnuts in a dry pan set over high heat to toast, shaking the pan occasionally, until they smell nutty and are lightly browned, 3 to 5 minutes. Remove and set aside to cool. Transfer the hazelnuts to a food processor fitted with a steel blade and grind until smooth.

Soak the bread in enough water to moisten. Remove and squeeze out the liquid. Crumble the bread into a medium saucepan and add the ground hazelnuts, tomato paste, lemon juice, oil, crème fraîche, and mahlab cherry pit powder. Press the garlic through a garlic press and stir into the mixture. Stir in enough water to make a smooth sauce. Set the pan over medium-low heat and bring to a low simmer. Transfer the meatballs to the sauce and heat, stirring gently. Serve warm.

> *Kitchen Note*
> *The name for this dish,* **al-bunduq**, *is derived from the Levantine Arabic. The Spanish term for meatballs in the Desert Southwest is* **albondigas**. *The recipe honors these origins with seasonings of fennel, coriander, and za'atar, or the rarer kamouneh.*

Main Dishes

Aromatic Lamb and Bulgur
(Kibbe, Kibbeh)

Iran, Iraq, Jordan, Lebanon, Palestine, and Syria

Serves 4 to 6

There are as many family recipes for kibbe as there are Lebanese grandmothers willing to show how to shape ground lamb (or beef) mixed with onion, bulgur, and spices. Gary's aunt would place her palm under Gary's hand to guide him in creating these oblong meatballs for roasting.

Our modification of the traditional recipe does not require an elder's guidance. Instead of making meatballs, we pat the mixture into a baking dish. The result is a fragrant meatloaf crowned with yogurt, basil, and pine nuts.

You'll find the recipe for kibbe spice, aka kamouneh, on page 165. This spice is also commercially available online (see page 183).

1 tablespoon extra-virgin olive oil, plus more for the dish and for drizzling
1 cup (182 g) fine bulgur
1 pound (454 g) ground lamb
⅓ cup grated white onion
2 teaspoons sea salt
Generous pinch freshly ground black pepper
1 generous tablespoon kamouneh (see page 165)
¼ cup (36 g) pine nuts, plus more for garnish
Yogurt for serving
Coarsely chopped fresh basil leaves for serving

Preheat the oven to 350°F (180°C). Lightly grease a 9-by-13-inch (23-by-33-cm) baking or casserole dish.

Put the bulgur into a colander and rinse under cold running water. Transfer to a medium bowl, add enough water to cover the grain, and soak for 20 minutes. Drain well. Transfer to a large bowl and add the lamb, onion, salt, pepper, and kamouneh. Work in the pine nuts and oil.

Pat the meat mixture into the prepared baking dish, drizzle a little oil over the meat, and scatter the pine nuts on top. Bake until the top is golden, 35 to 45 minutes. Serve warm with a dollop of yogurt and the basil.

Sheet Pan Chicken in a Spiced Nut Crust
(Pollo en Pepitoria, Pollo in Crosta)

Latin America and Spain

Serves 4

This Spanish classic traveled west to North America, where ground nuts are often used for coating meats. The time-honored technique inspired this recipe for an easy sheet pan chicken that's juicy and succulent with a crisp crust.

1 cup (50 g) panko breadcrumbs
1 cup (114 g) pecans or hazelnuts, finely chopped
¼ cup (15 g) chopped fresh parsley or cilantro or a mix
1 teaspoon smoked paprika
2 teaspoons coarse salt
Freshly ground black pepper
1 large egg
⅓ cup (82 g) plain whole-milk yogurt
4 boneless, chicken breasts, about 3–4 ounces (174 g) each
½ cup (60 g) fine cornmeal
16 dates, pitted and thinly sliced, for garnish
Chopped fresh cilantro for garnish

Preheat the oven to 400°F (200°C). Line a rimmed baking sheet with parchment paper.

In a flat bowl, stir together the panko, nuts, parsley, paprika, salt, and pepper to taste. In a separate bowl, whisk together the egg and yogurt. Dust the chicken with the cornmeal, then dip in the yogurt-egg mixture. Allow the yogurt-egg to drip off, then coat the chicken with the nut-panko mixture.

Arrange the chicken on the prepared baking sheet and roast until the juices run clear and the meat is no longer pink, 25 to 30 minutes. A digital meat thermometer should read 165°F (75°C).

Remove the chicken and allow it to rest before slicing and serving, garnished with the dates and cilantro.

Goat Tagine with Apricots, Pineapple, and Warm Spices
(Tagine Maeiz, Maroc Maeiz)

Algeria, Libya, Morocco, and Tunisia

Serves 4 to 6

Tagines are the most celebrated stews in the Maghreb. The Daija (Moroccan) word *tagin*, which comes from the Arabic and Aramiac term *tazin*, for "saucepan," refers to the beautiful cone-shaped cookware of Morocco and adjacent Algeria.

Goat meat is just right for this tagine. The flavor is a tad grassier and sweeter than lamb and works well with warm spices, briny olives, and the anise notes of fennel. Pineapple adds a bright finish. If goat is unavailable, choose lamb. You'll know the dish is ready when the meat is fork tender and lush. We like to add couscous to the tagine before it goes into the oven so that it absorbs the juices and flavors to create a one-pot dish.

1 cup (130 g) dried apricots
2 pounds (908 g) goat meat, cut into 2-inch (5 cm) pieces
Sea salt
Freshly ground black pepper
3 tablespoons olive oil
1 medium onion, chopped
1 stem fennel fronds, diced
12 green olives, pitted and sliced
2 garlic cloves, chopped
2 teaspoons orange zest
1 teaspoon ground cumin
1 teaspoon ground ginger
1 teaspoon ground cinnamon
½ teaspoon ground turmeric
Water from cooked apricots plus water or vegetable stock to equal 2 cups (480 ml)
2 teaspoons honey
½ cup (90 g) couscous
¼ cup (60 ml) orange blossom water
6 pineapple rings or sliced pineapple
1 tablespoon toasted sesame seeds for garnish
Chopped fresh cilantro for garnish

Put the apricots in a small pot and add enough water to cover by about 2 inches (5 cm). Set over high heat, bring to a boil, turn off the heat, and allow the apricots to soak and plump, about 10 minutes. Drain and reserve the cooking water.

Preheat the oven to 350°F (180°C). Sprinkle the meat with salt and pepper.

Film a large skillet with about 2 tablespoons of the oil and set over medium-high heat. Sauté the onion, fennel, olives, garlic, orange zest, cumin, ginger, cinnamon, and turmeric until the onion is translucent and the spices are fragrant. Add the apricot water and stock, and honey. Stir in the couscous and simmer until the couscous plumps, 8 to 10 minutes. Remove from the heat and allow to cool.

Add the remaining 1 tablespoon oil to a tagine or large deep pot and add the couscous mixture, orange blossom water, plumped apricots, and goat meat. Lay the pineapple rings over the ingredients. Cover the pot and bake until the meat is very tender and the liquid has been absorbed, 1½ to 2 hours, checking midway through. Serve garnished with the sesame seeds and cilantro.

Kitchen Note
A tagine is a two-part vessel that condenses steam so the food cooks gently to preserve its nutrients, color, and flavor. You can replicate the tagine by transferring the ingredients to a casserole dish, Dutch oven, or deep pot, then placing parchment paper over the ingredients and covering with a secure lid.

Sticky Lamb Ribs

(Braai)

China, Kazakhstan, Korea, Mongolia, Tajikistan, and Uzbekistan

Serves 4

We're not sure why lamb ribs are unappreciated by home cooks and restaurant chefs. When slathered with a bold, sticky glaze, they are finger-licking delicious. You'll find variations of this recipe along the Spice Road in western China's Xinjiang Province, Kazakhstan, and the other "stans" of western Asia. In this recipe, the ancho chile powder and paprika give the ribs a bit of smoke and heat, and the vinegar adds snap. You can prepare the ribs and sauce separately, refrigerate 8 to 10 hours, and then finish them both the next day.

¼ cup (60 ml) olive oil or sesame oil
½ cup (120 ml) honey
3 garlic cloves, smashed
2 teaspoons ancho chile powder
1 tablespoon smoked paprika
2 teaspoons ground cumin
2 teaspoons sea salt
½ cup (120 ml) rice wine vinegar
Zest and juice of 1 orange
3 pounds (1.36 kg) (2 racks) lamb spareribs

In a medium bowl, whisk together the oil, honey, garlic, chile powder, paprika, cumin, salt, vinegar, and orange zest and juice.

Put the ribs into a large plastic bag and add the marinade. Seal the bag, pressing out the excess air. Place this on a plate and refrigerate at least 4 hours or overnight (8 to 10 hours).

Preheat the oven to 300°F (150°C). Put the ribs in a shallow baking dish and cover tightly with aluminum foil. Pour the marinade into a saucepan.

Bake the ribs until the meat is very tender, 3½ to 4 hours. Toward the end of that time, set the marinade over medium-high heat, bring to a boil, lower the heat to a simmer, and reduce the liquid by half, 10 to 15 minutes.

Remove the ribs, spoon off excess fat, and brush or spoon about ¼ cup (60 ml) of the sauce over the ribs. Return to the oven and roast uncovered until the ribs are caramelized and sticky, 15 to 20 minutes longer. Remove the ribs from the oven and let sit for about 5 minutes, then cut into individual ribs and serve the remaining sauce on the side.

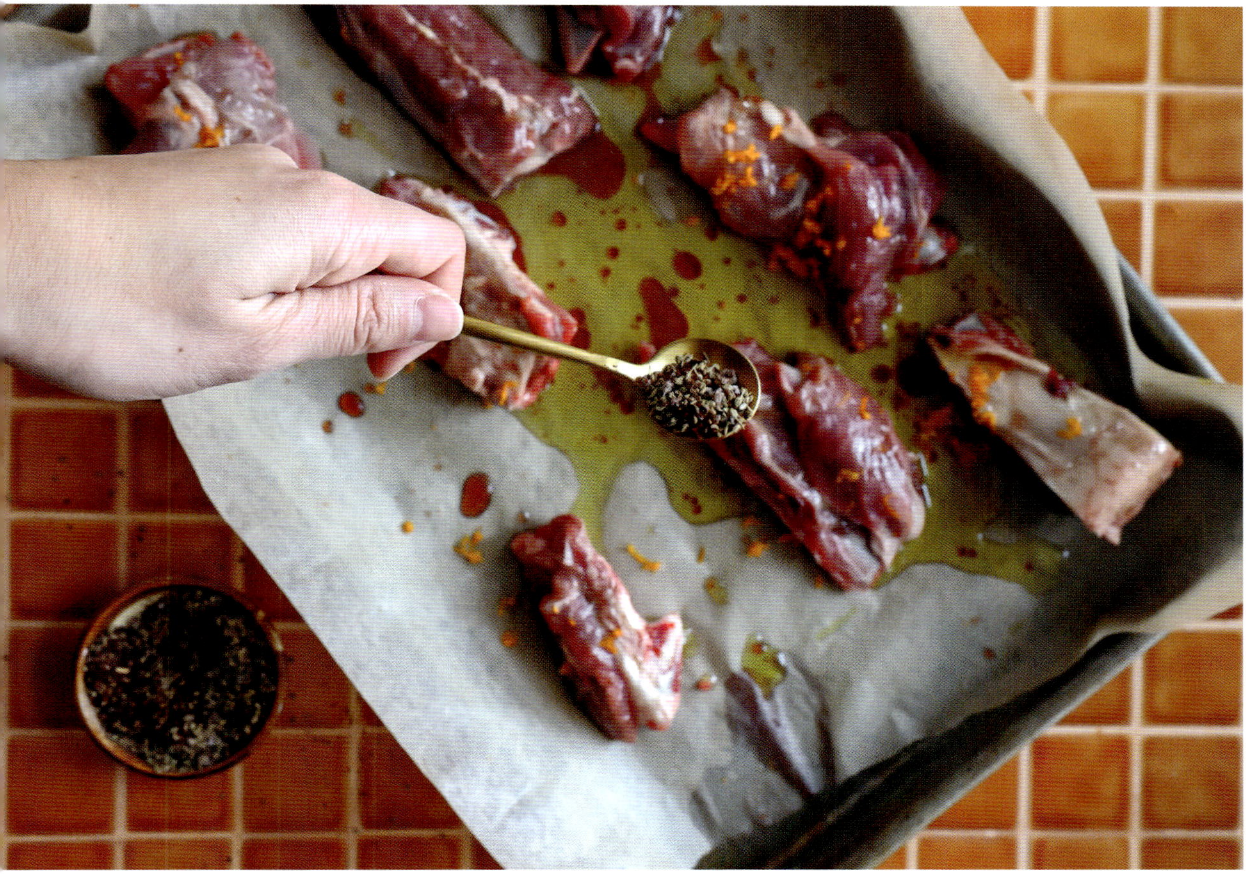

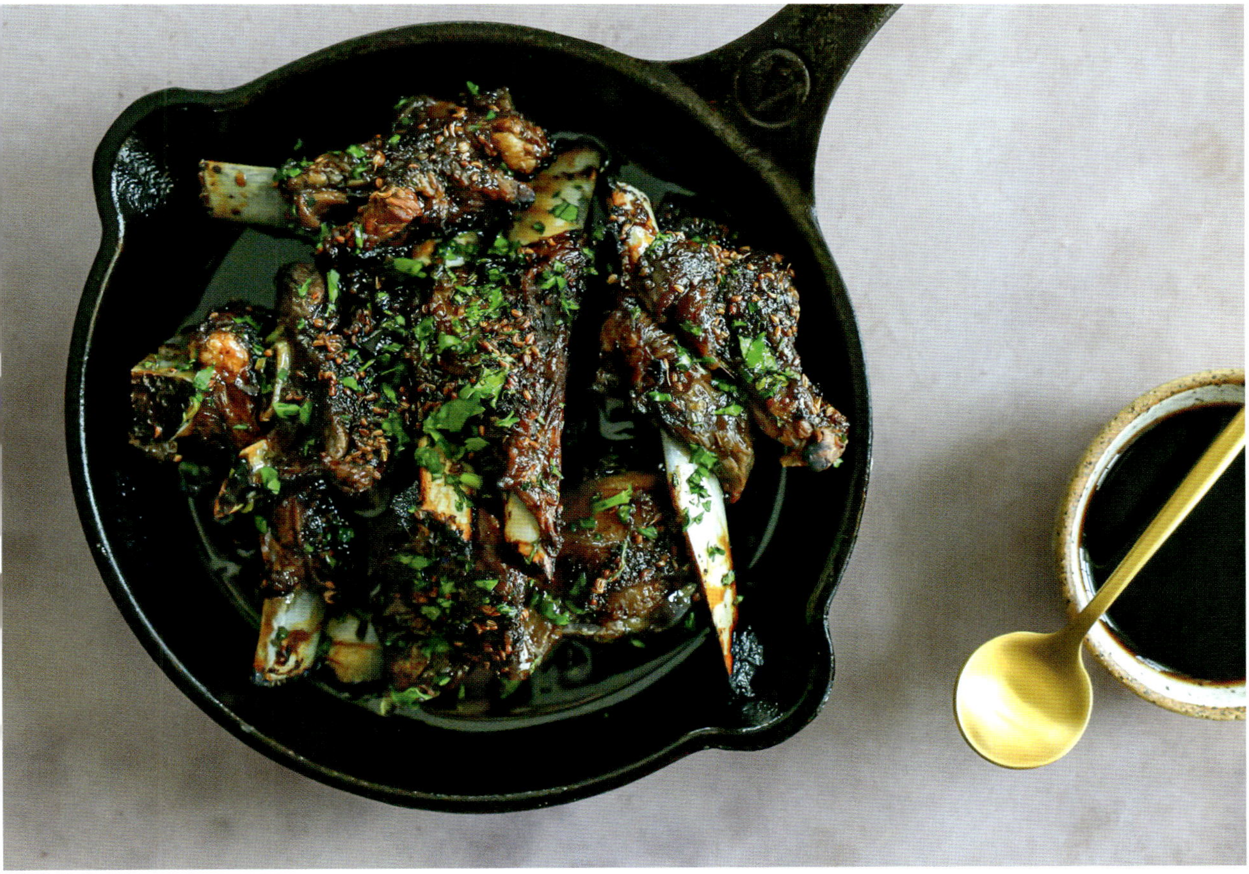

Lamb Kebabs with Moroccan Spices and Pomegranate Molasses Glaze

(Alambre, Kebab, Kebabk, Kabob, Pincho, Pinchito, Shish Kabob)

Southern Spain, Iran, Iraq, Lebanon, Mexico, Morocco, and Turkey

Serves 4

Skewered meat—lamb, beef, goat, and chicken—grilled over a wood fire is one of the most beloved dishes in desert regions. The Arabic word *kebab* originally referred to fried meat—usually lamb—but as the dish spread across the globe, grilling and baking became just as common. The Turkish term *shish kebab* is universal for skewered meats, though in Spanish they're often referred to as *alambres de carne asada*.

The layers of meat, onions, and vegetables cook quickly over fire to be crisp and juicy. Here they're seasoned with tart sumac and warm cumin (from the ras el hanout), and then lightly brushed with a tangy-sweet pomegranate glaze. Serve these over rice or couscous, or wrapped in a flour tortilla and topped with our Cilantro-Pistachio Pesto (page 45) or a bright salsa.

1½ pounds (681 g) leg of lamb, trimmed of fat and cut into 1-inch (2.5 cm) chunks
1 medium zucchini, cut into 1-inch (2.5 cm) slices
1 large bell pepper or Anaheim pepper, seeded and cut into 1-inch (2.5 cm) chunks
1 small onion, cut into 1-inch (2.5 cm) chunks
Up to 2 tablespoons olive oil
1 tablespoon Ras el Hanout (see page 169)
1 tablespoon sumac
Generous pinch coarse salt
2 tablespoons pomegranate molasses
Chopped mint for garnish

Place the lamb and vegetables in a shallow dish, add enough oil to coat, and season with the ras el hanout, sumac, and salt. Set aside to marinate while you prepare the grill. Heat the grill to medium.

Thread the meat alternately with the vegetables on the skewers, pressing the pieces together. Grill the meat a few inches from the heat until well browned on all sides and well done, 5 to 10 minutes. Brush the meat with the pomegranate molasses right before removing from the grill.

To serve, arrange the skewers on a platter and garnish with the mint.

Kitchen Note
Ras el hanout is also available online and in the spice aisle of most supermarkets and co-ops.

Persian Duck in Tart Fruit Sauce
(Khoresh-e Fesenjān)

Iran, Tajikistan, and Turkey

Serves 2 to 4

In this updated version of a Persian classic, seared duck breasts glisten under a gorgeous crimson pomegranate glaze. The traditional Persian dish—called *Khoresh-e Fesenjān* in Farsi—varies through the Islamic world. Sometimes it's made with chicken squab or quail and then glazed with a fruit syrup of choice.

Scoring the skin of the duck (but not cutting through to the flesh) allows the fat to render as it cooks, low and slow, to become succulent and tender. Serve the duck over rice, drizzled with the sauce.

1 cup (240 ml) pomegranate juice
1 cinnamon stick
1 cup (240 ml) duck or chicken stock
1 thyme sprig
1 teaspoon ground cumin
¼ cup (60 ml) pomegranate molasses
1 to 1½ pounds (454 to 681 g) duck breast
Coarse salt
Freshly ground black pepper
Pomegranate seeds for garnish

Put the juice, cinnamon stick, stock, thyme, cumin, and molasses into a saucepan. Set over medium heat and stir occasionally until the ingredients become smooth and glossy, about 5 minutes. Set aside.

With a sharp knife, score the duck breast skin in a tight crosshatch pattern with cuts about ⅛ inch apart, being careful not to expose the duck flesh.

Season both sides of the duck with salt and pepper. Place the duck breast, skin side down, in a large, cold sauté pan. Place the pan over medium-low heat and press the duck down with a smaller pan to keep the edges from curling up. Drain out the rendered fat as the duck cooks until most of it has been rendered and the skin is golden brown and the duck reaches 125°F (52°C) on a digital thermometer, about 15 minutes.

Increase the heat to medium to continue browning the skin, about 1 minute; flip and cook on the flesh side until the temperature reaches 130°F (54°C), another 1 to 2 minutes. Continue cooking to 140°F (60°C) for medium or 155°F (68°C) for well done. Remove the duck from the pan and set aside.

Pour the pomegranate sauce into the pan, increase the heat, and scrape up any browned bits sticking to the bottom. Bring to a boil and then lower the heat and simmer until the liquid reduces to a sticky rich sauce, thick enough to coat the back of a spoon. Remove from the heat and season with salt and pepper. Slice the duck and serve drizzled with the sauce and garnished with pomegranate seeds.

Upside-Down Rice, Vegetable, and Chicken Casserole
(Maqluba)

Israel, Jordan, Palestine, and Syria

Serves 6 to 8

Maqluba literally translates to "upside down," and is one of the most ancient of the Middle Eastern dishes. Originally, this was a shepherd's dinner that could be prepared in the morning before taking the goats and sheep out to forage; its pot was sealed with a lid and buried in the sand atop coals so that no intruders could steal it during the day. Some historians claim that it is the precursor of both paellas and tagines of the Mediterranean regions. These days, this rustic casserole is served in high-end restaurants throughout the Middle East, and when it's flipped onto a silver platter, the diners applaud. It deserves the same recognition when served to family and friends at home. The colorful blend of ingredients is boldly seasoned and hearty, which is perfect for a crowd. Serve it with whole-milk yogurt or kefir.

- 2 eggplants, cut into ¼-inch (.6 cm) slices
- 2 teaspoons sea salt, plus more for the eggplant
- 1½ cups (297 g) basmati rice
- 1 to 2 tablespoons olive oil
- 6 boneless skin-on chicken thighs
- 1 white onion, cut into chunks
- Freshly ground black pepper
- 2 bay leaves
- 4 cups (960 ml) water
- 2 to 3 tablespoons butter, plus more for greasing the pan
- 1 small cauliflower, cut into florets
- 4 Roma tomatoes, cut into ½-inch-thick (1.25 cm) slices
- 5 garlic cloves, cut in half
- 1 teaspoon ground turmeric
- 1 teaspoon ground cinnamon
- 1 teaspoon ground allspice
- 1 teaspoon ground coriander
- 1 teaspoon ground cumin
- 1 teaspoon ground cardamom
- ½ teaspoon freshly ground black pepper
- ¼ teaspoon ground cloves
- ¼ cup (36 g) pine nuts, toasted, for garnish
- Whole-milk yogurt or kefir for serving

Kitchen Note
If the list of spices feels too long, feel free to substitute Turkish Baharat (page 164).

Lay the eggplant slices on paper towels and sprinkle both sides with a little salt; allow to drain for about 20 minutes, then pat dry.

Put the rice into a colander and rinse well under cold water. Transfer it to a large pot and add 1 teaspoon of the salt and enough water to cover the rice. Let the rice soak for 30 minutes.

Film a large skillet with some oil and set over medium-high heat. Sear the chicken on all sides until golden, about 2 to 3 minutes per side. Then add the onion, a few grinds of pepper, bay leaves, and water. Bring to a boil, cover, reduce the heat, and simmer for about 20 minutes. Remove the meat from the pan and set it aside. Strain and reserve the stock.

In a medium skillet set over medium heat, melt 2 tablespoons of the butter and sauté the cauliflower in batches, being careful not to crowd the pan, until it's nicely browned, 3 to 5 minutes. Remove and set aside. Then, adding more butter if needed, sauté the eggplant until browned on both sides, 3 to 5 minutes.

Wipe out the large skillet and line the bottom with a circle of parchment paper. Lightly grease the parchment and the sides of the pan with a little butter. Arrange the tomato slices in one layer on the bottom, overlapping, then the eggplant slices, cauliflower pieces, and chicken. Drain the rice and spread it over the final layer and scatter the garlic over all.

Measure out 3 cups (720 ml) of the reserved chicken stock and stir in all of the spices plus the remaining 1 teaspoon salt. Pour this over the rice and then gently press everything down with your hands. Make sure the stock covers all the rice and ingredients. (Add a little more stock if needed.)

Set the skillet over medium heat and bring to a simmer, cover, decrease the heat to low, and cook for 30 minutes. Do not peek! Remove the skillet from the heat. Remove the lid, quickly lay a clean dish towel over the ingredients, then seal with the lid. Leave for 10 minutes to rest.

Remove the lid and towel, invert a large round serving plate over the skillet, and quickly invert the pan and plate, holding on to both sides. Leave the pan on the plate for about 3 minutes, then carefully lift it off. Garnish with the pine nuts and serve with whole-milk yogurt or kefir alongside.

Main Dishes ▪ 89

Spiced Orange Chicken
(Pollo a la Naranja)

Spain and US Desert Southwest

Serves 4 to 6

Seville oranges give this quick sheet pan dinner a tangy punch. The oranges, also called bitter or sour oranges, originated in Andalusia and reflect the historic trade relationship between Portugal and Spain.

If Seville oranges are not available, substitute navel oranges with a mix of orange juice and rice wine vinegar.

⅓ cup (80 ml) Seville orange juice or ¼ cup (60 ml) fresh orange juice mixed with 2 tablespoons rice wine vinegar
¼ cup (60 ml) extra-virgin olive oil
1 teaspoon ground cumin
1 teaspoon smoked paprika
½ teaspoon ground coriander
½ teaspoon ground cardamom
Pinch sea salt
Pinch freshly ground black pepper
1 pound (454 g) boneless, skinless chicken thighs, cut in half
4 to 5 orange slices, cut in half
¼ cup (33 g) pitted black olives
¼ cup (34 g) pitted dates
Chopped fresh cilantro or parsley for garnish
Cooked white or brown rice for serving

In a large bowl, whisk together the juice, oil, cumin, paprika, coriander, cardamom, salt, and pepper. Add the chicken to the bowl and turn to evenly coat. Cover and marinate for about 10 minutes or cover and refrigerate 8 to 10 hours or overnight.

Preheat the oven to 425°F (220°C). Line a rimmed baking sheet with parchment paper. Spread out the chicken on the prepared baking sheet and tuck the orange slices under and around the chicken. Roast until the chicken is light brown, about 20 minutes, rotating the pan halfway through. Pour the reserved marinade over the chicken and toss in the olives and dates. Continue roasting until the chicken's juices run clear when pierced with a knife and the meat registers 165°F (75°C) on an instant-read thermometer, 8 to 10 more minutes. Remove and allow the chicken to rest a few minutes before serving drizzled with the pan juices and garnished with the cilantro. Serve with rice.

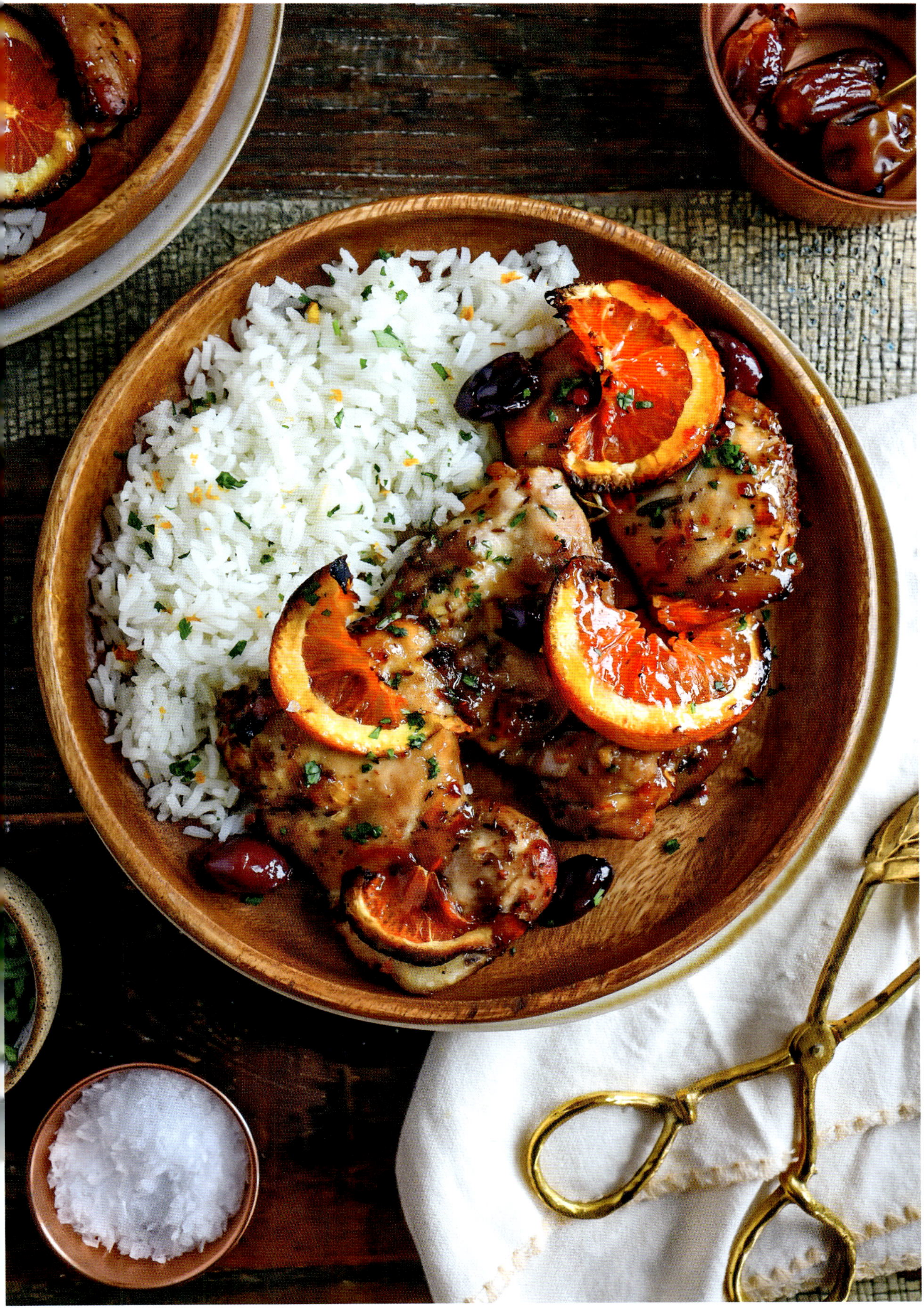

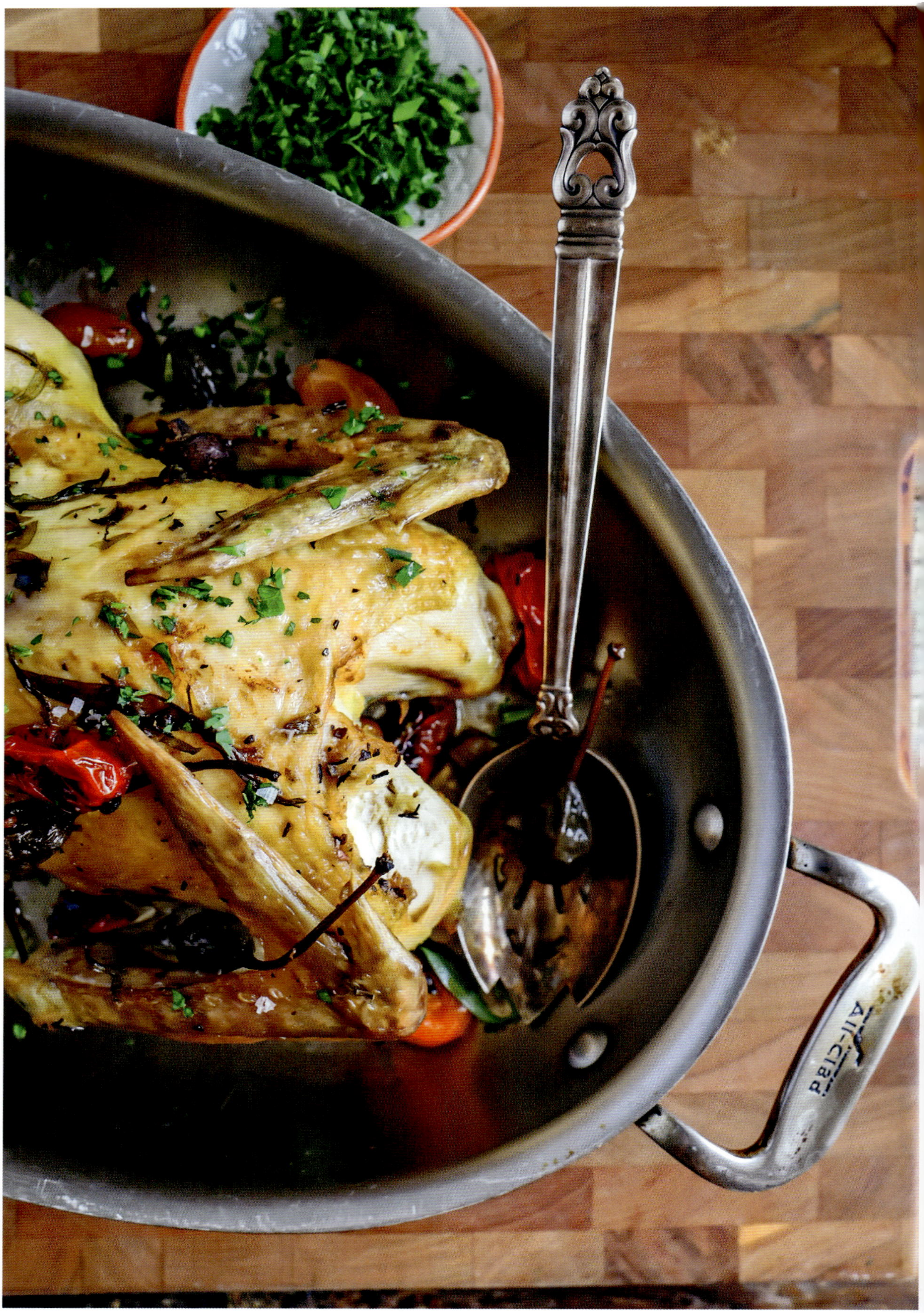
All-Clad

Roast Chicken with Tarragon and Capers
(Pollo Asado con Estragón, Poulet à l'Estragon)

France, Mexico, Spain, and US Desert Southwest

Serves 4 to 6

The tarragon of Mexico and the US Southwest is similar to the Spanish and French tarragons with their earthy, minty, and lemony notes, but its flavor is bolder and muskier with hints of cinnamon and allspice. This recipe is a desert spin on the classic tarragon roast chicken. For bursts of tang, we've tossed in capers. If you have access to juniper, you can substitute pickled juniper berries. Serve this over rice or with plenty of rustic bread to sop up all the lovely juices.

1½ tablespoons finely chopped fresh tarragon, plus 5 large sprigs
2 teaspoons coarse salt, plus more as needed
1 teaspoon freshly ground black pepper
1 teaspoon lemon zest
2 tablespoons extra-virgin olive oil
1 chicken (3½ to 4 pounds [1.59 to 1.82 kg])
¼ cup (30 g) capers, drained, or pickled juniper berries (see Note)
1 tablespoon chopped fresh parsley leaves for garnish

Preheat the oven to 450°F (230°C).

In a small bowl, whisk together the tarragon, salt, pepper, lemon zest, and oil and smear over the chicken, tucking a little under the skin. Scatter the juniper berries over and around the chicken.

Place the chicken, breast side up, in a roasting pan or on a rimmed baking sheet. Stuff the cavity of the chicken with the tarragon sprigs. Roast for 30 minutes.

Baste the chicken with the pan juices. Continue roasting until the chicken's juices run clear when the skin is pierced with a knife, 20 to 30 more minutes. The chicken is done when a digital thermometer inserted into the thigh reaches 165°F (75°C).

Transfer the chicken to a serving platter and allow it to rest for 8 to 10 minutes before carving and serving, drizzled with the juices and garnished with parsley.

> **Kitchen Note**
> *To pickle juniper berries, combine 1 cup (240 ml) rice vinegar with ½ cup (46 g) berries in a jar or covered container. Set in a sunny spot for a good 2 weeks. Store in a covered container for up to 6 months. Use in lieu of capers.*

Stuffed Mexican Peppers in Yogurt Walnut Sauce

(Chiles en Nogada)

Mexico and US Desert Southwest

Serves 4 to 8

Chiles en nogada is Mexico's national dish for good reason! Showcasing the colors of the Mexican flag (green, white, and red), it was created in 1821 to recognize Mexico's independence from Spain.

Chiles en nogada resembles the Lebanese *sheikh el mahshi-bil-laban*. In the Lebanese version, tiny eggplants are filled with a similar mixture of dried fruits, olives, and meat, topped with a creamy nut sauce, and garnished with pomegranate seeds.

In this version, we've opted to focus on Mexican chiles and have given the traditional method a slight tweak. Instead of frying the peppers, they are first roasted in a broiler and then finished in a warm oven.

- 8 large poblano chiles
- 2 tablespoons olive oil
- 1 pound (454 g) ground dark-meat chicken or turkey
- 1 medium white onion, chopped
- 4 garlic cloves, chopped
- 1 cup (118 g) chopped tart apple
- ½ cup (85 g) dried raisins, plumped in hot water to cover
- 1 tablespoon chopped fresh oregano, or 1 teaspoon dried
- ½ teaspoon ground cinnamon
- ¼ teaspoon ground clove
- ¼ cup (60 ml) dry sherry
- 1 small can (14 ounces [397 g]) fire-roasted tomatoes with their juices
- ¼ cup (25 g) chopped pistachios
- ¼ cup (36 g) chopped pitted green olives
- ¼ cup (15 g) chopped fresh parsley, plus more for garnish
- 1 teaspoon grated lemon zest
- 1 tablespoon fresh lemon juice
- Salt
- Freshly ground black pepper
- Pomegranate seeds for garnish

WALNUT SAUCE

- ½ cup (64 g) raw walnuts
- 1 cup (245 g) whole-milk yogurt
- ¼ cup (29 g) queso fresco

Preheat the broiler to high. Put the peppers on a baking sheet and broil until the skins are blackened, turning them several times, about 10 minutes total. Remove and cover with a clean dish towel to steam until cool. Rub the skin from the peppers (don't worry if all of it doesn't come off). Cut a horizontal slit down the middle and remove and discard the ribs and seeds.

Film a large skillet with the oil and spread the ground meat out in an even layer. Cook, undisturbed, until lightly browned, about 3 minutes. Toss and continue cooking, breaking up the meat with the back of a spoon and scraping up any browned bits, until the meat is lightly browned. Stir in the onion and garlic, and continue cooking until the onion is tender, about 2 minutes. Stir in the apples, raisins with their juices, oregano, cinnamon, clove, sherry, and tomatoes and stir, scraping up any brown bits clinging to the bottom of the pan. Simmer until the liquid is reduced and the stuffing is firm. Stir in the pistachios, olives, parsley, lemon zest, and lemon juice. Season with salt and pepper and adjust the flavors to taste. Set aside.

Reduce the oven to 200°F (95°C). Place the peppers bottom side up on a rimmed baking sheet and fill each with equal amounts of the stuffing, pressing the filling into the peppers but not so much that they burst. Place in the oven to hold until ready to serve.

To make the sauce: Process together the walnuts, yogurt, and cheese in a blender or food processor, until smooth but still a bit chunky.

Serve the peppers drizzled with the sauce and garnished with the pomegranate seeds and parsley.

Tajín Grilled Chicken
(Pollo con Tajín a la Parilla)

Mexico and US Desert Southwest

Serves 4 to 6

In this recipe, Tajín, the Mexican seasoning of dried chile and dehydrated lime juice, adds zip to chicken thighs on the grill. Serve the chicken with any of our dips, sauces, or condiments (see pages 36–51), Blue Corn Bread (page 146), or Pomegranate Arugula Salad (page 130). Perfect for a backyard BBQ.

Vegetable oil for the grill
8 boneless, skinless chicken thighs, about 2 pounds (908 g)
2 to 3 tablespoons extra-virgin olive oil
1 tablespoon Tajín Clásico
Coarse salt
Chopped fresh cilantro for garnish

Prepare a grill for a medium-high direct heat. Clean the grates and brush with vegetable oil. Generously coat the chicken with the olive oil and season with the Tajín and salt to taste. Grill the chicken, turning, until cooked through and charred a bit, with juices running clear, 7 to 8 minutes per side. The internal temperature should reach 165°F (75°C) on a digital meat thermometer. Remove from the grill, sprinkle with cilantro, and serve.

Turkey in Pumpkin Seed Sauce
(Guajolote en Mole Verde con Pepitas)

Mexico and US Desert Southwest

Serves 4 to 6

Not all moles are made with chocolate and not all have an ingredient list three pages long. This version is fast and bold, and it's wonderful with roast turkey or chicken. Serve it over rice or with a side of our Blue Corn Bread (page 146).

1½ cups (179 g) raw pumpkin seeds (pepitas)
1 teaspoon ground cumin
2 cups (480 ml) chicken or turkey stock
¼ cup (60 ml) vegetable oil
1 cup (150 g) diced onion
2 garlic cloves, smashed
1 pound (454 g) tomatillos, husked and halved
10 leaves romaine lettuce, chopped
4 jalapeño peppers, seeded and diced
2 cups (120 g) chopped fresh cilantro
2 teaspoons dried oregano, preferably Mexican
4 cups (454 g) cooked shredded turkey or chicken meat
Coarse salt
Freshly ground black pepper

Set a large heavy skillet over medium heat, add the pumpkin seeds, and toast, stirring, until they deepen in color, about 3 minutes. Cool. Transfer the seeds to a food processor and grind into a fine powder. Transfer to a bowl and stir in the cumin and 1 cup (240 ml) of the stock to make a thick paste.

Pour the oil into a Dutch oven or a large heavy pan. Set over medium-high heat. When the oil shimmers, add the seed paste and fry, stirring and scraping, until it becomes a deep golden color, 6 to 7 minutes. Remove from the heat.

In a food processor, puree the onion, garlic, tomatillos, and ½ cup (120 ml) of the stock until smooth. Add the romaine, jalapeños, cilantro, and oregano and pulse until chunky.

Return the Dutch oven to medium heat. Transfer the puree to the pot and stir in the remaining ½ cup (120 ml) stock, shredded meat, and salt to taste. Bring to a simmer, stirring occasionally, for about 20 minutes. Taste and adjust the salt, and add black pepper to taste.

Turkey Tacos
(Tacos de Guajolote)

Mexico and US Desert Southwest

Serves 4

Wild turkeys strut across Gary's orchard near the Arizona–Sonoran border. In Minneapolis, where Beth lives, bold toms stop traffic as they emerge from the woods.

This recipe for turkey *carnitas*, or "little meats," can be made with any meat, but it's a great way to dispatch a leftover Thanksgiving turkey or a roast chicken. Be sure to sizzle the meat until it's nicely browned and super crisp. Serve on corn tortillas and top with your favorite prepared or homemade salsa, chopped onions, cilantro, and lime.

2½ to 3 cups (284 to 341 g) cooked shredded dark turkey meat
1 teaspoon dried oregano
½ teaspoon ground cumin
Coarse salt
Freshly ground black pepper
Zest and juice of 1 navel orange
1 tablespoon fresh lime juice
1 white onion, chopped
5 garlic cloves, smashed
1 cinnamon stick, broken into 2 pieces
1 bay leaf
¼ cup (60 ml) sunflower oil or any neutral oil
Warmed corn tortillas
Chopped white onion, chopped fresh cilantro, lime wedges, and cranberry salsa (optional toppings)

In a nonstick skillet, combine the turkey, oregano, cumin, and salt and pepper to taste, and toss to coat the pieces. Add the orange zest and juice, lime juice, onion, garlic, cinnamon stick, and bay leaf and toss together. Drizzle the oil over the meat. Set over medium-high heat, bring to a boil, reduce the heat, and simmer until the liquid evaporates.

Increase the heat and cook the turkey, pressing it down on the skillet, until it begins to brown. Break it up and continue cooking, stirring, until the pieces brown and become crisp, 8 to 10 minutes. Remove and serve with tortillas, garnished with the desired toppings.

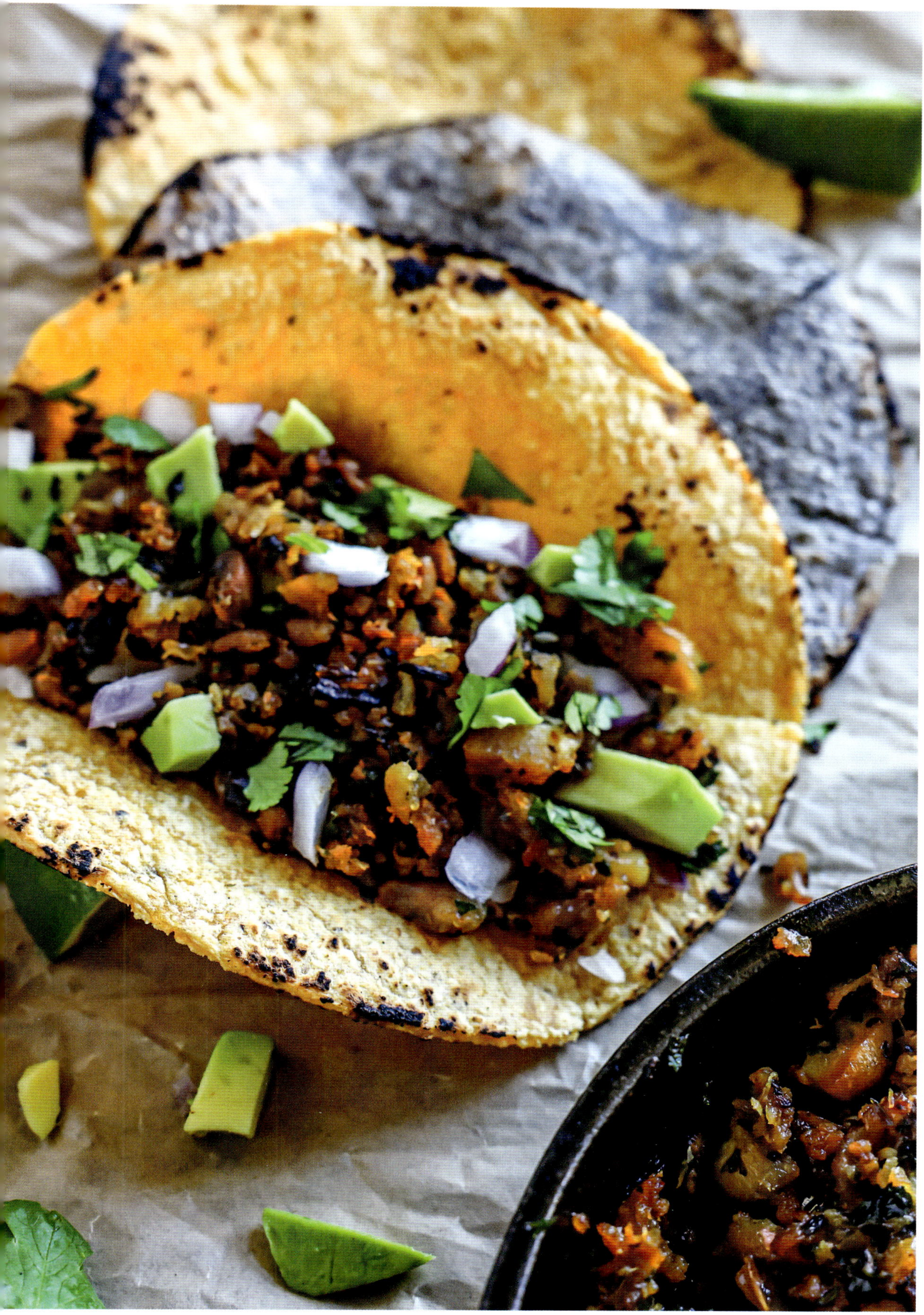

Sea Scallops in Tamarind Glaze
(Escalopa en Salsa de Tamarindo)

Baja California, East Africa, East Indies, and Mexico

Serves 2 to 4

The coastal areas of Baja, Sonora, Ecuador, Peru, the Indian sub-peninsula, the Arabian peninsula, and eastern Africa are home to tamarind trees and shellfish. Here, the pods from the tamarind tree make a wonderful sticky-sweet-tangy paste, perfect for glazing plump scallops. This recipe comes from the area near the Sea of Cortez, where Gary's beach cabin is located, which is close to beds of the round hatchet scallops. The tamarind sauce works equally well with shrimp, clams, and fish. Be cautious, as scallops are easily overcooked. Serve over rice.

4 tablespoons ghee
1 large white onion, diced
10 garlic cloves, mashed
3 cups (180 g) chopped fresh cilantro
2 large Roma tomatoes, peeled and diced
3 tablespoons fenugreek seeds
¼ cup (15 g) chopped fresh holy basil or 2 tablespoons dried
2 teaspoons curry powder
½ teaspoon freshly ground black pepper
½ teaspoon Aleppo pepper
⅔ cup (160 g) tamarind paste
1½ pounds (681 g) West Coast (aka calico) scallops or small bay scallops

Film a large skillet with 2 tablespoons of the ghee and set over medium heat. Add the onions and garlic and sauté until translucent, 5 to 8 minutes. Stir in the cilantro, tomatoes, fenugreek, basil, curry powder, black pepper, Aleppo pepper, and tamarind paste. Reduce the heat and simmer for about 20 minutes. Cover and set aside.

Heat the remaining 2 tablespoons ghee in another large skillet over medium heat. Add the scallops and sear quickly, about 2 minutes per side. Pour the tamarind sauce over the scallops and toss to coat.

Shrimp with Wild Sea Greens and Potatoes
(Revoltijo)

Mexico

Serves 4

Revoltijo means "jumble" or "scramble," and this traditional Mexican dish is made with romeritos, a wild, salt-tolerant green that's been harvested since pre-Colonial times. The plant resembles rosemary but tastes like salty spinach and is extremely nutritious. Rich in fiber, iron, potassium, and vitamins A and C, it's known to support healthy digestion. Because it's so perishable, fresh romeritos is not readily available; fresh baby spinach makes a fine substitute. Serve over cooked rice.

1 tablespoon vegetable oil

½ cup Mexican Mole Chile Seed Paste (page 168)

1½ cups (360 ml) water or chicken stock

1 pound (454 g) baby potatoes, cooked

1 cup (86 g) nopales (see page 134), cleaned and sliced ½ inch (1.25 cm) thick

1 cup romeritos or baby spinach, washed and drained

1 pound (454 g) shrimp, tails removed

Film a large pot with the oil and set over medium heat. Add the mole paste and water and stir until the paste has dissolved and the sauce is smooth. Add the potatoes, nopales, and romeritos and toss to coat with the mole. Cook until the nopales are tender, about 10 minutes. Add the shrimp and continue cooking until they turn pink, about 5 minutes.

Kitchen Note
Sea blights, such as romeritos, are enjoyed as fresh greens and used as a cure for gastric ulcers. Commercially available in Mexican delis in the United States, they are served at Christmas and Lenten holidays. Because this plant thrives in salty conditions, it may help mitigate the salinity that limits commercial crop production.

Grilled Fisherman's Catch with Chermoula
(Pescado Marinado con Chermoula)

Argentina, Canary Islands, Caribbean, Morocco, and Venezuela

Serves 4 to 6

The fish used here is lightly marinated in lemon, sour orange juice, and sweet paprika before being tossed on the grill. Use skin-on fillets, because they won't fall apart or dry out. The chermoula sauce is akin to adobo, mojo picon, and other salsas from subtropical regions. This recipe is not as piquant as it is citrusy, floral, and herby. Store extra chermoula in a covered container in the refrigerator for up to a month. It's lovely on chicken, stirred into soups, and whisked into mayonnaise.

CHERMOULA

Makes about 1½ cups

4 garlic cloves, smashed
1 bunch flat-leaf parsley and tender stems, chopped
Grated zest of 1 large lemon
3 tablespoons ground coriander
2 teaspoons smoked paprika
1 teaspoon ground cumin
1 teaspoon achiote (annatto) paste
1 teaspoon coarse salt
¾ cup (180 ml) neutral oil (grapeseed, sunflower, etc.)

To make the chermoula: Put the garlic, parsley, lemon zest, coriander, paprika, cumin, achiote, and salt into a blender or food processor. Pulse to combine the ingredients. With the motor running, add the oil in a slow, steady stream. Transfer to a bowl and set aside.

GRILLED FISH

½ cup (120 ml) extra-virgin olive oil
¼ cup (60 ml) fresh lemon juice
2 tablespoons sour orange juice or syrup
1½ cups (216 g) chopped red onion
3 garlic cloves, smashed
¼ cup (15 g) chopped fresh cilantro, plus more for garnish
2 teaspoons sweet paprika
2 teaspoons coarse salt
1 teaspoon ground cumin
1 teaspoon freshly ground black pepper
½ teaspoon Aleppo pepper
1 to 1½ pounds (454 to 681 g) skin-on sea bass (or other white fish) fillets
Vegetable oil for the grill

To prepare the fish: In a small bowl, whisk together the olive oil, lemon juice, orange juice, onion, garlic, cilantro, paprika, salt, cumin, achiote, black pepper, and Aleppo pepper.

Lay the fish fillets in a baking dish big enough to hold them. Pour the marinade over the fish and turn the fish over several times to make sure they are thoroughly coated. Refrigerate for 15 minutes.

Prepare a hot grill. Grease the grill grate with vegetable oil. Set the fish on the grill, skin side down. Partially cover and grill until the fish is cooked through and flaky, 7 to 8 minutes. Remove and place on a platter, skin side up. Drizzle with the chermoula and serve extra alongside.

Pan-Roasted Fish with Olive-Caper Relish
(Smaka bi Zaytun-Kebbar, Samke Harra)

Egypt, Lebanon, Morocco, Palestine, and Turkey

Serves 4

Choose a firm white fish for this recipe—cod, halibut, sole, or monkfish. The combination of olives and capers is fitting in that both span the range of desert oases across the Old World, from western China's Gobi and Taklimakan to southern Morocco's Sahara. In the ocean-side cafes in Byblos and Tripoli, where Gary has been hosted by kin, it's simply called *semke harra*: spicy grilled fish. It's delicious served over lemon rice or our Millet Polenta with Blistered Tomatoes (page 107), with a side of Spinach with Spices and Yogurt (page 137).

¼ cup (60 ml) extra-virgin olive oil
1 tablespoon dried oregano
2 tablespoons red wine vinegar
¼ cup (36 g) finely diced onion
2 tablespoons minced kalamata olives
2 tablespoons minced green olives
1 tablespoon drained capers
2 tablespoons chopped fresh parsley
¼ teaspoon ground cumin or ajwain (see page 108)
Sea salt
Freshly ground black pepper
1 to 1¼ pounds (454 to 568 g) firm white fish (cod, halibut, monkfish)
Toasted pine nuts for garnish
Lemon wedges for serving

Pour 3 tablespoons of the oil into a small saucepan and set over low heat. Add the oregano, turn off the heat, and steep the oregano in the oil for 5 minutes.

Whisk in the vinegar, onion, olives, capers, parsley, and cumin. Season with salt and pepper to taste. Transfer the relish to a dish and set aside.

Film a large cast-iron skillet with the remaining 1 tablespoon oil and set over medium-high heat. Season the fish with salt and pepper and place in the pan. Cook until golden brown on one side, about 3 minutes. Turn and continue cooking until done, another 3 to 4 minutes.

Transfer the fish to a platter and spoon some of the relish over the fish. Garnish with the pine nuts and lemon wedges. Pass additional relish alongside.

Borderland Ranch-Style Beans
(Frijoles de la Olla)

Mexico and US Desert Southwest

Serves 4 to 6

Ranch-style beans are the ultimate comfort food for breakfast, lunch, and dinner throughout western Texas, New Mexico, Arizona, and northern Mexico. They are a mainstay, like fava beans are in Arab countries. Historically, they were slow cooked in clay pottery on coals overnight, hence the name *frijoles de la olla*. This is "anything goes" kind of cooking. We like to season the beans with ancho chile peppers, Mexican oregano, and plenty of cumin, and add a little fire-roasted mesquite pod powder to the dish to give it a warm, smoky, herbaceous taste.

Serve the beans over rice with a dollop of sour cream or shredded queso fresco. Anasazi, pinto, or black beans work well here. Cilantro or epazote makes a wonderful garnish.

---

1 to 2 dried ancho chiles, rinsed
5 cups (1.2 L) hot water
2 tablespoons olive oil or vegetable oil
1 onion, chopped
5 garlic cloves, smashed
1 teaspoon coarse salt
1 teaspoon freshly ground black pepper
2 tablespoons dried oregano (preferably Mexican)
1 tablespoon ground cumin
1 teaspoon ground coriander
½ teaspoon roasted mesquite pod powder
1 teaspoon paprika
12 ounces (340 g) dried Anasazi, pinto, black, or other beans (except kidneys), rinsed and picked over
Finely chopped fresh cilantro or epazote for garnish

Rip the chiles into pieces and discard the stems and seeds. Place in a dry skillet, set over medium heat, and toast, turning, until fragrant, about 5 minutes. Transfer to a blender with the hot water. Process until smooth.

Film a heavy saucepan or Dutch oven with the oil. Add the onion and garlic and cook, stirring, until the onion is translucent and tender, about 5 minutes. Add the salt, pepper, oregano, cumin, coriander, mesquite pod powder, and paprika and continue cooking for about 30 seconds.

Stir in the beans, the ancho puree, and enough water to cover the beans by about 1 inch (2.5 cm). Set over high heat, and bring to a boil. Reduce the heat to a simmer, cover, and cook the beans until very tender, stirring occasionally and adding more water if they look to be drying out, 4 to 5 hours.

Using a fork, mash some of the beans against the side of the pot to thicken the mixture. Season with salt and pepper. Serve warm, garnished with cilantro.

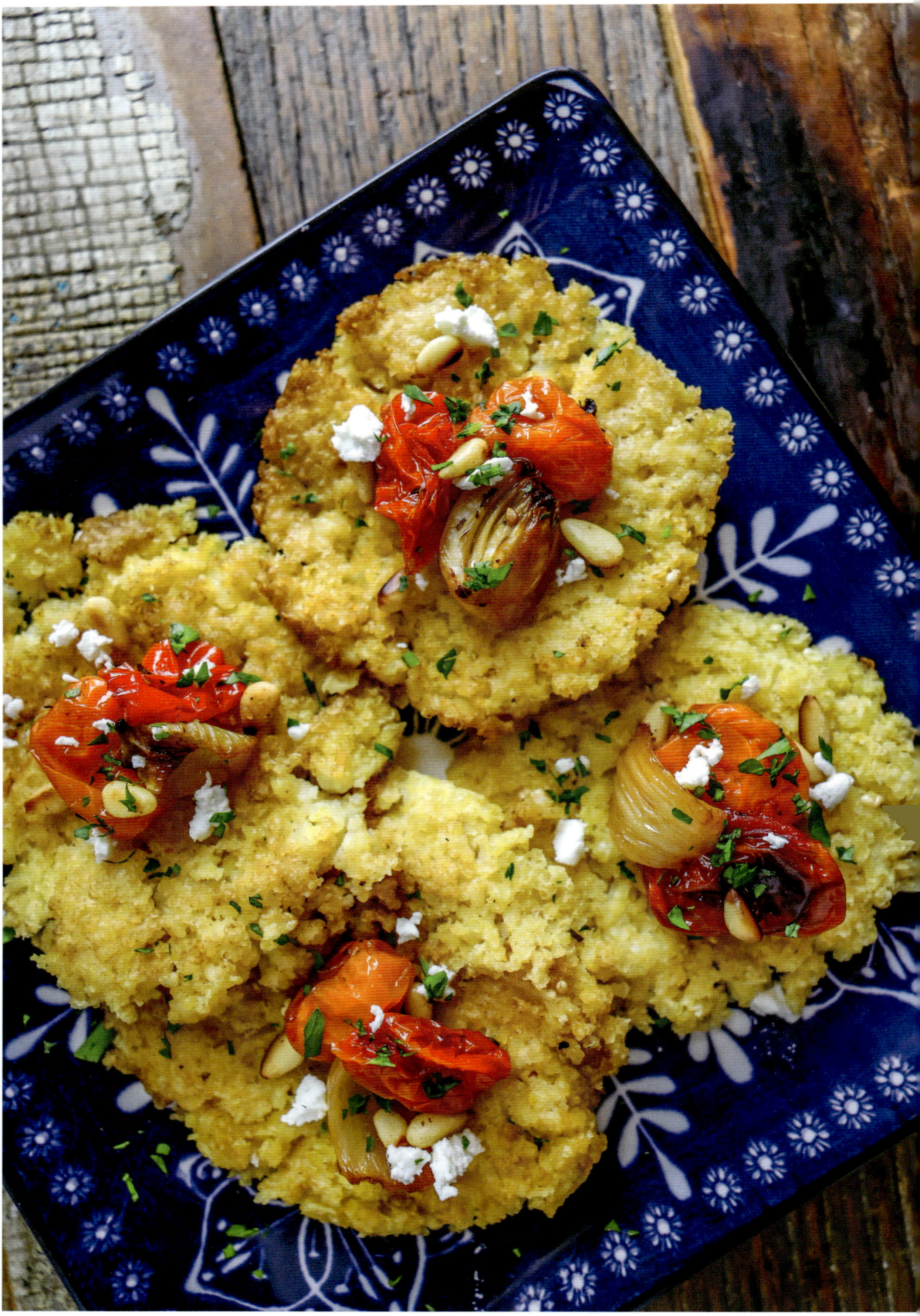

Millet Polenta with Blistered Tomatoes
(Polenta di Mijo con Pomodoro)
North Africa and Sicily

Serves 2 to 4

Millet, a tiny grain, is a nutritional powerhouse. Slightly sweet, a bit nutty, it's high in protein, fiber, and antioxidants as well as B vitamins, calcium, iron, potassium, and zinc. Plus, it's gluten free. A pantry staple throughout Africa, China, and India, it has been cultivated for over 7,000 years, making it one of the oldest cereal crops. And it makes a fabulous polenta. Surprisingly, it was grown on the banks of two iconic desert rivers—the Nile and the Colorado of Grand Canyon fame—through the 1930s. We would do well to return to it.

1 cup (206 g) millet
3½ cups (840 ml) water
Coarse salt
2 pints (454 g) cherry tomatoes
1 small onion, diced
2 to 3 tablespoons extra-virgin olive oil, plus more for drizzling
Freshly ground black pepper
Minced parsley for garnish
Crumbled feta cheese for garnish (optional)
Pine nuts for garnish (optional)

Put the millet, water, and a generous pinch of salt into a medium pot. Set over high heat and bring to a boil. Reduce the heat to a simmer, cover, and cook, stirring occasionally, for 20 to 30 minutes, checking to be sure the millet isn't sticking to the bottom of the pot. The millet is cooked when the liquid is absorbed and the millet resembles a thick polenta. Remove from the heat and allow to stand, stirring once or twice, until cool enough to handle, 20 to 30 minutes.

While the millet is simmering, preheat the oven to 400°F (200°C). Line a baking sheet with parchment paper. Spread the tomatoes and onions on the prepared baking sheet, drizzle with just enough oil to lightly coat, and sprinkle with a little salt and pepper. Roast until the tomatoes have burst and shrunk and the onions are nicely browned, 15 to 20 minutes, shaking the pan occasionally. Remove and tent with foil to keep them warm.

With dampened hands, shape the millet into cakes about 3 inches (7.5 cm) in diameter and an inch (2.5 cm) or so thick. Film a large skillet with the oil and set over medium-high heat. Working in batches so as not to crowd the pan, fry the cakes until the bottoms are browned, 3 to 5 minutes. Carefully flip the cakes with a spatula and cook until the other side is browned, another 3 to 5 minutes.

Serve the millet cakes topped with the roasted tomatoes and parsley. Sprinkle with feta and pine nuts, if using.

Spiced Red Lentils
(Misir Wat, Masoor Dal, Ades Hererra)

Egypt, Eritrea, Ethiopia, India, Morocco, Pakistan, and Sri Lanka

Makes about 3½ cups

Lentils are a key ingredient in Ethiopia's most popular dishes. This one relies on ajwain, an assertive spice with notes of thyme, cumin, and anise that brings a variety of dishes to life. If time allows, mix up a batch of niter kibbeh, the spiced clarified butter that is a staple in every Ethiopian kitchen. Serve with flatbread.

¼ cup (60 ml) Niter Kibbeh (recipe follows), butter, or oil
2 onions, chopped
1 tablespoon peeled and grated fresh ginger
5 garlic cloves, smashed
1 teaspoon ajwain
3 tablespoons sweet paprika
1 tablespoon smoked paprika
2 cups (384 g) lentils, picked through and rinsed
5 cups (1.2 L) water, plus more as needed
Sea salt
Freshly ground black pepper

Melt the niter kibbeh in a large pot set over medium-high heat. Add the onions, ginger, and garlic and cook until the onions begin to caramelize, about 5 minutes. Stir in the ajwain and the paprikas and cook until you have a red paste that is darkening in color, 30 seconds to 1 minute.

Stir in the lentils and water and increase the heat to bring the mixture to a boil. Reduce the heat to a simmer, cover, and cook the lentils until they are falling apart, 20 to 25 minutes, stirring so they do not stick to the pan and adding more water if necessary. Season with salt and pepper, taste, and adjust the flavors.

Niter Kibbeh

Makes 1 pound (454 g)

1 pound (454 g) unsalted butter, cubed
¼ cup (36 g) diced onion
6 garlic cloves, minced
2 tablespoons peeled and grated fresh ginger
1 cinnamon stick
3 to 4 cardamom pods (preferably black)
3 whole cloves
1 teaspoon whole black peppercorns
1 teaspoon fenugreek seeds
1 teaspoon ground coriander
1 teaspoon dried oregano
½ teaspoon ground cumin
¼ teaspoon ground nutmeg
¼ teaspoon ground turmeric

Place all the ingredients in a medium saucepan and set over very low heat. Bring to a simmer and cook, watching, until it begins to foam. Continue cooking, stirring frequently, for about 35 minutes. Strain the mixture into a jar and discard the whole spices. Allow the mixture to cool, then cover and store in the refrigerator up to six months.

> **Kitchen Note**
> *Niter kibbeh, the Ethiopian spiced clarified butter, is easy to make. Keep it in a covered jar in the refrigerator to spice up a range of dishes. If you don't have time to gather and and measure out the individual spices called for, substitute an equal amount of garam masala or curry powder.*

Poached Eggs in Spicy Tomatoes
(Shakshuka, Menemen)

Algeria, Egypt, Libya, Tunisia, and Turkey

Serves 6

It's as fun to say "shakshuka" as it is easy to make. Originating in North Africa, it's popular throughout the Middle East. Versatile and adaptable, it can be scaled up or down for breakfast, brunch, dinner, or a late-night snack. The origin of the word is debated, but it probably comes from the Arabic for "mixture"—for cooking eggs in onions, tomatoes, and sweet peppers. As with any homey, comforting dish, the proportions and seasonings are really up to the cook. Serve this over toasted pita or roll into a lavash.

3 tablespoons extra-virgin olive oil, plus more for finishing
1 medium onion, chopped
1 large red bell pepper, seeded and chopped
1 small chile pepper, seeded and chopped
2 garlic cloves, smashed
1 tablespoon smoked paprika
1 teaspoon ground cumin
One 28-ounce (794 g) can diced fire-roasted tomatoes with their juices
Coarse salt
Freshly ground black pepper
¼ cup (15 g) chopped cilantro, plus more for garnish
6 eggs
Chopped black olives for garnish

Film a large skillet with the oil and set over high heat. When the oil begins to shimmer, add the onion, bell pepper, and chile pepper in an even layer and cook, without stirring, until the vegetables become browned and are beginning to char, about 5 minutes. Stir and continue cooking until they are soft and slightly charred all over, another 4 minutes. Stir in the garlic, paprika, and cumin then stir in the tomatoes. Reduce the heat and simmer until the mixture thickens, about 10 minutes. Season to taste with salt and black pepper, and stir in the cilantro.

Using a large spoon, make a well near the perimeter of the pan. Break an egg directly into the well and spoon a little sauce over the edges of the white to partially submerge and contain it, leaving the yolk exposed. Repeat with the remaining eggs, working around the pan. Season with a little more salt. Cover, reduce the heat, and cook until the egg whites are set and the yolks are runny, 5 to 8 minutes. Garnish with more cilantro and the olives.

> **Kitchen Note**
> *The quantities here are for six servings, while the photo shows a meal for one. Adjust the amounts accordingly.*

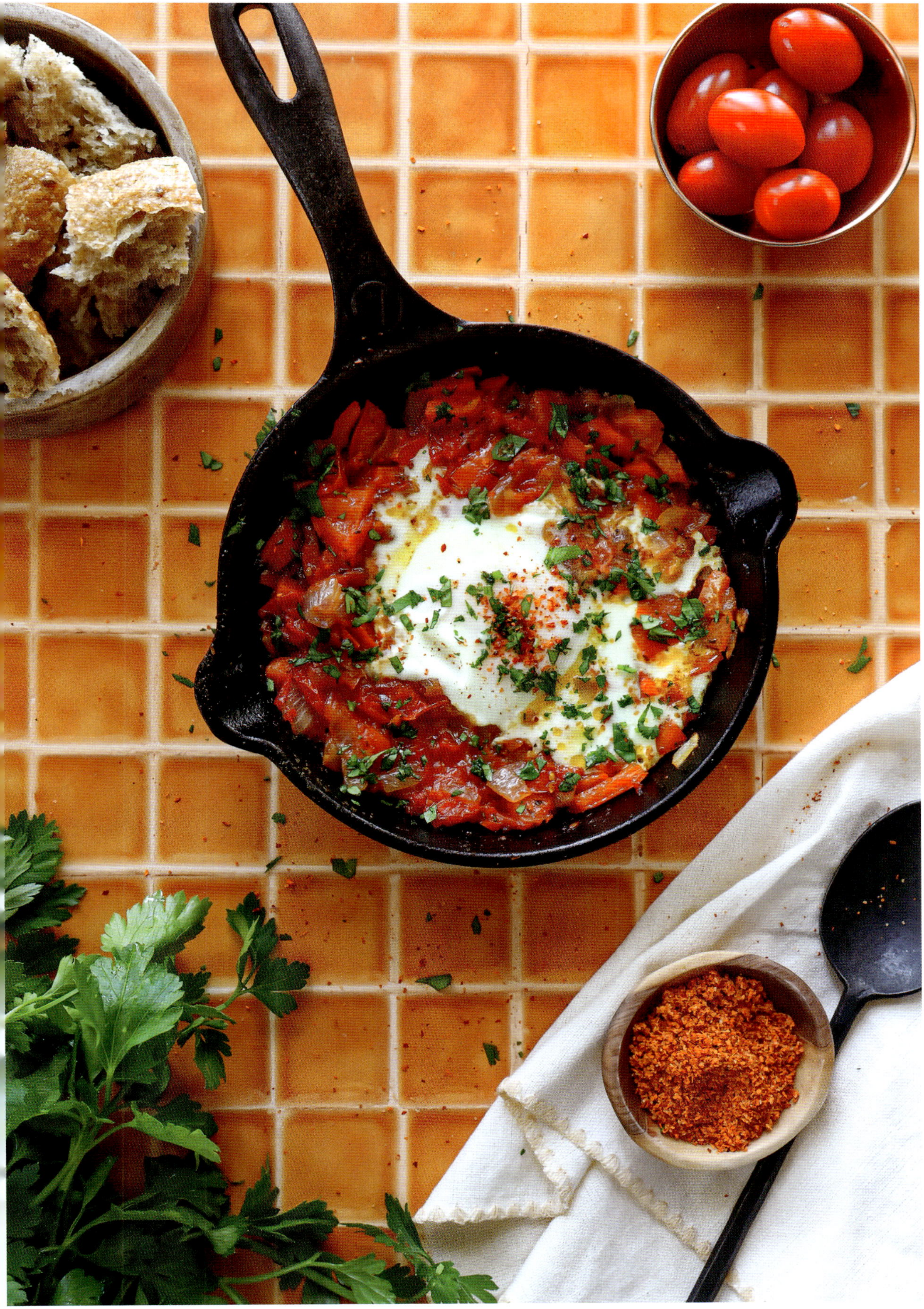

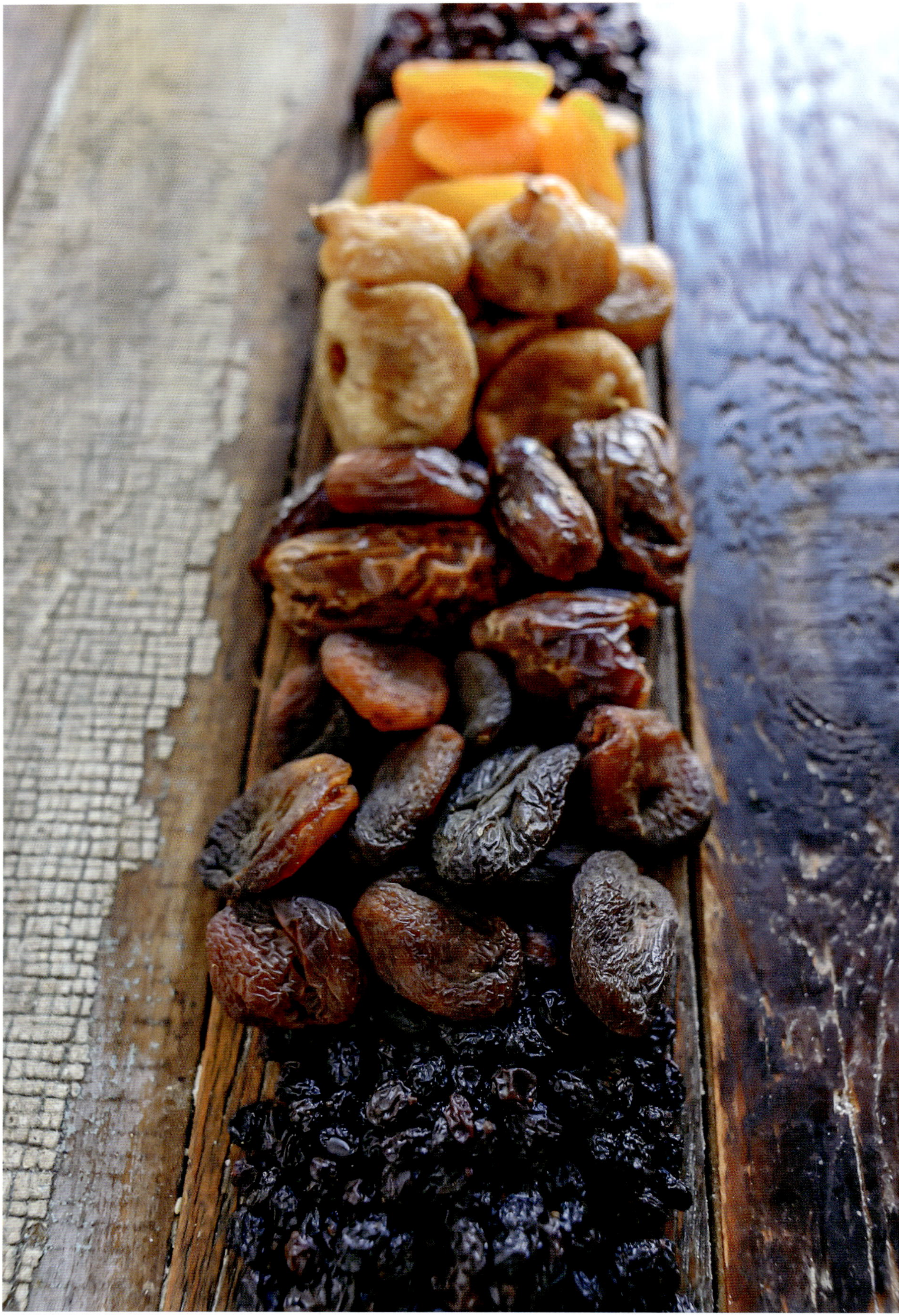

Chapter 11

Soups and Stews

Soup may not be the dish that leaps to mind when you think about desert cuisine. But nights can get chilly once the sun goes down. Plus, these soups are focused on simplicity and comfort. They can be easily expanded to serve many and are often made from the odds and ends of a delicious meal. The cold soups offered here are perfect for lunch in the blasting midday heat.

Tunisian Chickpea Stew	114
Avocado Soup	116
Brilliant Tomato Harissa Soup with Favas	117
White Bean Chili	118
Chicken and Okra Stew	120
Cold Pistachio-Saffron Soup of Yogurt, Apricots, and Rose Water	121
Festive Spicy Beef Stew	122
Lamb and Chickpea Stew	124
White Gazpacho	125
Watermelon and Cactus Fruit Gazpacho	126
Lamb and Spinach Stew	127

Tunisian Chickpea Stew
(Lablabi, Lablebi Harira)

Libya and Tunisia

Serves 4

Lablabi, a Tunisian chickpea soup, is a warming comfort food with plenty of punch. Seasoned with harissa, it is finished with tangy lemon and chopped olives. For brunch, serve it with a dollop of plain whole-milk Greek yogurt or top with a soft-boiled egg and a mound of herbs. Enrich the soup with a final swirl of good olive oil and serve with plenty of flatbread for dunking.

3 tablespoons extra-virgin olive oil
1 onion, diced
1 carrot, diced
Coarse salt
6 garlic cloves, smashed
1 tablespoon ground cumin
1 to 2 tablespoons harissa (see page 167)
2 cans (14 ounces [800 g]) chickpeas with their liquid or 3 cups (800 g) cooked chickpeas with stock (see Note)
1 can (14 ounces [397 g]) fire-roasted diced tomatoes with juices
1 cup (240 ml) bean or vegetable stock
2 tablespoons fresh lemon juice, plus more as needed
½ cup chopped sun-dried tomatoes in oil plus 1 tablespoon additional oil
1 teaspoon honey
Chopped olives for garnish

Film a Dutch oven with the oil and set over medium heat. Add the onion, carrot, and a pinch of salt. Sauté, stirring, until tender, about 8 minutes. Stir in the garlic and cumin and cook to release the aromas, about 1 minute. Stir in the harissa to taste.

Add the chickpeas with their liquid, the canned tomatoes with their juices, and the stock. Season with salt, increase the heat, bring to a boil, and reduce the heat to a simmer. Cook, stirring occasionally, until the liquid has reduced and thickened and the chickpeas are warmed through, 10 to 15 minutes. Stir in the lemon juice, sun-dried tomatoes and their oil, and honey. Taste and adjust the seasonings. Serve garnished with chopped olives.

Kitchen Note
To cook dry chickpeas, put 1½ cups (250 g) chickpeas into a large pot or bowl and add enough water to cover by 4 inches (10 cm). Soak 8 to 10 hours. Drain the chickpeas. Transfer to a heavy pot and add enough water to cover the chickpeas by 4 inches (10 cm). Add ½ whole onion, 3 garlic cloves, 1 small carrot, 1 small celery stalk, 2 bay leaves, 5 parsley sprigs, and 5 whole peppercorns. Bring to a boil, reduce the heat to a simmer, cover, and cook until the chickpeas are tender, 50 minutes to 1 hour. Transfer the chickpeas to a colander, reserving the cooking liquid, and discarding the solids.

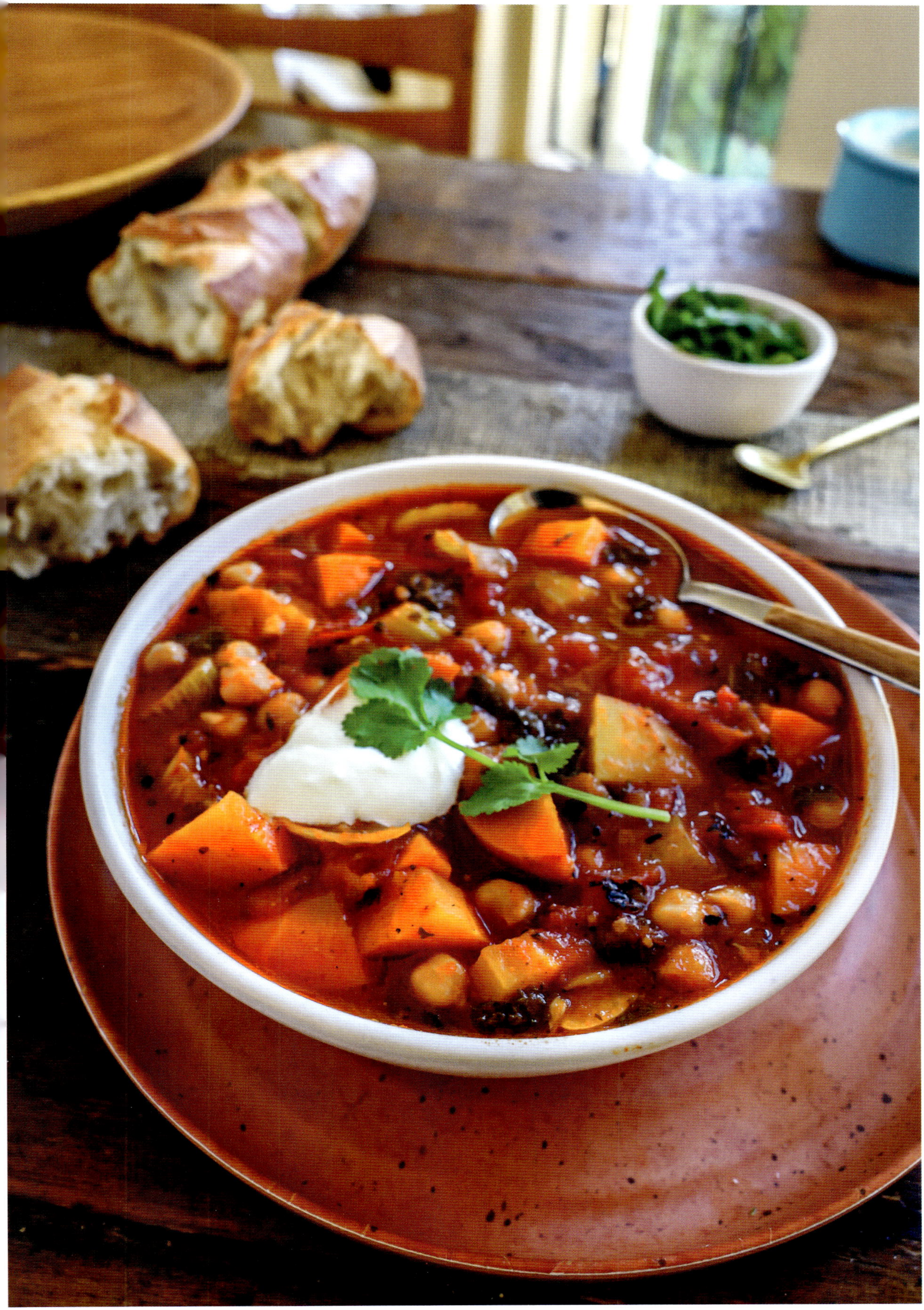

Avocado Soup
(Sopa Fria de Aguacate)

Mexico

Serves 4 to 6

This easy, cooling soup makes fast use of avocados on a hot summer day. Serve with corn tortillas or chips and call it lunch.

½ cup (120 ml) cold water, plus more as needed
2 large ripe avocados, halved, pitted, and peeled
1½ cups (368 g) plain whole-milk yogurt or kefir
¼ cup (60 ml) fresh lime juice
¼ cup (60 ml) extra-virgin olive oil
½ cup (30 g) chopped cilantro, plus more for garnish
1 small jalapeño, seeded and diced (optional)
Sea salt
Freshly ground black pepper
Crumbled queso fresco for garnish (optional)
Chile powder for garnish (optional)

Put the water, avocados, yogurt, lime juice, oil, cilantro, and jalapeño (if using) into a blender and puree until smooth. Season to taste with salt and pepper. Transfer to a covered container and chill well.

When ready to serve, if the soup is too thick, thin with a little ice-cold water. Pour into chilled soup bowls or chilled glasses and garnish with more cilantro, queso fresco, and chile powder if desired.

Brilliant Tomato Harissa Soup with Favas
(Harira, Zuppa di Ful Madamas)
Algeria, Egypt, Morocco, and Lebanon

Serves 4 to 6

This is a simple everyday recipe that doesn't require hours and hours of seasoning. It gets a punch from harissa, the North African chile paste. Thanks to the beans, the soup thickens quickly. It's wonderful topped with toasted pita and feta.

3 tablespoons extra-virgin olive oil
1 onion, diced
1 large carrot, diced
6 garlic cloves, smashed
1 generous tablespoon ground cumin
1 to 2 tablespoons harissa (see page 167)
3 cups (510 g) cooked fava beans or chickpeas plus ½ cup (120 ml) of cooking liquid (see Note)
2 cups (490 g) canned diced tomatoes
Sea salt
Freshly ground black pepper
2 tablespoons fresh lemon juice
Chopped green olives for garnish
Chopped fresh cilantro for garnish

Film a large Dutch oven or soup pot with the oil and set over medium heat. Add the onion, carrot, garlic, and cumin and cook until the vegetables become tender, 5 to 8 minutes. Stir in the harissa to taste and cook another minute.

Stir in the beans and cooking liquid along with the tomatoes. If the soup seems too thick, add a little water to reach the desired consistency. Season with salt and pepper, increase the heat, and bring to a boil. Reduce the heat and simmer, stirring occasionally, about 5 minutes. Stir in the lemon juice. Serve garnished with the olives and cilantro.

Kitchen Note
To cook dry beans, place dried beans in a bowl and add enough water to cover by 4 inches (10 cm). Soak 8 to 10 hours. Drain the beans, transfer to a pot, and add enough water to cover by 4 inches (10 cm). Set over high heat, bring to a boil, reduce the heat to a simmer, cover, and cook the beans until tender, 40 minutes to 1½ hours, adding more water to the pot as needed.

White Bean Chili
(Sopa de Chile con Frijoles Blancos)

Mexico, El Salvador, and US Desert Southwest

Serves 6

There is really no such thing as the best chili. Every cook, every family, and every town has a favorite recipe that's as personal and soul-warming as a hug. Whether it's made with beef, turkey, chicken, red beans, black beans, or white beans, like this one, a good chili is hearty and fragrantly spiced.

- 2 cups (416 g) dried white beans (such as cannellini or navy)
- 3 tablespoons olive oil
- 3 yellow or white onions, diced
- 1 medium fennel bulb, trimmed and diced
- 3 garlic cloves, smashed
- 1 jalapeño pepper, seeded and diced
- 10 cups (2.4 L) vegetable or chicken stock, plus more as needed
- ¼ cup (15 g) chopped fresh parsley
- 1 bay leaf
- 1 tablespoon fresh thyme leaves or 1 teaspoon dried
- 1 tablespoon fresh oregano leaves or 1 teaspoon dried
- 3 tablespoons ground cumin
- Salt
- Freshly ground black pepper
- 1 cup (176 g) fresh or frozen corn kernels
- 1 tablespoon fresh lime juice
- ¼ cup (15 g) finely chopped fresh cilantro, plus more for garnish
- 1 cup (245 g) Greek yogurt or sour cream

Put the beans in a large pot or bowl and add enough water to cover the beans by 3 inches (7.5 cm). Soak for at least 6 hours or overnight (8 to 10 hours). Drain and reserve.

Film a Dutch oven or large deep, heavy pot with the oil and set over medium-high heat. Add the onions and fennel and sauté until soft, about 5 minutes. Add the garlic and jalapeño and continue cooking until fragrant, 3 to 5 minutes.

Add the drained beans to the pot along with the stock, parsley, bay leaf, thyme, oregano, cumin, and a sprinkle of salt and black pepper. Bring to a simmer and cook, stirring occasionally, adding more stock if needed, until the beans are tender and the mixture has thickened, about 90 minutes. Add the corn. Season with the lime juice and more salt and black pepper as needed.

In a small bowl, stir 2 tablespoons of the cilantro with the yogurt. Serve the chili garnished with a dollop of the herbed yogurt and the remaining cilantro.

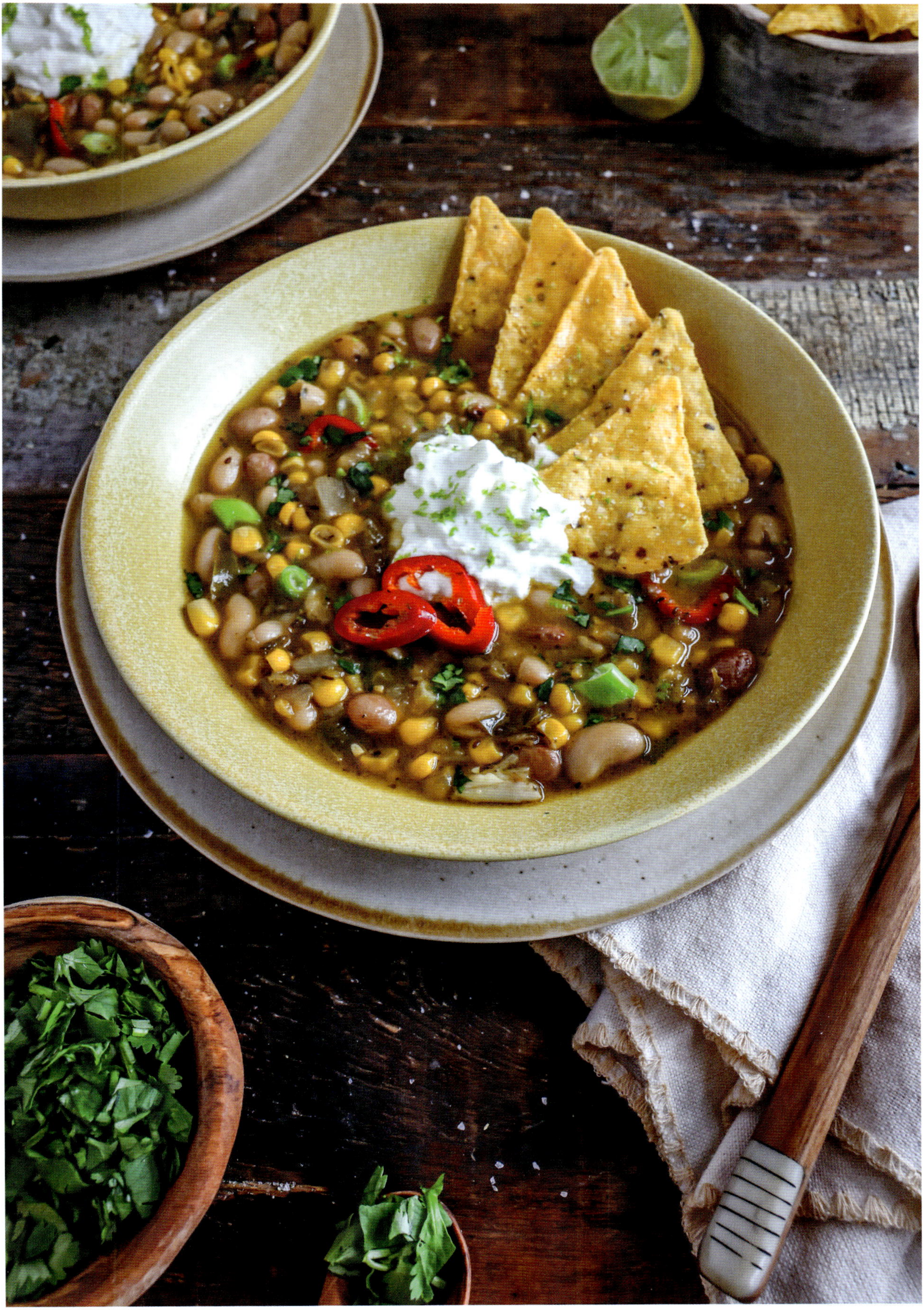

Chicken and Okra Stew

(Kotopoulo me Bamies, Shorbet Bamia bi Lahme)

Greece, Lebanon, Syria, and Turkey

Serves 4 to 6

Okra, beloved throughout the US South, is a staple in Middle Eastern countries. In Turkey and Greece, okra goes by its Arabic name, *bamyeh* or *bamyies*. Here it's tossed with lemon and salt to marinate for about an hour to reduce the "slime" factor. Look for the smallest pods you can find. Serve over rice with toasted pita.

- 2 pounds (908 g) okra, stems removed
- 2 teaspoons coarse salt, plus more as needed
- ¼ cup (60 ml) fresh lemon juice
- ¼ cup (60 ml) extra-virgin olive oil
- 4 to 5 pounds (1.82 to 2.27 kg) boneless chicken, cut into pieces
- 1 medium onion, chopped
- 3 garlic cloves, smashed
- 2 teaspoons dried Greek oregano
- 1 teaspoon ground cumin
- One 16-ounce (454 g) can fire-roasted diced tomatoes
- 1 cup (240 ml) chicken stock or water

Rinse the okra under cold running water. Transfer to a bowl and sprinkle with the salt and lemon juice. Set aside for 1 hour.

Pour the oil into a Dutch oven and set over medium-high heat. Working in batches, cook the chicken until it browns on all sides, 15 to 20 minutes. Remove the chicken to a dish. Add the onion, garlic, oregano, cumin, tomatoes, and stock to the pot and stir to scrape up any browned bits clinging to the bottom of the pot. Return the chicken to the pot, increase the heat and bring to a boil, and reduce to a simmer. Partially cover and cook until the chicken is tender and the internal temperature of the dark meat has reached 170°F (77°C) on a digital meat thermometer, about 1 hour.

Brush any excess salt from the okra and add to the pot. Cook until tender, about 10 minutes. Taste and season with salt as needed.

Cold Pistachio-Saffron Soup of Yogurt, Apricots, and Rose Water

(Asheh Pesteh, Crema de Pistache, Crema de Pistacchio, Tarator)

Bulgaria, Greece, Iran, Israel, and Italy

Serves 4 to 6

This classic Persian soup makes a lovely light dessert on a hot summer day or a light lunch when paired to a crisp green salad with a snappy vinaigrette. Make it at least 3 hours ahead so it has time to cool and the flavors marry. If you prefer a smooth soup, puree it in a blender before serving.

- 2 tablespoons boiling water
- ¼ teaspoon saffron threads
- ½ cup (64 g) shelled, peeled pistachios (or hazelnuts or cashews), coarsely chopped, plus a little more for garnish
- 2 tablespoons honey, plus more as needed
- 1 cup (130 g) chopped dried apricots
- 2 teaspoons rose water, plus more as needed
- ¼ cup (61 g) whole-milk Greek yogurt or labneh
- Pinch sea salt

In a small dish, combine the boiling water and saffron threads. Set aside.

Put the pistachios, honey, apricots, and rose water in a medium pot and cover with about 3 inches (7.5 cm) of cold water. Set over high heat, bring to a boil, turn off the heat, and allow the apricots to plump. Add the saffron threads. Transfer the mixture to a serving bowl, allow to come to room temperature, and stir in the yogurt. Add salt to taste. Cover and cool for at least 3 hours or overnight (8 to 10 hours). Serve garnished with pistachios.

Festive Spicy Beef Stew
(Estofado, Guacabaqui, Wakabaki)

Mexico, Philippines, Puerto Rico, Spain, and US Desert Southwest

Serves 6 to 8

A cherished dish of the Yaqui Pueblos of the Sonoran Desert, this is the stew of big family gatherings, best made ahead so the flavors marry. It is an Indigenous American adaptation of *estofados,* game soups found throughout much of the Spanish-speaking world. The Yaqui originally used white-tailed deer instead of beef or oxtail. This dish is hearty and comforting and guaranteed to cure whatever ails you, from a broken heart to a hangover. The beef is slowly braised in an aromatic sofrito with tomatoes to become silky and sumptuous. Serve over rice with corn bread to sop up all the fabulous juices.

ADOBO SAUCE

2 teaspoons extra-virgin olive oil
2 teaspoons white wine vinegar
3 garlic cloves, smashed
1 teaspoon dried oregano (preferably Mexican)
1 teaspoon coarse salt
½ teaspoon freshly ground black pepper

STEW

2 pounds (908 g) beef chuck roast, trimmed of fat and cut into 2-inch (5 cm) pieces
3 tablespoons olive oil, plus more as needed
1 small bell pepper, seeded and diced
4 garlic cloves, smashed
1 onion, chopped
2 teaspoons ground cumin
2 teaspoons sweet paprika
1 teaspoon ground turmeric
¼ cup (15 g) chopped fresh cilantro
Sea salt
Freshly ground black pepper
1 cup (240 ml) beef stock, plus more as needed
One 14.5-ounce (411 g) can chopped fire-roasted tomatoes with their juices
3 bay leaves
1 carrot, chopped
1 celery stalk, chopped
1 pound (454 g) Yukon Gold potatoes, scrubbed and chopped

To make the adobo sauce: With a mortar and pestle, pound together the oil, vinegar, garlic, oregano, salt, and pepper. Set aside.

To make the stew: Pat the meat dry and put into a medium bowl; add the adobo and turn to coat. Cover and marinate for at least 30 minutes at room temperature or in the refrigerator for 8 to 10 hours.

Film a Dutch oven or large heavy pot with the oil and set over high heat. Working in batches to prevent crowding, add the beef and cook, flipping often, to brown evenly on all sides. Transfer to a clean bowl and set aside.

Lower the heat to medium, add a little more oil, and stir in the bell pepper, garlic, onion, cumin, paprika, turmeric, cilantro, and salt and pepper to taste, and cook until fragrant, about 30 seconds. Stir in the stock, scraping up any browned bits clinging to the bottom of the pan, then add the tomatoes and bay leaves. Nestle the meat into the pot, bring to a simmer, reduce the heat to low, and cook for an hour, stirring occasionally.

Stir in the carrot and celery and cook for 1 more hour, adding more stock or water if needed. The meat should cook until it falls apart when pressed with the back of a fork.

Add the potatoes and cook, covered, until tender, another 30 minutes. Taste and adjust the seasonings.

Lamb and Chickpea Stew
(Carne de Cordero en la Olla, Harira)

China, Greece, Lebanon, Iran, and Morocco

Serves 4 to 6

This ancient stew dates back to the early 14th century in western China, Central Asia, and the Far East. In fact, it traverses all arid-land geography and is perhaps the most widely diffused desert dish on the planet. It's wonderful for a dinner party, so feel free to double the recipe. It's best served with rice to soak up all those fragrant juices.

1⅓ pounds (604 g) lamb shoulder or stew meat, cut into 1-inch (2.5 cm) pieces
Sea salt
Freshly ground black pepper
3 tablespoons olive oil, plus more as needed
1 onion, coarsely chopped
¼ cup (15 g) chopped fresh cilantro
½ cup (120 ml) lamb or chicken stock, plus more as needed
½ cup (123 g) diced tomatoes, canned or fresh
1 teaspoon finely crushed mastic paste or powder (optional)
1-inch (2.5 cm) piece fresh ginger, peeled and grated
½-inch (1.25 cm) piece fresh turmeric, peeled and grated
½ teaspoon ground cumin
1 teaspoon malagueta pepper
1 teaspoon dried oregano
¼ teaspoon freshly grated nutmeg
Pinch saffron threads (optional)
2 cups (328 g) cooked, drained chickpeas
1 tablespoon fresh lemon juice
4 cups (120 g) fresh spinach
Lemon wedges for garnish

Generously season the lamb cubes with salt and black pepper.

Film a Dutch oven or large deep skillet with the oil and set over medium-high heat. When the oil is hot, add the lamb and sauté until well browned on all sides, 5 to 8 minutes. Remove and set aside.

Add the onion and cilantro to the pot and sauté until the onion is translucent, 3 to 5 minutes.

Stir in the stock and tomatoes, scraping up any browned bits clinging to the bottom of the pot. Stir in the mastic (if using), ginger, turmeric, cumin, malagueta pepper, oregano, nutmeg, and saffron, if using.

Cover, lower the heat, and simmer until the lamb is very tender, 1 to 1½ hours, adding more stock if the level of the liquid looks too low. Stir in the chickpeas and lemon juice, then the spinach, and simmer until cooked through. Serve with the lemon wedges.

White Gazpacho
(Gazpacho Blanco de Ajo, Tharid)
Saudi Arabia and Spain

Serves 6

This elegant cold soup, thickened with bread and almonds, is brightened with sherry vinegar. The blanched almonds give it a floral, nutty fragrance while the garlic provides its complexity. Be sure to chill the soup thoroughly before serving so that the flavors meld and develop. Garnish with a drizzle of peppery olive oil, sliced green grapes, and a shower of chopped fresh mint.

1 cup (145 g) blanched almonds
3 cups (720 ml) cold water
2 garlic cloves, smashed
½ pound (227 g) crustless rustic bread, cut into pieces
Coarse salt
1 to 2 teaspoons sherry vinegar
1 tablespoon extra-virgin olive oil, plus more for garnish
Sliced green grapes, for garnish
Chopped mint, for garnish

Put the almonds, water, and garlic into a blender and process on high speed until milky, scraping down the sides as needed.

Add the bread and process until very smooth. Season with salt and vinegar, then blend in the oil. Transfer the soup to a covered container and refrigerate until well chilled, at least 2 hours or overnight (8 to 10 hours).

Serve the gazpacho very cold, garnished with a drizzle of oil, grapes, and mint.

Watermelon and Cactus Fruit Gazpacho
(Gazpacho de Sandía, Muk)
Mexico and Spain

Serves 6 to 8

The word *gazpacho* is derived from the Arabic for "soaked bread." This cold soup is also called *tharid* and *mukarrah*. The most familiar versions focus on ripe summer tomatoes, but here, the flavors of Old World watermelons are paired with two kinds of cactus fruit now available in many stores, prickly pear and dragon fruit, for a refreshing fusion of the Old and New Worlds.

4 cups diced, seeded watermelon (about 2½ pounds [1.14 kg])
2 cups diced small Lebanese (Beit Alpha) mini cucumbers or Armenian melon cucumber (1½ to 2 pounds [681 to 908 g])
¼ cup (36 g) diced red onion
¼ cup (45 g) dragon fruit (see Notes)
¼ cup (37 g) diced prickly pear (about 1 prickly pear) or ¼ cup prickly pear pulp (see Notes)
1 medium red bell pepper or 3 mini red bell peppers, cored, seeded, and diced
¼ cup (15 g) minced fresh purple basil
¼ cup (15 g) minced fresh spearmint, plus more for garnish
3 tablespoons sherry vinegar
3 tablespoons extra-virgin olive oil
2 cups (70 g) slightly stale cubed bread
1 teaspoon ground cumin
Sea salt
Freshly ground black pepper
Minced jicama for garnish

Put the watermelon, cucumbers, onions, dragon fruit, prickly pear, bell pepper, basil, spearmint, vinegar, oil, bread, and cumin in a blender and process until you have your desired consistency. Season to taste with salt and black pepper. Chill for at least an hour or overnight (8 to 10 hours). Serve garnished with spearmint and jicama.

Kitchen Notes
To prepare the prickly pear pulp, wearing protective gloves, hold the prickly pear on a cutting board. Slice off both ends. Make one long vertical slice down the body and slip your finger into the slice and grab hold of the skin, peel it back, and discard. Dice the prickly pear. Prickly pear puree is also available online (see page 183).

To prepare the dragon fruit, slice the dragon fruit in half and scoop out the slightly firm flesh with a spoon. Be sure to store any leftover dragon fruit in a sealed container. It will stay fresh for at least 2 weeks in the refrigerator.

Lamb and Spinach Stew
(Sabzi)
Afghanistan

Serves 6

This is one of the traditional New Year's dishes in Afghanistan. The green hue symbolizes spring's arrival and hope. The lamb cooks until tender in a flavorful broth of onion, garlic, and chile, and is finished with cilantro and garlic chives. Serve over rice.

1 cup (240 ml) vegetable oil
1 onion, chopped
2 garlic cloves, smashed
1 red chile, thinly sliced
2 pounds (908 g) boneless lamb stew meat, cut into 2-inch (5 cm) chunks
Coarse salt
4 cups (960 ml) water
1½ cups (90 g) chopped fresh cilantro
½ cup (24 g) chopped garlic chives
2½ pounds (1.14 kg) fresh spinach, stems removed, chopped

In a large heavy pot or Dutch oven, heat ½ cup (120 ml) of the oil over medium-high heat and add the onion, garlic, and chile. Cook, stirring frequently, until golden brown, about 10 minutes. Add the lamb and cook until lightly browned on all sides, about 5 minutes. Add 1 tablespoon salt and the water, stirring to scrape up any browned bits clinging to the bottom of the pot, and skim any scum that rises to the top. Reduce the heat to a simmer, cover, and cook until the lamb is very tender, 1½ to 2 hours.

In a large skillet, heat the remaining ½ cup (120 ml) oil over medium heat. Add the cilantro and garlic chives and fry, stirring occasionally, about 5 minutes. Add the spinach and toss together.

Using a slotted spoon, add the lamb to the skillet. Add 1 cup (240 ml) of the lamb broth and stir to combine. Reduce the heat to low and simmer until the flavors have mingled, about 15 minutes. Taste and adjust the seasonings.

> **Kitchen Note**
> *Allow the excess lamb broth to cool and then transfer it to a covered container and store in the refrigerator for up to a week, or freeze.*

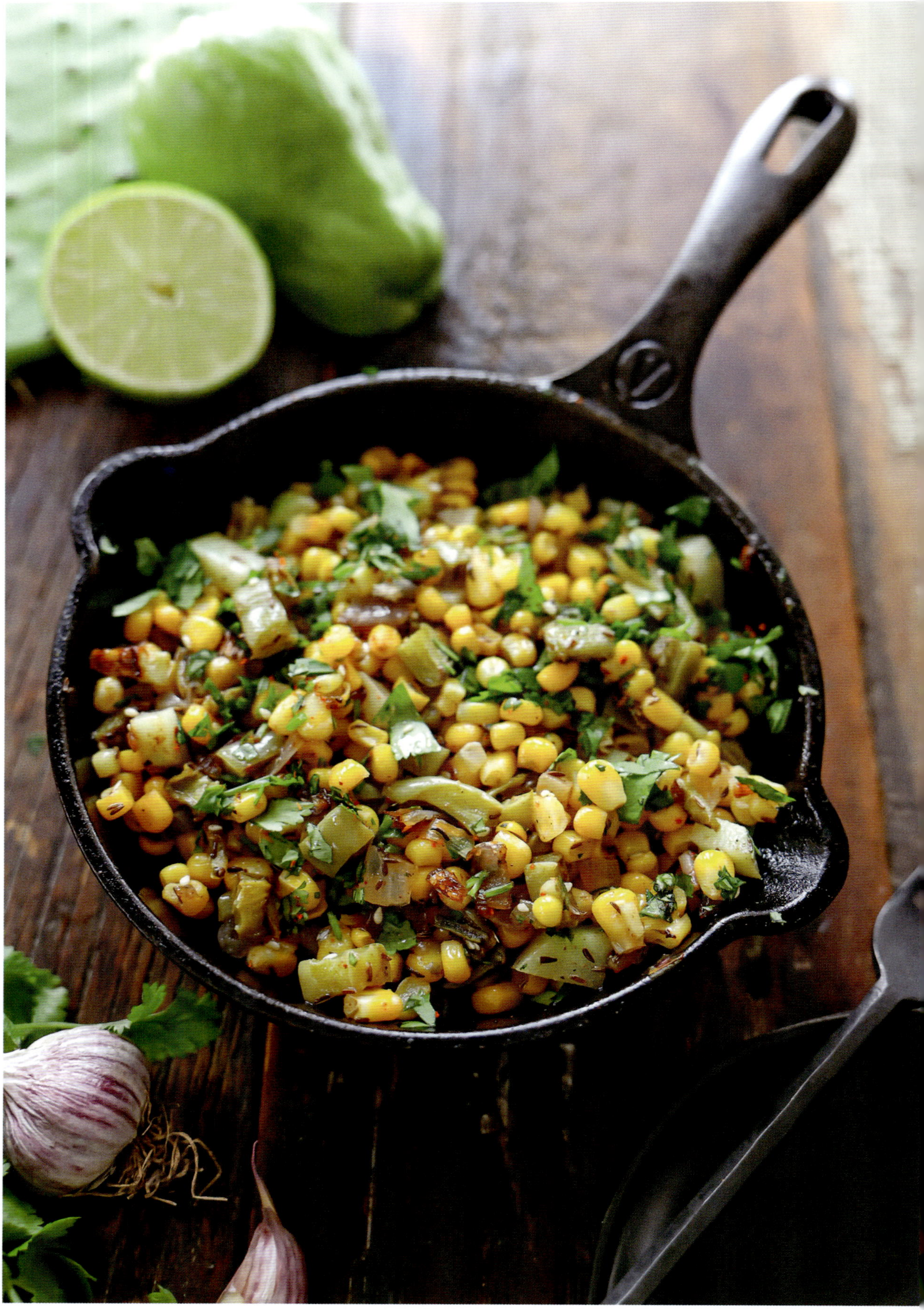

Chapter 12

Salads

Exceptionally flavorful and wholesome, these salads showcase the desert's bounty and the wisdom that continues to guide the region's cuisine. The recipes here focus on freshness and are ready in minutes.

Pomegranate Arugula Salad	130
Brilliant Citrus Salad	131
Parsley, Mint, Cilantro, and Bulgur Salad	133
Desert Succotash	134
Za'atar-Roasted Cauliflower	135
Chayote and Melon Salad	136
Spinach with Spices and Yogurt	137
Mixed Citrus and Radish Salad	138
Jicama, Orange, and Avocado Salad	139
Watercress, Tomato, and Toasted Pita Salad with Sumac and Mint	140

Pomegranate Arugula Salad
(Ensalada de Granada y Rúcula)

Israel, Mexico, and Spain

Serves 4

A toss-up of spicy arugula and tangy-sweet pomegranate gives this salad a peppery-tangy-sweet kick. Use dandelion greens whenever they're in season for a sunny, robust flavor.

¼ cup (60 ml) pomegranate molasses
Juice of ½ lemon
2 tablespoons honey
2 tablespoons white wine vinegar
¾ cup (180 ml) extra-virgin olive oil
Sea salt
Freshly ground black pepper
6 cups (120 g) arugula
½ cup (28 g) torn dandelion greens (optional)
½ cup (87 g) pomegranate seeds
¼ cup (28 g) crumbled feta cheese
¼ cup (29 g) toasted pecans

In a small bowl, whisk together the molasses, lemon juice, honey, and vinegar. Then slowly whisk in the oil. Season to taste with salt and pepper.

In a large bowl, toss together the arugula, dandelion greens (if using), and pomegranate seeds, and drizzle in enough of the dressing to lightly coat. Lightly toss in the feta. Serve topped with the pecans.

Brilliant Citrus Salad
(Leemoone Taktouka)

Jordan and Morocco

Serves 4

Moroccan salads are not just mixtures of lettuces doused with dressings. Rather than being served at the end of the meal, European-style, salads like this bright and lively one make a great appetizer to excite the palate.

3 navel oranges
1 pink grapefruit
Coarse salt
1 shallot, chopped
1 rosemary sprig
3 tablespoons extra-virgin olive oil
1 tablespoon fresh lime juice
¼ teaspoon honey (optional)
Coarsely ground black pepper
Pinch red pepper flakes
¼ cup (36 g) chopped black kalamata olives
¼ cup (44 g) pomegranate seeds

Peel and then cut the oranges and grapefruit into discs or half-moons and place in a bowl. Sprinkle with a pinch of salt. Add the shallot and rosemary and cover to rest for 1 hour or in the refrigerator overnight (8 to 10 hours).

In a small bowl, whisk together the oil, lime juice, and honey, if using. Drizzle over the salad. Grind a little black pepper over the salad and add some red pepper flakes. Scatter the olives and pomegranate seeds over all. Serve cold or at room temperature.

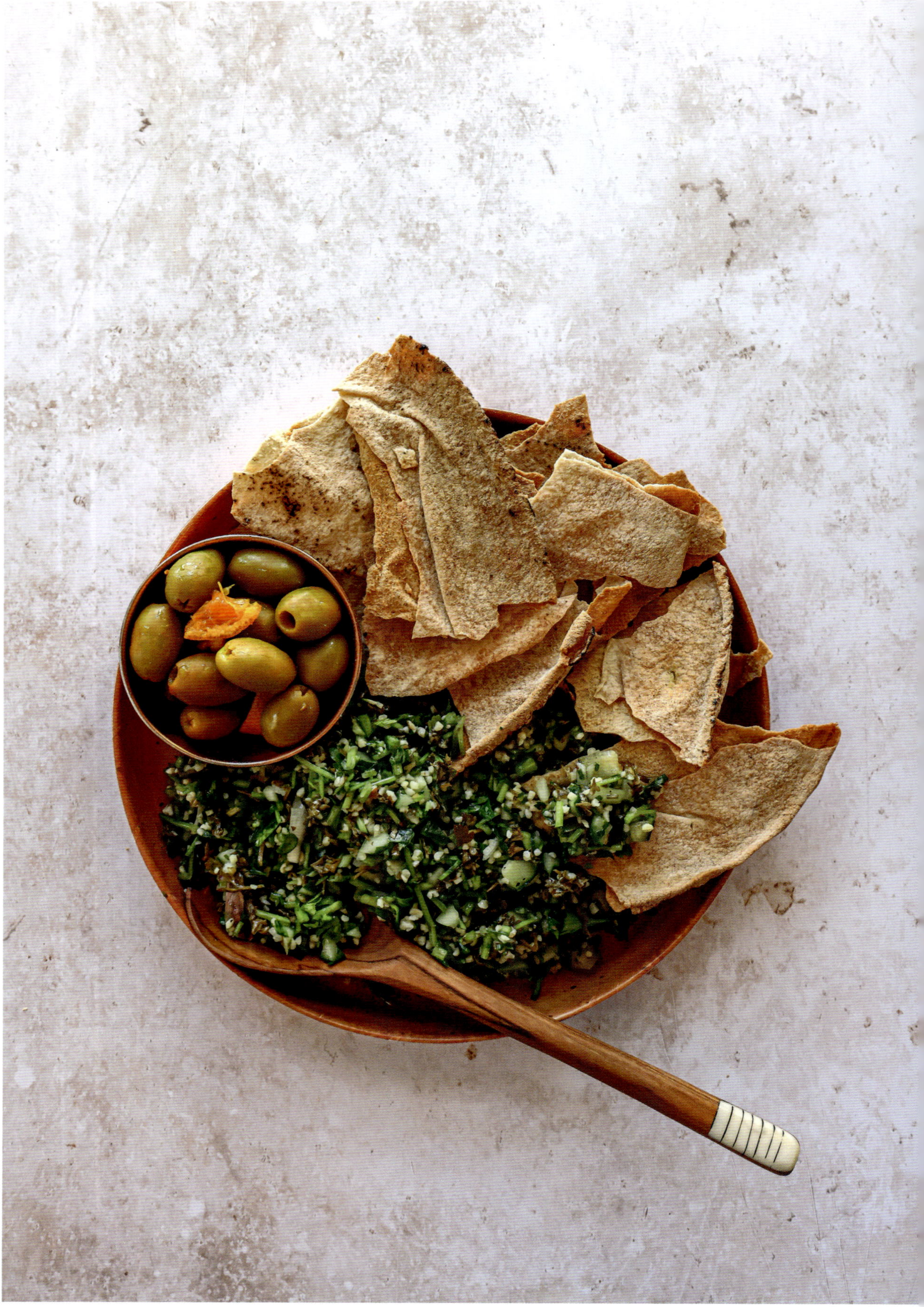

Parsley, Mint, Cilantro, and Bulgur Salad
(Tabbouleh, Tabouli)

Israel, Jordan, Lebanon, Palestine, and Syria

Serves 4 to 6

This light, bright Lebanese salad is an edible garden. Served as an appetizer, it often includes blistered tomatoes. Here we've opted for lots of greens since the salad's Arabic name shines the light on the parsley rather than the bulgur wheat. In fact, you can even make it with quinoa.

¼ cup (34 g) fine bulgur wheat
1 small garlic clove, minced
Juice of 2 lemons
2 cups (120 g) finely chopped fresh flat-leaf parsley
1 cup (60 g) finely chopped fresh cilantro
½ cup (17 g) finely chopped purslane or watercress
¼ cup (15 g) finely chopped fresh mint
1 bunch scallions, chopped
Coarse salt
¼ cup (60 ml) extra-virgin olive oil

Place the bulgur in a bowl and add enough water to cover by ½ inch (1.25 cm). Soak for 20 minutes, until slightly softened. Drain in a fine-mesh strainer and press the bulgur to squeeze out any excess water.

Transfer to a large bowl, toss with the garlic, lemon juice, parsley, cilantro, purslane, mint, and scallions, and sprinkle in some salt. Chill for about 2 hours so the bulgur absorbs the liquid.

Add the oil, toss, and adjust the seasonings to taste.

Desert Succotash
(Guisado de Elote y Nopalitos)

Mexico and US Desert Southwest

Serves 4

Nopales, paddles of the prickly pear cactus, taste a little like green beans, but are slightly tangier. They make a fine match to sweet corn in this lively succotash.

2 tablespoons olive oil
2 nopalitos, thorns scraped off, cut into small dice
1 cup (132 g) diced chayote squash
2 cups (304 g) corn kernels, fresh or thawed frozen
½ cup (72 g) diced red onion
1 tablespoon minced garlic
1 teaspoon ground cumin
1 teaspoon dried oregano
1 teaspoon sumac
½ teaspoon ancho chile powder
½ cup (30 g) chopped fresh cilantro, plus more for garnish
1 tablespoon fresh lime juice, plus more as needed
Sea salt
Freshly ground black pepper

Film a large heavy skillet with the oil, set over medium heat, and sauté the nopalitos and squash, stirring often until tender, about 5 minutes. Add the corn, onion, garlic, cumin, oregano, sumac, and chile powder, and continue cooking until the vegetables are tender. Stir in the cilantro and season with the lime juice, salt, and pepper to taste. Serve garnished with more cilantro.

Za'atar-Roasted Cauliflower
(Arnabit bi Za'atar)

Iran, Iraq, and Morocco

Serves 4 to 6

Just a drizzle of honey amplifies the warm spices in this simple dish. It's a wonderful side to roast chicken or lamb, or as an entrée served over cooked grain and topped with Greek yogurt and chopped cashews.

1 head cauliflower, about 1½ to 2 pounds (681 to 908 g), broken into florets
1 medium carrot, sliced into coins
2 to 3 tablespoons olive oil
Generous pinch coarse salt
Generous pinch freshly ground black pepper
Up to 3 tablespoons honey
1 tablespoon za'atar spice, plus more as needed
¼ cup sliced green olives
Chopped fresh cilantro or parsley for garnish
Lemon wedges for serving

Preheat the oven to 400°F (200°C). Line a baking sheet with parchment paper. In a large bowl, toss the cauliflower and carrot with enough olive oil to generously coat, along with the salt and pepper. Spread the cauliflower and carrot out on the prepared baking sheet and roast, shaking the pan occasionally, until the cauliflower is nicely browned, 20 to 25 minutes. Transfer to a serving bowl and toss with enough honey to lightly coat and then add the za'atar. Taste and adjust the seasonings. Garnish with olives and cilantro. Serve with lemon wedges on the side.

Chayote and Melon Salad
(Ensalada de Chayote y Melón)

Eastern Mexico and Jamaica

Serves 4

This Jamaican-inspired salad of crisp chayote squash and melon is just right for a hot summer day. Make sure you serve it cold. Chayote goes by many other names: alligator pear, choco, and, in Louisiana, merlitón. It also pairs well with green Persian melon, watermelon, or avocado.

1 small cantaloupe or honeydew melon, halved, seeded, and thinly sliced
1 chayote squash, peeled, halved, seeded, and finely sliced
1 small shallot, diced
40 fresh mint leaves
Extra-virgin olive oil
Splash of fresh lime juice
Sea salt
Freshly ground black pepper
⅓ cup (41 g) roasted pistachios (see Note) for garnish

In a large bowl, toss together the melon, chayote, shallot, and mint leaves. Drizzle in enough olive oil to generously coat the vegetables, then toss in the lime juice, salt, and pepper to taste. Chill and then serve topped with the roasted pistachios.

Kitchen Note
To roast pistachios, spread the nuts out on a roasting pan and roast in a 350°F (180°C) oven until they smell toasty, 3 to 5 minutes. Remove and allow to cool before using as a garnish.

Spinach with Spices and Yogurt
(Sbankh, Spanek)

Jordan, Lebanon, and Palestine

Serves 4 to 6

Throughout the Middle East, you'll find a range of subtly spiced dishes topped with tangy yogurt. You can turn this into a soup by adding vegetable or chicken stock. Serve with flatbread.

1 cup (245 g) whole-milk Greek-style yogurt or strained plain yogurt
1 garlic clove, minced
Generous pinch sea salt
Generous pinch freshly ground black pepper
2 tablespoons extra-virgin olive oil
1 tablespoon pine nuts
⅛ teaspoon ground cloves
⅛ teaspoon ground allspice
¼ teaspoon ground coriander
¼ teaspoon ground cinnamon
9 to 10 cups (300 g) fresh spinach, torn

In a small bowl, stir together the yogurt, garlic, and a generous pinch of salt and pepper. Set aside.

Film a wide, heavy skillet with the oil, set over medium heat, and add the pine nuts. Cook, stirring, until they begin to color, 2 to 3 minutes. Remove from the oil with a slotted spoon and set aside. Add the spices to the oil and cook for about 15 seconds, then add the spinach and toss until it's coated with the oil to wilt, 15 to 30 seconds. Toss in the pine nuts, transfer to a serving dish, and top with the seasoned yogurt.

Mixed Citrus and Radish Salad
(Shlada Fijl wa Latsheen)

Morocco

Serves 4 to 6

The combination of tangerines, tart blood oranges, and sweet Cara Caras with zesty radishes (red or watermelon) is a study in color, texture, and contrasting tastes. Orange blossom water bumps up the floral notes.

2 tangerines or mandarins
2 blood oranges
2 navel or Cara Cara oranges
2 tablespoons fresh lemon juice
2 tablespoons orange blossom water
1 teaspoon honey
Generous pinch ground cinnamon
Pinch cayenne pepper
2 tablespoons hazelnut oil or pistachio oil
10 ounces (283 g) radishes, sliced thin
1 tablespoon chopped fresh mint, plus more for garnish
Sea salt
Freshly ground black pepper

Using a sharp knife, peel the tangerines and oranges over a bowl to catch the juices, being careful to remove all the bitter white pith. Whisk in the lemon juice, orange blossom water, honey, cinnamon, cayenne, and hazelnut oil.

Cut in between the orange section membranes to release the sections into the bowl. Toss in the radishes and mint. Season to taste with salt and freshly ground black pepper. Cover and refrigerate until cold. Serve garnished with mint.

Jicama, Orange, and Avocado Salad
(Ensalada de Jicama)
Mexico and US Desert Southwest

Serves 4 to 6

This refreshing toss-up of Desert Southwest flavors helps douse the spicy heat of cayenne. You can make this salad more substantial by adding crumbled queso fresco or a mild feta.

3 Cara Cara oranges
3 tablespoons fresh lime juice
2 tablespoons extra-virgin olive oil
Pinch cayenne pepper
1 small jicama, peeled, quartered, and diced into 1-inch (2.5 cm) pieces
2 avocados, quartered and thinly sliced
¼ cup (15 g) chopped fresh cilantro
Sea salt
Freshly ground black pepper

Using a sharp knife, peel the oranges over a large bowl to catch the juices, being careful to remove all of the bitter white pith. Cut in between the membranes to release the sections. Squeeze the membranes for more juice. Whisk in the lime juice, oil, and cayenne. Toss in the jicama and avocado, then the cilantro. Season to taste with salt and black pepper.

Watercress, Tomato, and Toasted Pita Salad with Sumac and Mint
(Fattoush)

Jordan, Lebanon, Palestine, and Syria

Serves 4 to 6

Fattoush, from the Arab root *fattah*, for "bread," simply means "bread salad." It is something that the Prophet Muhammad reputedly savored with soups every day, except when fasting. Although often made with romaine lettuce in the US, versions with watercress or purslane, or both, are terrific. The key spice is the sweet-sour sumac powder called *simmaq*. We harvest three kinds of sumac where we live, and we love to dress any salad with this zingy spice.

- 6 cups (258 g) watercress or purslane, roots and thick stems trimmed
- ½ cup (30 g) finely chopped fresh parsley
- 1 tablespoon sumac
- 2 tablespoons fresh lemon juice
- 1 garlic clove, finely chopped
- ¼ teaspoon coarse salt, plus more as needed
- ¼ cup (60 ml) extra-virgin olive oil
- 1 pound (454 g) grape or Roma tomatoes, cut in half, or chopped heirloom tomatoes
- 2 Persian cucumbers, sliced into rounds
- ½ red onion, very thinly sliced
- ¼ cup (15 g) roughly torn fresh mint leaves
- 3 pita breads, toasted and broken into 1- to 2-inch (2.5 to 5 cm) pieces
- Sea salt
- Freshly ground black pepper

In a blender, process 1 cup of the watercress, the parsley, sumac, lemon juice, garlic, and salt. With the motor running, add the oil in a slow, steady stream.

In a large bowl, toss the remaining watercress with the tomatoes, cucumbers, onion, mint, and toasted pita. Add the dressing and toss with your hands, breaking up the tomatoes and really melding all the flavors. Season with salt and pepper to taste.

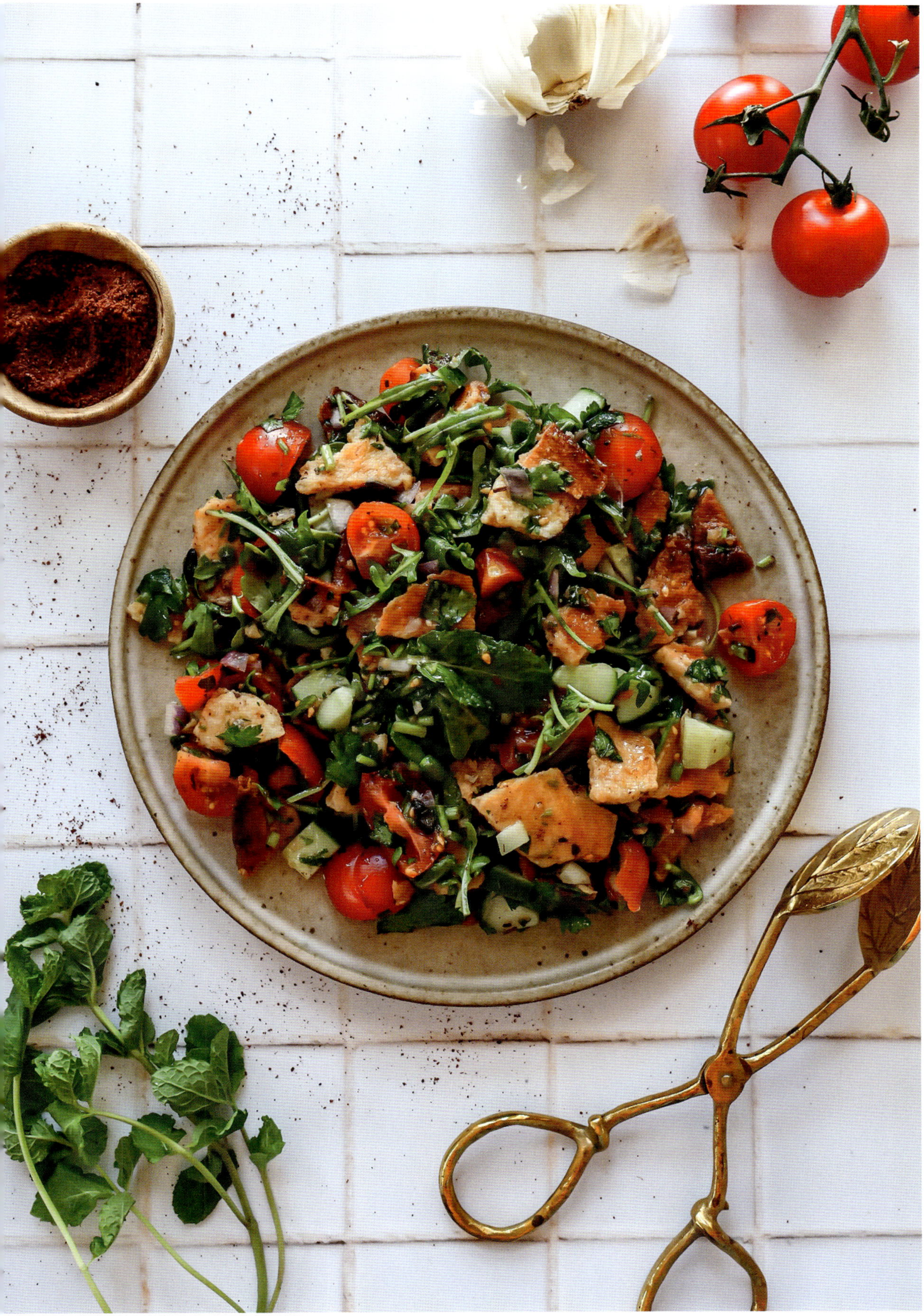

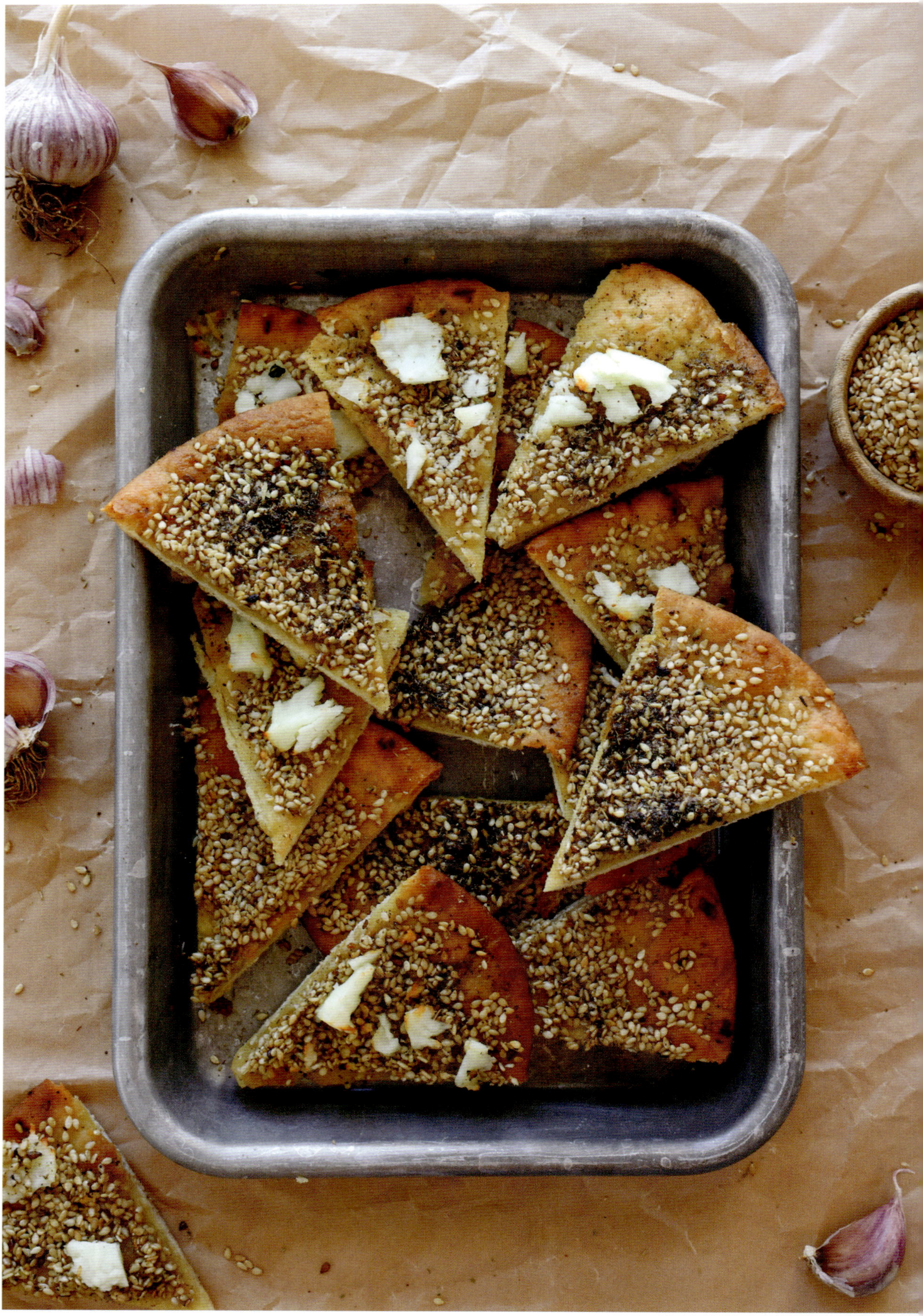

Chapter 13
Breads

Bread is a staple in many desert cuisines and is eaten with every meal. In many homes, bread is considered a gift from the gods, and if a piece falls to the ground, it is picked up, kissed, and eaten. Bread, dates, and salt are symbols of hospitality, especially in hot, dry regions, and are often brought as gifts to a host or to bless a just-married couple.

Pocket Flatbreads	144
Za'atar Lavash	145
Blue Corn Bread	146
Holiday Seed Bread	148
Savory Egg Bread	149

Pocket Flatbreads
(Khubz, Pita)

Greece, Lebanon, Syria, and Turkey

Makes 4 flatbreads

Savory flatbreads are beloved throughout desert regions, where they are easily cooked over an open fire. In this recipe, baking soda and baking powder replace yeast, and the kefir adds body and tang. It's best to give the dough a rest before baking off. Finish each loaf with a seasoning of choice and perhaps some cheese or a swirl of oil, and serve with any of our dipping sauces for an appetizer (see page 35), or use them to wrap up meats and veggies.

2 cups (240 g) all-purpose flour, plus more for dusting
¾ teaspoon baking powder
¼ teaspoon baking soda
2 teaspoons coarse salt, plus more to finish
½ teaspoon sugar
⅓ cup mixed seeds, such as sesame, nigella, mustard, and coriander
4 scallions, thinly sliced
1 cup (240 ml) cold kefir or buttermilk
Up to ¼ cup (60 ml) olive oil

In a medium bowl, whisk together the flour, baking powder, baking soda, salt, sugar, seeds, and scallions. Make a well in the center then add the kefir and stir with a wooden spoon to make a shaggy dough. Transfer the dough onto a lightly oiled surface and knead it gently into a ball. Place the ball in a lightly greased bowl, cover, and let rest for at least 30 minutes or up to an hour. Preheat the oven to 300°F (150°C).

Transfer the dough to a lightly floured surface and divide it into 4 pieces. Using a floured rolling pin, roll out each ball to ⅛ inch thick and about 6 inches (15 cm) long and 4 inches (10 cm) wide.

Lightly film a large, heavy skillet with oil and set over medium-high heat. When the oil is very hot, add the flatbread a piece at a time and cook until charred on one side, about 3 minutes, then flip and continue cooking another 2 to 3 minutes. Transfer to a baking sheet, sprinkle with salt, and hold in a warm oven while you cook the remaining pieces. Serve warm.

Za'atar Lavash
(Manaqueesh, Manoushe)

Jordan, Lebanon, Palestine, and Syria

Makes 6 flatbreads

These simple flatbreads are popular throughout the Arab world—especially in Lebanon, Syria, Jordan, and Palestine, where they're enjoyed at breakfast. Traditionally topped with za'atar, they're delicious with feta, roasted peppers, and thick yogurt. Experienced bakers stretch the dough by hand, but a rolling pin works, too. The key ingredient is a good extra-virgin olive oil.

3½ cups (420 g) all-purpose flour
1 cup (113 g) whole-wheat flour
1 teaspoon salt
Generous pinch sugar
2 teaspoons instant yeast
1 to 2 cups (240 to 480 ml) lukewarm water
½ cup (120 ml) extra-virgin olive oil, plus more as needed
¾ cup (144 g) Lebanese Za'atar Spice Blend (page 170), for topping

In a large bowl, stir together the flours, salt, and sugar. Add the yeast and 1 cup (240 ml) of the water and knead in the bowl. Gradually knead in another ¼ cup (60 ml) of water, adding a little more at a time, until the dough comes together in a sticky ball. Let the dough rest for 5 minutes, then continue kneading until it's very supple and elastic, another 7 minutes.

Rub the dough ball with oil, cover the bowl with plastic wrap and set aside until the dough doubles in size, 45 minutes to 1 hour.

In a small bowl, stir together the za'atar spice mix and ½ cup (120 ml) of the oil. Set aside.

Grease several baking sheets or line with parchment paper. Divide the dough into 6 equal portions, roll these into spheres, and place on the prepared baking sheets about 1 inch (2.5 cm) apart. Cover loosely with a damp tea towel so the dough doesn't dry out. Let rise until doubled in size, about 30 minutes. Preheat the oven to 500°F (260°C).

Flatten the dough spheres into thin circles, 7 to 8 inches (18 to 20 cm) in diameter, and, using your fingers, press indentations into the dough. Spread the za'atar mixture over the doughs, leaving a narrow border along the perimeter, and press it into the dough.

Bake until the breads are golden at the edges and the topping is bubbling, 5 to 7 minutes. Transfer to a wire rack to cool.

Blue Corn Bread
(Pan de Maiz Azul)
Mexico and US Desert Southwest

Serves 10 to 12

Blue cornmeal gives this cornbread its haunting corn flavor and lavender hue, but yellow or white cornmeal will work equally well. You can find blue cornmeal in co-ops and online. Store it in the refrigerator or freeze.

12 tablespoons unsalted butter
⅓ cup (80 ml) honey or maple syrup
2¼ cups (540 ml) buttermilk
3 large eggs
3½ cups (546 g) blue, yellow, or white cornmeal
1½ tablespoons baking powder
1½ teaspoons coarse salt
½ teaspoon baking soda
1 small red bell pepper, seeded and diced
1 cup (152 g) corn kernels, fresh or thawed frozen
¼ cup (32 g) pepitas (optional)

Preheat the oven to 375°F (190°C). In an 11- or 12-inch (27 or 30 cm) ovenproof skillet (cast iron preferred), melt the butter over medium heat, swirling to lightly coat the sides of the pan. When the foam subsides and the butter begins to turn brown (1 to 2 minutes; watch closely that it does not burn) remove it from the stove and pour into a large bowl.

In the same bowl as the butter, whisk in the honey, buttermilk, and eggs then whisk in the cornmeal, baking powder, salt, and baking soda. Stir in half of the bell pepper and ¾ cup (115 g) of the corn kernels, and the pepitas (if using).

Reheat the pan on the stove for a few minutes. Pour the batter into the pan, scatter the remaining bell pepper and corn on top, and bake until the top is darkened and split and a toothpick inserted into the center emerges clean, 30 to 40 minutes. Remove and allow to stand about 5 minutes before serving.

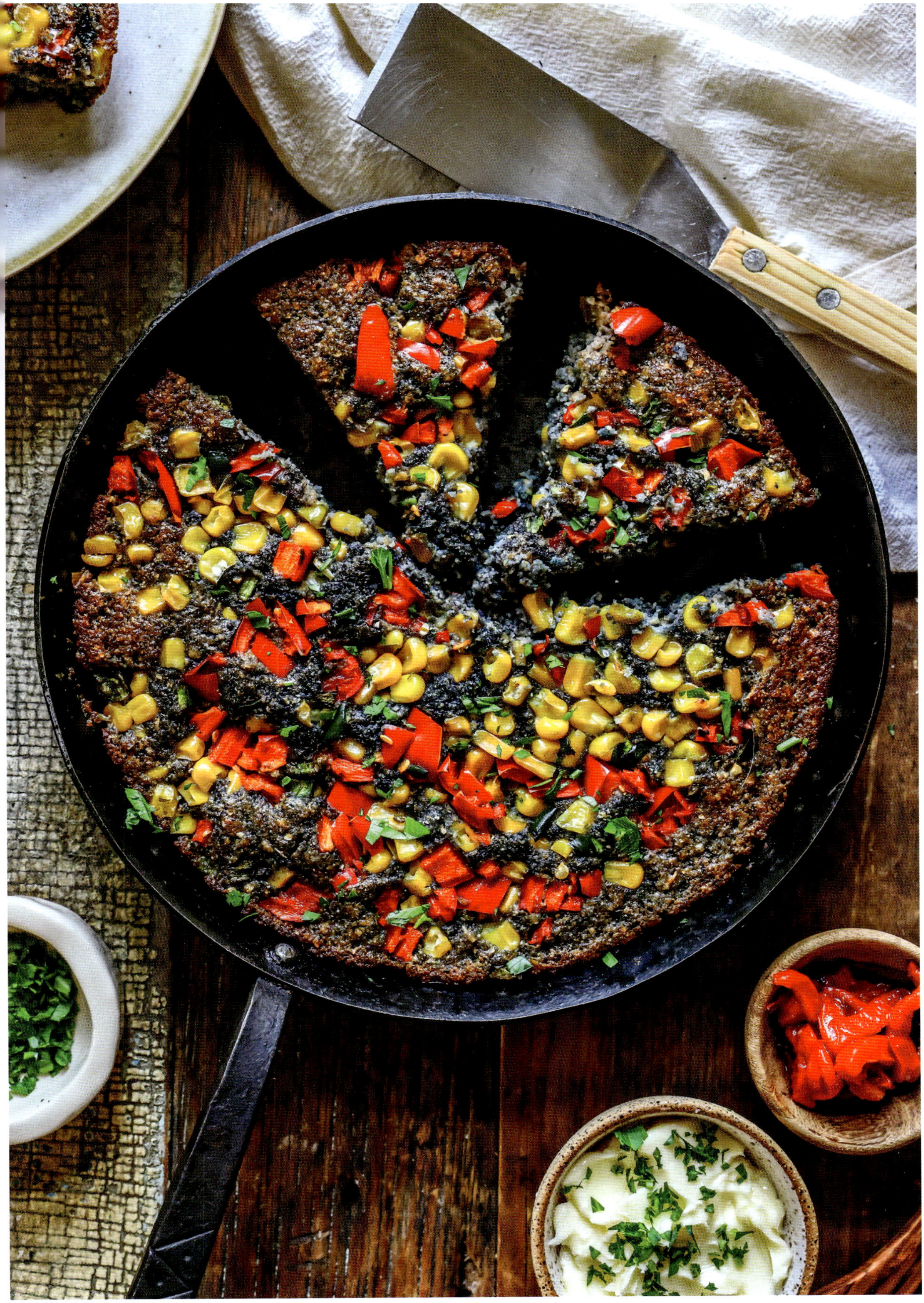

Holiday Seed Bread
(Pan de Semita)

Mexico, Morocco, Spain, and US Desert Southwest

Makes 4 loaves

This festive seed bread provides a clue to where Muslims and Jews settled in the Americas. The bread and bread pudding (aka *capirotada*) are served at Passover, Easter, and Ramadan. It is a symbol of *convivencia* (voluntary conviviality) by the worshippers of those three faiths. We like to think of it as a taste of hope.

3½ cups (420 g) white Sonora wheat bread flour, plus more for dusting
1 cup (213 g) dark brown sugar
1 teaspoon ground anise seed
1 teaspoon ground cinnamon
2¼ teaspoons active dry yeast
½ cup (57 g) chopped almonds or pecans
2 teaspoons sea salt
⅓ cup (80 ml) virgin coconut oil
1½ cups (360 ml) warm water
½ cup (85 g) currants or golden raisins, plumped in orange juice
2 tablespoons unsalted butter, softened

In a large bowl, mix together the flour, ½ cup (56 g) of the brown sugar, anise, cinnamon, yeast, nuts, and salt. Add the coconut oil, 1¼ cups (300 ml) of the warm water, and the currants and juice. Turn the dough out onto a lightly floured surface and knead until it's soft and pliable. Liberally butter the insides of a large bowl. Place the dough in the greased bowl, cover with a clean towel, and set aside to rise until doubled, about 1 hour. Mix the remaining ½ cup (56 g) brown sugar with the remaining ¼ cup (60 ml) warm water to make a stiff glaze.

Line a baking sheet with parchment paper. Punch the dough down and divide into four pieces and shape each into a round. Space the rounds on the prepared baking sheet. Cover with a clean towel and set aside to rise for 20 minutes. Preheat the oven to 350°F (180°C).

Press lightly down on the rounds. Brush with the brown sugar glaze. Bake until golden, about 20 minutes. Remove, transfer to a wire rack, and cool slightly before serving.

Savory Egg Bread
(Challah)

Algeria and Morocco

Makes 2 round loaves

The Mizrahi and Sephardic Jews from North Africa and the Middle East bake a challah that's distinctly different from the braided sweet bread familiar to most Americans. This leaner, less sweet, more savory loaf goes beautifully with tagines, mezes, and salads.

¼ cup (36 g) sesame seeds, plus 2 tablespoons for garnishing
1 tablespoon caraway seeds
1 tablespoon cumin seeds
1 envelope (2¼ teaspoons) active dry yeast
¾ cup plus 2 tablespoons (210 ml) warm water
5 cups (600 g) bread flour, plus more for dusting
2½ tablespoons extra-virgin olive oil, plus more for oiling the bowls and pans (optional)
1 tablespoon honey
2 whole large eggs
1 tablespoon coarse salt
Cornmeal for dusting (optional)
2 egg yolks

Put the sesame seeds, caraway seeds, and cumin seeds into a skillet and set over moderate heat to toast until fragrant, 1 to 2 minutes. Transfer to a plate to cool.

In a small bowl, combine the yeast with the 2 tablespoons warm water and let stand until thoroughly moistened, about 5 minutes.

In a large bowl, stir together the flour, oil, remaining ¾ cup (180 ml) warm water, the honey, and eggs. Stir until a very soft dough forms. Stir in the salt, yeast mixture, and seed mixture until thoroughly combined and the dough is subtle and smooth. Using oiled hands, transfer the dough to a large oiled bowl. Cover the bowl with a clean towel and let stand until the dough has doubled in size, 1½ to 2 hours.

Line two small baking sheets with parchment paper or lightly oil and dust with cornmeal. Turn the dough out onto a lightly floured work surface and press to deflate. Cut the dough in half and let rest for 5 minutes. Roll each piece into a long rope. Coil each rope to create a loaf, tucking the ends of the rope underneath to finish the coil. Repeat with the second rope.

Transfer each loaf to a prepared baking sheet and cover with a clean kitchen towel. Let stand until the loaves have doubled, about 1 hour. Preheat the oven to 400°F (200°C).

In a small bowl, whisk the egg yolks with 1 tablespoon of water. Brush the egg wash over the loaves and sprinkle with the remaining 2 tablespoons sesame seeds. Bake the loaves until they're golden and sound hollow when tapped, 30 to 35 minutes. Transfer to a wire rack and allow to cool before slicing.

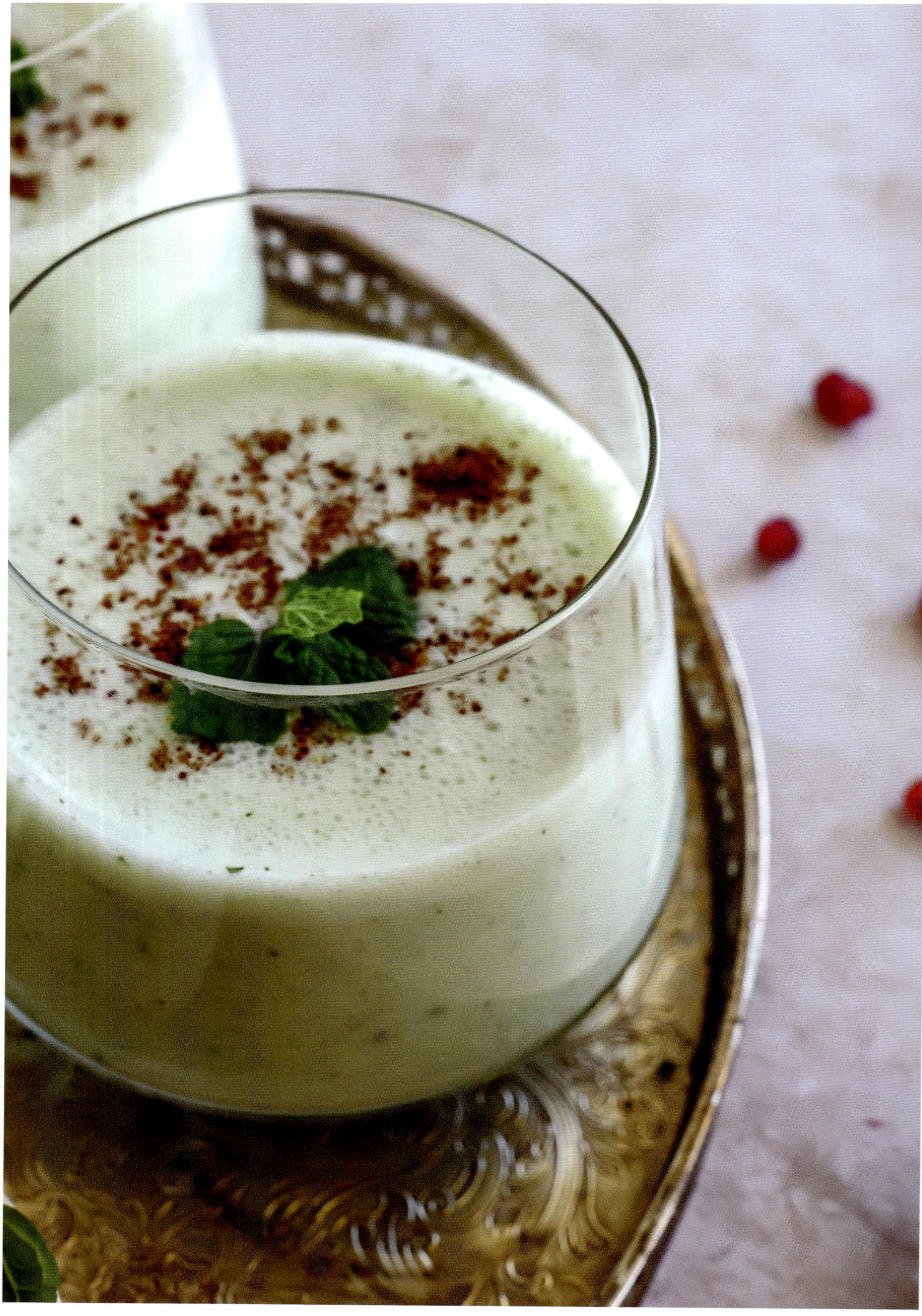

Chapter 14

Drinks and Desserts

Desert cuisine tends to walk that intoxicating balance between rich, heady aromas and fresh, bright flavors. The magic of these cocktails is that they work with, not against, the primary bold tastes. While we call for distilled liquors from the different countries of origin, feel free to turn them into nonalcoholic drinks by substituting sparkling waters or tonic water.

Desserts play a special role in traditional meals, serving as a source of pride for the family's cooks. Gestures of celebration, desserts tend to be luxurious, layered, and very sweet, brimming with nuts and honey, and scented with warm cinnamon, cardamom, nutmeg, and ginger.

Pineapple Margarita	152
Lebanese Cocktail	154
Cucumber-Rosemary Gin and Tonic	155
Desert Yogurt Smoothie	155
Phyllo Nut Pinwheels	156
Lebanese Rice Pudding with Rose Water and Mahlab Cherry Powder	158
Pine Nut and Anise Wedding Cookies	159
Canary Islands Pastries	160

Pineapple Margarita
(Margarita de Piña y Sotol)

Mexico and US Desert Southwest

Makes 2 drinks

The flavor of the luxurious pineapple blends harmoniously with a range of spirits, though most often with rum (think piña colada). This particular margarita uses the uniquely North American desert succulent named sotol, or desert spoon, that is distant kin of the agaves used in mezcal and tequila.

Pineapple cocktails are especially festive thanks to an enzyme called bromelain that breaks down protein and reacts with air to make bubbles when the juice is shaken.

You can make up a big batch for a crowd and hold it in the refrigerator. Not everyone loves the smoky notes of some sotols or mezcals, so feel free to use an artisanal Cascahuin Tahona Blanco tequila. Make a zero-proof cocktail (or mocktail) by omitting the alcohol and adding several extra splashes of fresh lime juice.

⅛ cup (30 ml) sotol (or a smoky mezcal or tequila); for a zero-proof version, use ⅛ cup (30 ml) fresh lime juice plus ¼ cup (60 ml) sparkling water
¼ cup (60 ml) fresh orange juice
2 tablespoons fresh lime juice
¾ cup (one 6-ounce [180 ml] can) pineapple juice
Coarse salt
Crushed ice
Lime slices for garnish
Grilled pineapple slices for garnish (see Note)

Put the sotol, orange juice, lime juice, and pineapple juice into a cocktail shaker and shake vigorously.

Pour about ¼ inch (.6 cm) of salt into a saucer. Lightly wet the rim of the glasses with water. Holding the glass at a 45-degree angle, run each glass rim around the salt. Set the glasses aside so that the salt hardens. Carefully fill the glasses with the crushed ice and then pour the margarita into the glasses. Garnish with the lime slices and grilled pineapple.

Kitchen Note
To grill the pineapple, remove the rind and cut the pineapple into 2-inch-thick (5 cm) pieces. To grill it on the stovetop, using tongs, hold each piece over a flame until it begins to char, 5 to 8 minutes. To grill in the broiler, preheat the broiler to high. Line a baking sheet with parchment paper. Arrange the pineapple on the parchment and place under the broiler, checking after 3 to 5 minutes. If it's beginning to char, flip and continue grilling another 3 to 5 minutes.

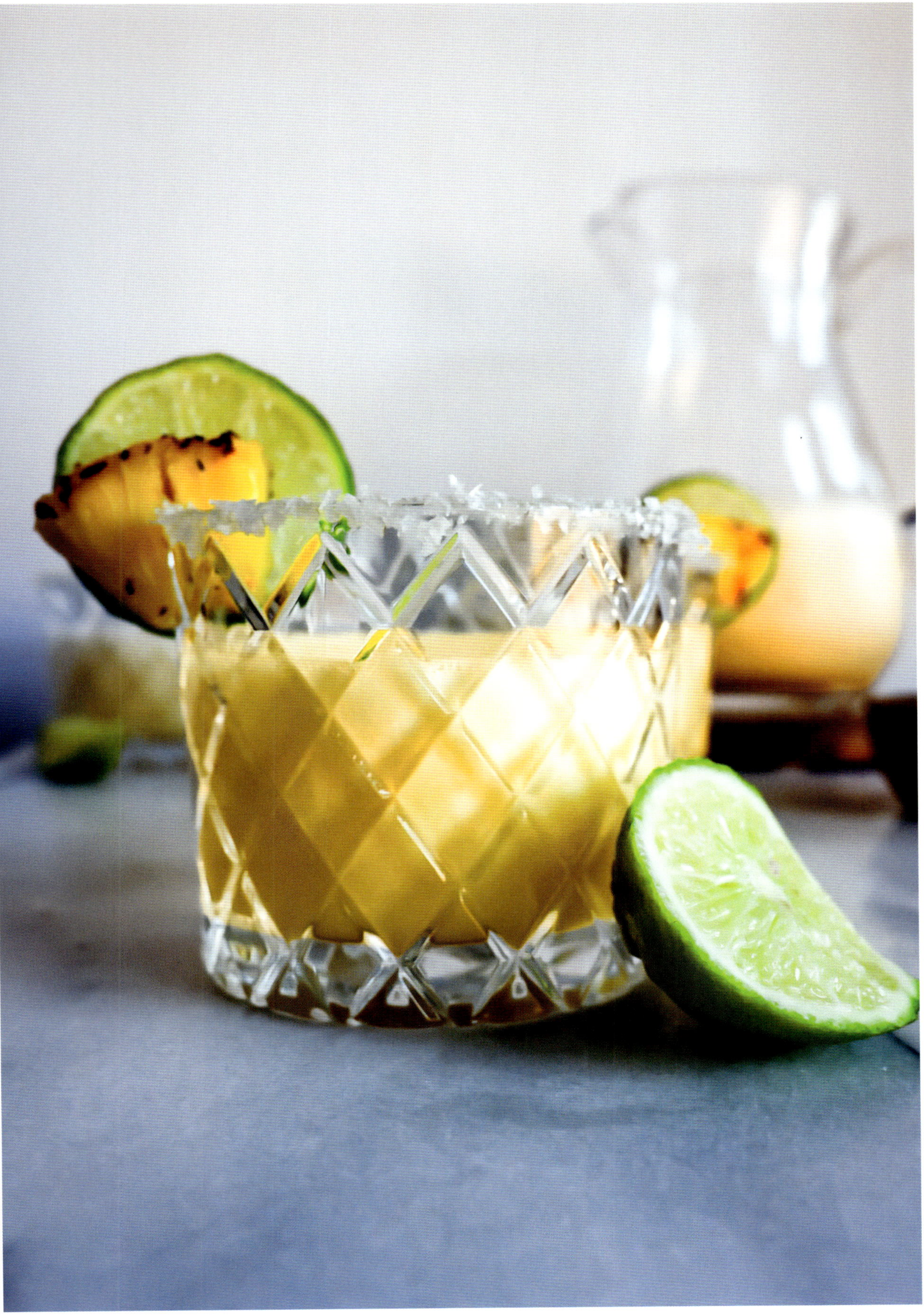

Lebanese Cocktail
(Arak Cocktail)
Lebanon

Makes 2 cocktails

Arak is an ouzo-like anisette that Gary's grandfathers and great uncles bootlegged in the United States during Prohibition. They'd learned the craft of making it in the Bekaa Valley of Lebanon, where it has been a local treasure for centuries. When Gary's father was a boy, one of his chores was to mash the grapes and anise seeds with his feet in the bathtub before he could go out to play baseball after school.

In this boldly seasoned cocktail, the ice-cold water turns the mixture into what Gary likes to call "a wonderous cloud of unknowing."

2 ounces (60 ml) arak or ouzo
1 ounce (30 ml) St-Germain elderflower liqueur, optional
½ ounce (15 ml) fresh lemon juice
¼ ounce (8 ml) coconut juice
Dash orange bitters
Dash ground cinnamon
Dash ground cardamom
Dash ground ginger
9 ounces (270 ml) ice-cold mineral water (such as Topo Chico)
Dash za'atar spice blend as garnish

Fill two glasses with ice cubes and pour half of the arak into each glass. Combine the St-Germain (if using), lemon juice, coconut juice, bitters, cinnamon, cardamom, and ginger in a shaker. At the last minute, whisk in the mineral water. Immediately pour into the prepared glasses, and finish with a sprinkle of za'atar.

Cucumber-Rosemary Gin and Tonic
(Kh'yar Kokitil)

Lebanon

Makes 2 cocktails

Those small, slightly sweet, and crisp Persian cucumbers (aka Beit Alpha or wild mikti cucumbers) are a perfect foil to the intense piney notes of rosemary. Look for the newer gins from Southern California and Arizona.

- 1½ ounces (45 ml) gin (such as The Botanist Islay Gin, Ventura Spirits, Canyon Diablo Desert Rain, Mojave, or Tanqueray Rangpur Gin)
- 1 Persian (or Beit Alpha or wild mikti) cucumber, skin on, grated
- 1 teaspoon fresh rosemary leaves
- 4½ ounces (135 ml) tonic water (such as Fever-Tree or Schweppes)
- 4 slices watermelon radish for garnish
- 2 rosemary sprigs for garnish

In a blender, process the gin, cucumber, and rosemary for 1 minute. Pour over a lowball glass filled with ice. Top with the tonic water and garnish with the watermelon radish and rosemary sprig.

Desert Yogurt Smoothie
(Ayran)

Egypt, Jordan, Lebanon, Palestine, and Turkey

Makes 2 drinks

Remarkably refreshing on a hot, dry day, this drink is wonderful for breakfast or as a quick snack. We often have it for dessert.

- 12 ounces (360 g) kefir
- 2 small cucumbers, diced (about 1 cup)
- 2 tablespoons rose water
- 2 tablespoons chopped fresh mint, plus 2 sprigs for garnish
- 2 tablespoons honey, or to taste
- 1 cup ice

Put all the ingredients into a blender and process. Serve icy-cold, garnished with a sprig of mint.

Phyllo Nut Pinwheels
(Baklava, Be'lewa)

Greece, Jordan, Lebanon, and Syria

Serves 8 to 10

Chock-full of nuts and laced with aromatics and honey, baklava is the iconic pastry of Greece, Turkey, and the Balkans. Be sure to thaw the phyllo in the refrigerator before working with it. And chill the syrup in advance of pouring it on top of the hot pastry. This technique allows the baklava to fully absorb all the honeyed goodness.

SYRUP

1 cup (198 g) granulated sugar
½ cup (120 ml) water
3 tablespoons honey
One 2-inch (5 cm) strip orange zest
1 cardamom pod

To make the syrup: combine the granulated sugar, water, honey, orange zest, and cardamom pod in a small saucepan. Set over low heat and bring to a simmer, stirring until the sugar has dissolved, 5 to 8 minutes.

Remove from the heat and allow to cool. Strain into an airtight container, cover, and refrigerate until chilled or overnight (8 to 10 hours).

PINWHEELS

12 ounces (340 g) toasted hazelnuts, pistachios, walnuts, or pecans
¼ cup (28 g) confectioners' sugar
Generous pinch ground cardamom
¼ teaspoon ground cinnamon
½ pound (½ package [(227 g)]) frozen phyllo dough, thawed (see Note)
½ cup (113 g) unsalted butter, melted

To make the pinwheels: Line a baking sheet with parchment paper.

In a food processor, pulse the nuts with the confectioners' sugar, cardamom, and cinnamon until ground.

Lay three sheets of the phyllo dough on a flat surface, stacked on top of one another, with one of the short sides close to you. Cover the remaining sheets with a damp kitchen towel as you work to keep them from drying out.

Generously brush the top layer of phyllo with the butter. Spread some of the nut mixture on the phyllo and pack it down. Roll the three phyllo sheets together away from you to form a log. Repeat with the remaining phyllo dough and nut mixture. Place the rolls seam side down on another baking sheet or flat pan and place in the freezer for about 12 minutes; this makes them easier to cut.

Preheat the oven to 350°F (180°C). Remove the rolls from the freezer and set on a cutting board. Using a serrated knife, cut them into 2-inch (5 cm) slices. Arrange the slices cut side up and spaced apart on the prepared baking sheet. Bake until golden brown, about 30 minutes.

Remove the pastries from the oven and immediately drizzle them with cold syrup. Arrange the pinwheels snugly, cut side up, in a serving dish. Allow this to cool completely before serving. Store in an airtight container in the refrigerator for up to a week or freeze for up to 1 month.

> **Kitchen Note**
> *Once the phyllo dough has thawed, you can remove any you don't need for the recipe; reroll, wrap in plastic, and refreeze for up to 2 months.*

Drinks and Desserts

Lebanese Rice Pudding with Rose Water and Mahlab Cherry Powder
(Riz bi Haleeb)

Lebanon and Syria

Serves 4

This pudding owes its sweetly elusive flavor and fragrance to mahlab, the crushed kernel of a Saint Lucie cherry.

1 cup (170 g) cooked rice
¼ cup (30 g) toasted pistachios
¼ cup (13 g) toasted, shredded coconut
1 cup (240 ml) coconut milk
1 cup (240 ml) water
¼ cup (60 ml) honey
1 teaspoon rose water
⅛ teaspoon sea salt
⅛ teaspoon mahlab
¼ teaspoon vanilla extract
¼ teaspoon almond extract
¼ teaspoon orange zest
1 teaspoon minced rose blossoms for garnish

In a medium saucepan, stir together the rice, pistachios, coconut, coconut milk, water, honey, rose water, salt, and mahlab. Set over medium heat for about 1 minute, then reduce the heat and simmer until thickened, 5 to 7 minutes, stirring frequently.

Remove from the heat and stir in the vanilla and almond extracts, and the orange zest. Let cool to room temperature and serve garnished with the rose blossoms.

Pine Nut and Anise Wedding Cookies
(Cap Ghazelle, Ghorayeba, Ghraybeh, Kourabiedes, Polvorones, Qurabiya)

Greece, Mexico, Morocco, Spain, and Turkey

Makes 2 dozen cookies

The origin of this cookie's name is unclear. Whatever the name—Mexican wedding cookies, Russian tea cakes, Christmas dreams, gazelle horns!—there's no doubt these rich, buttery, melt-in-your-mouth confections are delicious any time of year. A touch of anise lends a mild, dreamy flavor. Pine nuts add the creamy texture, but feel free to substitute hazelnuts, pecans, pistachios, or walnuts.

½ cup (72 g) pine nuts
1½ cups (173 g) confectioners' sugar
Generous pinch sea salt
1 cup (226 g) unsalted butter, at room temperature, cut into tablespoon-size pieces
½ teaspoon anise extract
1 teaspoon grated orange zest
1¾ cups (210 g) all-purpose flour, plus more for shaping

Put the pine nuts and 1 cup (115 g) of the sugar into a food processor and blend until the nuts are finely ground. With the motor running, add the salt and the butter, one chunk at a time. Add the anise extract and orange zest and continue to process until smooth. Pulse in the flour until you have a soft dough. Scrape the dough into a bowl and refrigerate for at least 1 hour or overnight (8 to 10 hours).

Preheat the oven to 350°F (180°C). Scoop the dough with a tablespoon and form into 1-inch (2.5 cm) balls with lightly floured hands. Roll the balls in the remaining sugar and place 1½ inches (3.75 cm) apart on ungreased baking sheets.

Bake until the cookies just begin to brown, about 15 minutes. Remove and let cool on a wire rack. Store in a covered container in refrigerator for up to 1 week.

Canary Islands Pastries
(Truchas Canarias Empanadas)

Canary Islands

Makes 36 small or 18 large empanadas

The Canary Islands, positioned at a crossroads of cultures, host a dynamic food scene that reflects the vibrant flavors of South America and North Africa. Empanadas are universal across the archipelago. These take their whimsical shape from the local trout—*truchas*. At Christmastime, the tiny pastries are stuffed with sweet potatoes, almonds, sugar, and spices.

This no-fail empanada dough calls for lard from a local butcher, not processed commercial lard. In its place, use a good-quality unsalted butter.

DOUGH

4 ounces (113 g) lard or unsalted butter, melted, plus more for brushing
2 cups (480 ml) water
1½ teaspoons fine salt
6 cups (720 g) all-purpose flour, plus more for dusting

SWEET POTATO FILLING

3 pounds (1.36 kg) sweet potatoes
3 tablespoons salted butter
3 teaspoons ground cinnamon
1 teaspoon ground nutmeg
Generous pinch ground ginger
1 to 2 tablespoons agave or honey
¼ cup (22 g) chopped toasted almonds
Sea salt
Freshly ground black pepper
1 to 2 tablespoons melted butter for brushing
1 to 2 tablespoons sugar for garnish

To make the dough: In a large bowl, stir together the melted lard, water, and fine salt. Gradually stir in the flour with a wooden spoon until the dough comes together. Transfer to a floured board and knead until firm and smooth, 1 or 2 minutes, dusting with more flour if it's too sticky. Wrap the dough in plastic and refrigerate for at least 1 hour.

To make the filling: Preheat the oven to 350°F (180°C). Line a baking sheet with parchment paper. Poke holes in the sweet potatoes with a fork or sharp knife and set on the prepared baking sheet. Roast until very tender, 45 minutes to 1 hour. Remove the potatoes and allow to come to room temperature.

Peel the sweet potatoes and mash in the butter, cinnamon, nutmeg, ginger, agave, and almonds along with the salt and pepper to taste. Adjust the seasonings as needed.

Divide the dough into 2-inch (5 cm) balls (or 4-inch [10 cm] balls for larger empanadas). On a lightly floured surface, roll out each ball into an oblong. Lay the pieces on the prepared baking sheet. Moisten the outer edge of each piece with water and lay about 2 tablespoons of the filling in the center of each. Wrap the dough around the filling to form an oval, and press the edges together. Fold the edge back and finish by pinching the dough and crimping with a fork. Gently nudge the dough into the shape of an arched fish.

Brush the tops with a little melted butter and sprinkle with sugar. Bake until golden, 10 to 15 minutes.

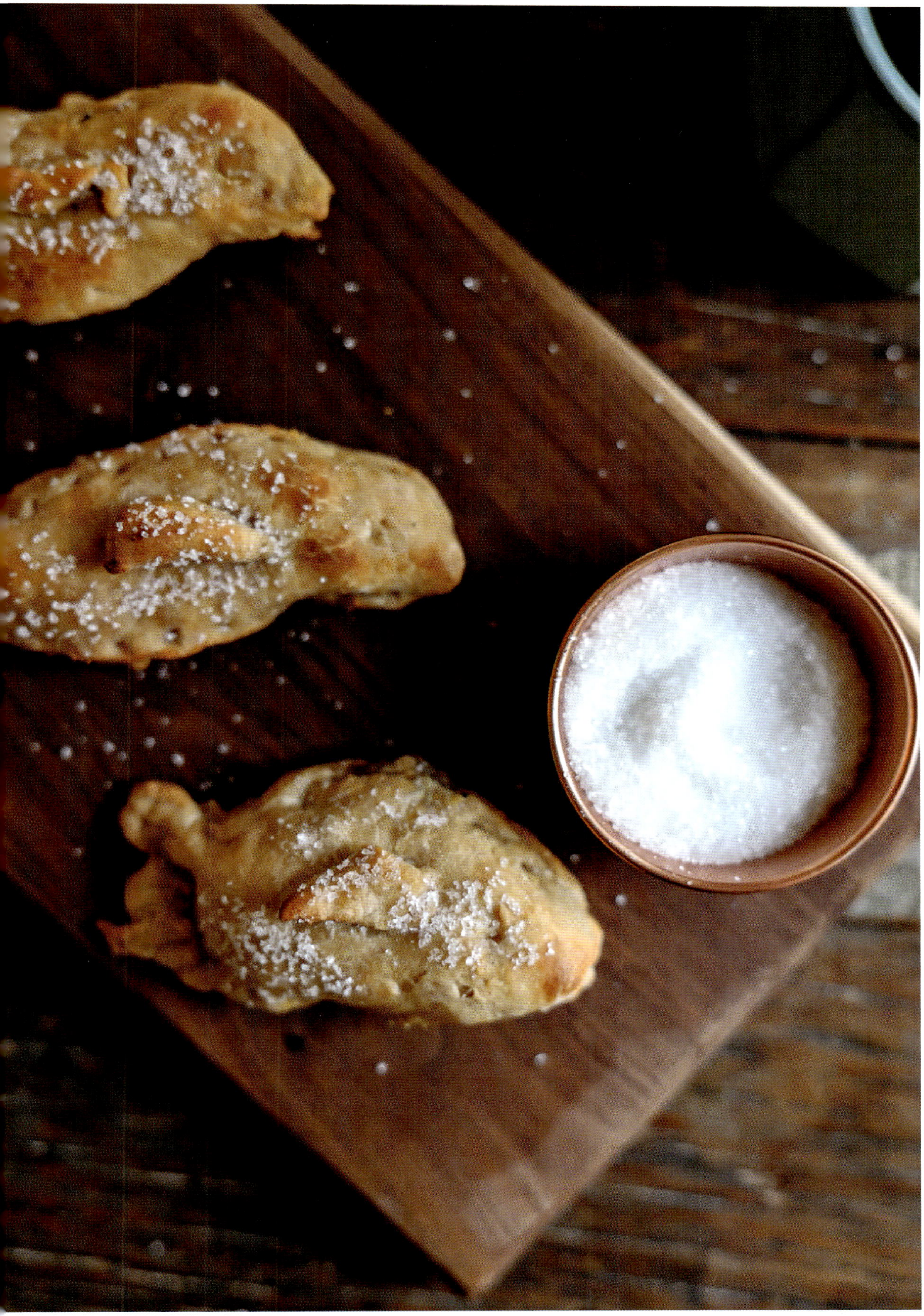

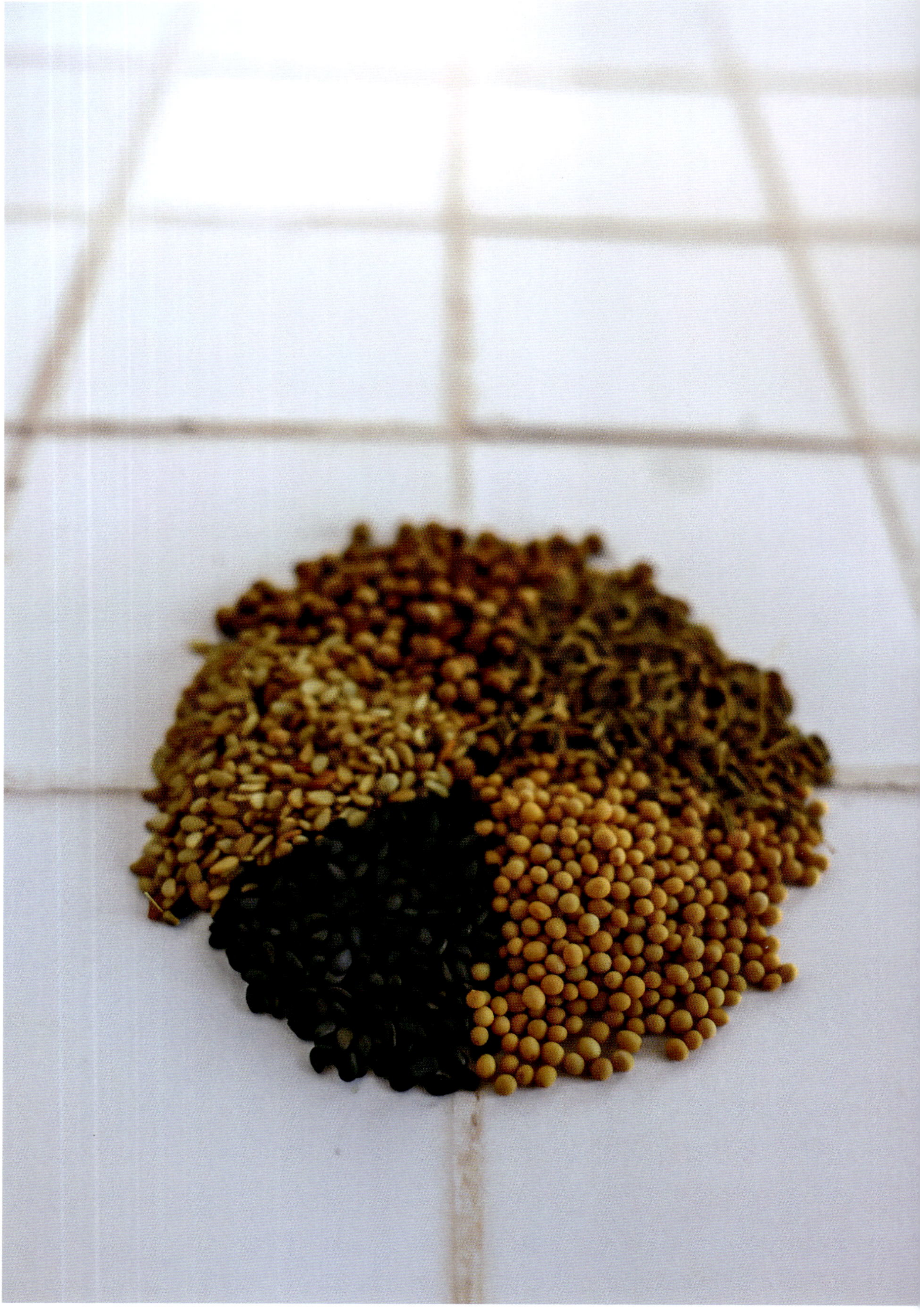

Chapter 15
Spice Blends

Blend these spices at home for maximum flavor, and to save time and money. Keep them in an airtight container in a cool, dark place for up to a year.

Turkish Baharat	164
Egyptian Dukkah Spice Mix	165
Lebanese Spice Blend	165
Kashmiri Spice Blend	166
North African Aromatic Harissa Chile Pepper Paste	167
Mexican Mole Chile Seed Paste	168
Moroccan Top of the Shop Spice Blend	169
Lebanese Za'atar Spice Blend	170

Turkish Baharat

Iran, Iraq, Lebanon, Syria, and Turkey

Scant 1 cup

Baharat simply means "spices" in Arabic, but it usually refers to a characteristic Middle Eastern ground spice blend used to season chicken, beef, fish, goat, lamb, mutton, pigeon, soups, and stews. Baharat is to Middle Eastern cuisine what garam masala is to Indian food. The Lebanese variant, called sabaa baharat, also includes ginger, spearmint, Aleppo pepper, or smoked paprika, here listed as options.

- 2 tablespoons black peppercorns
- 2 tablespoons dried spearmint (optional)
- One 2-inch (5 cm) cinnamon stick, broken into pieces
- 2 teaspoons allspice berries
- 2 teaspoons whole cloves
- 2 teaspoons cumin seeds
- 2 teaspoons rough-grated nutmeg
- 1 teaspoon peeled and grated fresh ginger (optional)
- 1 teaspoon cardamom seeds
- 1 teaspoon smoked paprika or Aleppo pepper (optional)

Place all the ingredients in a small glass bowl. Thoroughly mix with a slotted spoon or with your hands then transfer to a small skillet set over medium-high heat and toss until fragrant, about 2 minutes. Using a mortar and pestle, grind together, or grind in a blender for a minimum of 2 minutes. Sift through a screen or colander to remove any hard bits and store in a glass jar in a cool, dry, shaded place.

Egyptian Dukkah Spice Mix
(Duqqa, Du'ah, Do'a)
Egypt, Israel, Libya, and Palestine

Makes about 3⅔ cups

The Cairene Arabic term *dukkah* means to pound or crush with a mortar and pestle. Dukkah is a finely ground spice blend that was once made of ground coriander and salt, but its ingredients have diversified in recent times. It's most often used to season roasted nut and seed mixes, and it works nicely on fish, meats, salads, rice, and couscous.

11 ounces (300 g) almonds
11 ounces (300 g) hazelnuts
6 tablespoons sesame seeds
2 tablespoons ground cumin
1 tablespoon ground coriander
2 tablespoons sea salt

Preheat the oven to 400°F (200°C). Toast the almonds, hazelnuts, and sesame seeds for 7 minutes or until golden, then let cool. Pour into a small glass bowl and mix with the cumin, coriander, and salt. Add the mixture to a mortar, and, using a pestle, finely grind for 2 to 4 minutes. Sift through a screen or colander and store in a glass jar in a cool, dry, shaded place.

Lebanese Spice Blend
(Kamouneh)
Lebanon

Makes 1 cup

Kamouneh, also known as kibbe spice, is used in traditional lamb meatballs. It's also used to give a savory flavor to other meats and vegetables.

5 tablespoons ground allspice
2 tablespoons ground turmeric
2 tablespoons freshly ground black pepper
2 tablespoons ground cinnamon
1 tablespoon paprika
1 tablespoon ground coriander
1 tablespoon ground cumin
2 teaspoons cayenne pepper

In a small bowl, whisk all the ingredients together. Transfer to a covered jar and store in a cool, dry, shaded place.

Kashmiri Spice Blend
(Garam Masala)

Bangladesh, India, Nepal, Pakistan, and parts of the Caribbean

Makes about ¾ cup

In Hindustani, garam masala consists of hot, pungent, or savory spices. They're toasted first to enhance their aromas, and then added at the end of cooking certain *biryanis*, *tandooris*, *tikkas*, or other rice, vegetable, or fish dishes of Kashmir. This aromatic blend heightens the sensory pleasures of any meal. Garam masalas vary greatly among regions of the Indian subcontinent and are sometimes tagged with place-based or dish-based adjectives such as Kashmiri, Bengali, or Tandoori. In some Indian kitchens, as many as 32 spices, herbs, seeds, and nuts may be integrated into one blend, so ours is clearly a simplified version.

2 ounces (50 g) black cardamom seeds
2 ounces (50 g) cassia cinnamon, broken in pieces
2 ounces (50 g) black peppercorns
½ ounce (20 g) black cumin seeds (see Note)
½ ounce (20 g) whole cloves
1 teaspoon fennel seeds
4 blades (or broken aril fragments) of mace
¼ teaspoon ground nutmeg

In a small skillet set over medium heat, toss all the ingredients for 3 to 4 minutes, stirring constantly, until all deepen in color and begin to crackle and emit fragrances. Transfer the mixture to a small bowl and cool 3 to 5 minutes. In a mortar and pestle, spice mill, or food processor, grind the spices together then sift until you obtain the texture of finely ground black pepper for all the spices. Store in an airtight glass jar in a cool, dry, shaded place.

> **Kitchen Note**
> *Black cumin is often confused with nigella seeds, but they are entirely different plants with different flavors.*

166 ▪ *Chile, Clove, and Cardamom*

North African Aromatic Harissa Chile Pepper Paste
(Harissa, Hrous)

Algeria, Libya, Mauritania, Morocco, and Tunisia

Makes about ¾ cup

Harissa is a Maghrebi Arabic or Darija term related to the verbs "to crush" or "to pound" in a *heraz* spice grinder, mortar and pestle, or food processor. Ubiquitous in the cuisines of North Africa, harissa may have originated in Tunisia. It is peppery, savory, and warm, often causing those who eat it to sweat and then cool down as the sweat evaporates.

- 7 ounces (200 g) Baklouti or Aleppo chiles
- 7 garlic cloves
- 3 tablespoons fresh lemon juice
- 2 tablespoons extra-virgin olive oil (preferably Picholine)
- 1 tablespoon rose water or fine-ground rosebuds
- 2 teaspoons sea salt
- 1 teaspoon ground cumin
- 1 teaspoon ground coriander
- 1 teaspoon ground caraway

Deseed the chiles, remove their stems, and soak in water for 30 minutes. Drain, then combine with the other ingredients. Grind in a heraz or hand-cranked grinder, molcajete, or mortar and pestle. Sift through a screen or colander and store in a glass jar in a cool, dry, shaded place.

Mexican Mole Chile Seed Paste
(Mole Pipian)
Central and southwestern Mexico

Makes ½ to ¾ cup

Moles are closely related to the recaudo spice pastes of the Yucatán Peninsula and are ultimately a hybrid of Mesoamerican spice blends with adobos and mojos from the Caribbean and Atlantic islands. There are at least seven primary variants. This is a pumpkin seed paste–based one from the Altiplano of Querétaro and neighboring states. An amazing, perfectly balanced blend of East and West, it's sweet and savory and makes a wonderful spice rub for meats and poultry and converts to a sauce with the addition of tomatoes or tomatillos.

2 each ancho, mulato, and pasilla chiles
¼ cup (32 g) raw pumpkin seeds (pepitas)
2 tablespoons sesame seeds
½-inch (1.25 cm) Mexican cinnamon stick
½ teaspoon anise seeds
½ teaspoon whole cloves
1 teaspoon dried thyme
½ teaspoon dried Mexican oregano or oregano indio
2 black peppercorns
1 tablespoon unsweetened cocoa powder (optional)
2 dried Mexican bay leaves
1 to 2 teaspoons vegetable oil

Soak the chiles in warm water for 10 minutes. Remove and discard the seeds, stems, and inner veins.

In a small skillet set over medium heat, toast the pumpkin seeds, sesame seeds, cinnamon stick, anise seeds, cloves, thyme, oregano, peppercorns, cocoa powder, and bay leaves for 1 to 2 minutes until fragrant, stirring constantly. Transfer to a mortar and pestle, spice grinder, or food processor and pulse until you have a coarse grind. Drain the chiles, add them to the spice mixture along with the oil, and pulse until combined. Transfer to a covered container and store in the refrigerator for up to a week.

Moroccan Top of the Shop Spice Blend
(Ras el Hanout)

Algeria and Morocco

Makes ½ to ¾ cup

Our favorite spice blend, aka the "top of the shop," ras el hanout is insanely variable from spice keeper to spice keeper, chef to chef, and region to region, so much so that we hesitate to include just one recipe here. Like mole from Mexico, it's really a synthesis of spices from the Old World and the New.

1 tablespoon allspice berries
1 tablespoon black peppercorns
1 tablespoon coriander seeds
1 tablespoon cumin seeds
10 green cardamom seeds
1 teaspoon anise seeds
1 teaspoon nigella seeds
2 whole cloves
Two 1-inch (2.5 cm) Ceylon cinnamon sticks, broken into pieces
1 teaspoon ground ginger
1 teaspoon dried epazote
½ teaspoon dried lavender buds
2 teaspoons mace arils
2 teaspoons malagueta pepper
1 teaspoon grated nutmeg
1 teaspoon orris root (optional)
1 tablespoon dried Damask rosebuds
1 teaspoon ground turmeric

In a small skillet over low heat, toast the allspice seeds, peppercorns, coriander seeds, cumin seeds, anise seeds, and nigella seeds until just fragrant, about 2 to 4 minutes. Transfer the toasted spices, along with the remaining ingredients, into a spice mill, food processor, or mortar and pestle and grind all the ingredients together, then sift out any hard bits. Store in a in a glass jar cool, dry, shaded place.

Lebanese Za'atar Spice Blend
(Za'atar, Zatar, Zaetra, Zaitra)

Jordan, Lebanon, Palestine, and Syria

Makes about ¾ cup

Za'atar blends are heavenly on flatbreads, in marinades for meats, and (surprisingly) in cocktails. Curiously, the linguistic roots of the word *za'atar* refer to savory herbs that differ from region to region, and fist fights are said to have been sparked by arguments over what is truly "authentic."

- 4 teaspoons cumin seeds
- 4 teaspoons sesame seeds
- 2 teaspoons sea salt
- 4 tablespoons dried za'atar (*Origanum syriacum*), sifted
- 4 tablespoons dried savory or za'atar rumi (*Satureja thymbra*), sifted
- 4 tablespoons dried thyme (*Thymus vulgaris*) or zaetra
- 1 teaspoon dried basil, thyme, or calamint (*Acinos arvensis*)
- 4 tablespoons sumac

Dry-roast the cumin seeds in a small skillet over low heat, remove, and set aside. Add the sesame seeds to the pan and toast until golden. Grind them together with the salt in a mortar or blender, then add the two za'atars, thyme, basil, and sumac. Sift through a sieve and transfer to a covered container and store in a cool, dry, shaded place.

Acknowledgments

Heartfelt thanks to our families for letting us experiment on them during this project, including Beth's kin, Kevin, Matt, Kip, and Tim; and Gary's clan, Laurie, Jeremy, Jessica, Laura Rose, Dustin, Danny, and Deja. We are deeply inspired by Ashley Moyna Schwickert's photography and her ease of working with us.

Our appreciation goes out to Matthew Derr, our acquiring editor, Melissa Jacobson in design, and the rest of the crew at Chelsea Green, and to Margo and Ian, the founders of Chelsea Green. Gary thanks his longtime literary agent and sister-not-just-friend, Victoria Shoemaker, for continuing support.

We are grateful to Keefe Keeley and others at the Savanna Institute for first bringing us together, and to the International Sonoran Desert Alliance and its Sonoran Desert Inn and Conference Center for hosting us at its anniversary celebration, fragrance garden inauguration, and cook-off. Gratitude to Colin Khoury, Ben Naman, and Evan Pugh for hosting Gary and his wife, Laurie, on the San Diego Botanic Garden expedition to Morocco, where many folks—including Gary and Meryanne Loum-Martin, their daughter, Thaïs, and botanist Mohamed El Laoudi—guided us to spice markets and souks.

We'd also like to thank old friends, food writers, bakers, and chefs like Lucia Watson, Elizabeth Johnson, Marty and Darrold Glanville, Luke Peterson, Carmen Fernholz, the Bianco Brothers, Kamal Mouzawak, Michel Nischan, Derrick Widmark, DeJa Walker, Barbara Abdeni Massaad, Janos Wilder, Tammi Hartung, Moishe Basson, Emma and Jeff Zimmerman, Don Guerra, Ernesto Camou Healy, Eugene Anderson, Aglaia Kremezi, Mary Simeti, Betty Fussell, Deborah Madison, Alice Waters, Bill Steen, Rami Zurayk, Joseph Geha, and Diana Abu-Jaber, who continue to help and inspire us on our wayward paths.

Finally, we are indebted to many food scholars, fragrance scientists, and writers, including Rob Raguso, Stephen Buchman, Alejandro de Avila, Paul Buell, Betty Fussell, Bill Hansson, Sandor Katz, Cesar Ojeda Linares, Diana Kennedy, Harold McGee, and Paula Wolfert, who have widened our horizons through their seminal works. Bless you all.

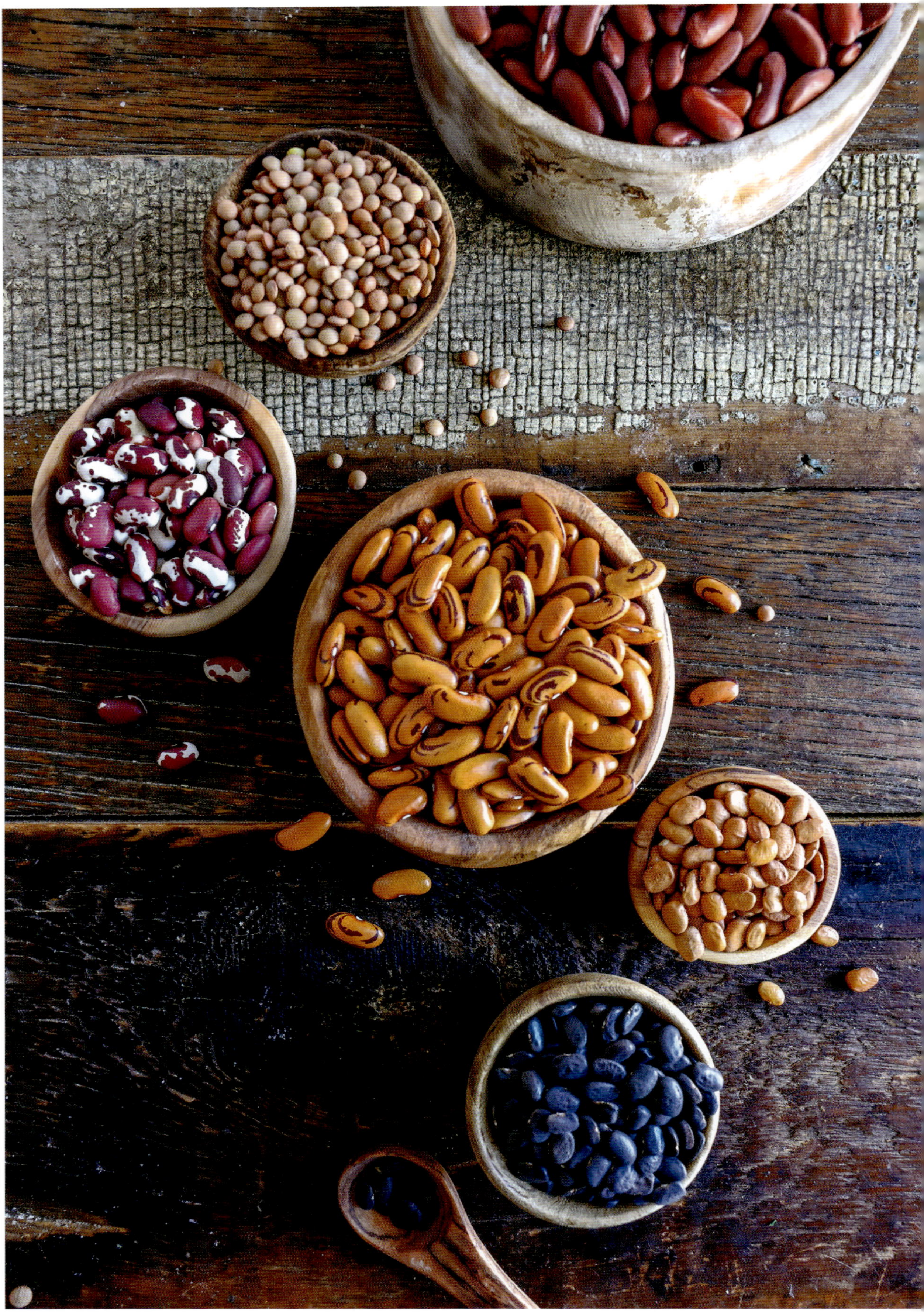

Appendix I

The Desert Pantry: An Introduction

Although some of the ingredients listed in this appendix may also grow in subtropical, tropical, or temperate climes, these plant products have deep roots in desert cuisines, where they are grown in the well-watered oases of true desert habitats or are traded in from adjacent regions. We have broken the listings into two larger categories—lesser-known and iconic—with subcategories of herbs and spices, beans and grains, syrups, infusions, and so forth. So as not to bore readers, the details of some commonly known icons, such as oreganos and tarragons, feature shorter descriptions. We have selected items with potent aromas and multiple antioxidants that scavenge free radicals to buffer the more daunting health impacts of climate change. These ingredients also feature compounds that provide antimicrobial, antibacterial, and anticarcinogenic properties. We won't detail the medicinal values of each herb or spice, for there is considerable redundancy among them, but rest assured that they provide tangible health benefits to those who wish to reduce the stresses caused by heat, damaging solar radiation, thirst, and inflammation that aggravate diseases of oxidative stress, such as diabetes, heart disease, and some cancers. Climate change is not merely increasing the frequency and severity of heatstroke, heat stress, severe thirst, and sunburn, it is also exacerbating the symptoms of chronic diseases. Consuming foods and spices high in antioxidants is but one of many means to protect yourself from the challenges of living in a hotter, drier world.

Lesser-Known Desert-Derived Ingredients

Herbs and Spices

AJWAIN (OR BISHOP'S WEED)

This warm, earthy spice smells slightly burnt when removed from its hard seed-like fruits, ones that are pale-brown and oval or oblong in shape. From Egypt, Persia, and India, it is dry-roasted, resulting in flavors akin to anise, caraway, oregano, and thyme. Cuminaldehyde and thymol are its primary volatile oils, but it is also rich in other phenols and in carotenoids such as lutein. In India, ajwain powder is infused into an aromatic butter called *tadka* to flavor lentil dals, curries, flatbreads, and pickles. In the parsley family, its scientific name is *Trachyspermum ammi*.

ALEPPO PEPPER

This Syrian heirloom chile combines fruity, tangy, sweet, and mildly piquant all in one delectable package. When it's sun dried and flaked, its burgundy color is intriguing, but its smoky powders are more remarkable. Its fragrances are reminiscent of cinnamon, cloves, cumin, and nutmeg. It is ideal for harissa, hummus bi tahini, fattoush salads, and soups. Store whole whenever possible, and use within a year, for it quickly loses its pungency. Aleppo pepper's antioxidants include capsaicin, beta-carotene, ascorbic acid, lutein, and xanthophyll. Like most other chiles in the Middle East, it goes by the scientific name *Capsicum annuum*.

ASAFETIDA

This deliciously stinky, sulfurous plant produces copious amounts of a sap that is harvested and dried into resinous, light brown chunks. They are ground into a yellow powder known as hing. It is turpentine-like, citrusy, peppery, and minty all at once. Coumarins and ocimene contribute to the iconic fragrance of asafetida. When heated, asafetida emits a complex, savory set of NAC-like (N-acetylcysteine) fragrances with notes of cabbage, onion, and garlic. Its pungency is used to enhance soups, stews, pickles, and sautéed vegetables. Asafetida is in the parsley family, and its scientific name is *Ferula asafoetida*.

CHILTEPIN

The fiery pea-sized fruits of this wild chile pepper change from a bright green as they mature to red, maroon, or black. Prized as a pickled condiment and flavoring, they are also sun dried, marinated, chopped, and embedded in fresh goat cheeses, or crushed and then eaten raw. In Sonora, Mexico, both sun-dried and *curtido* chiltepins are found on tables in every rural household. These tiny fruits harbor at least five antioxidants, including capsaicin and other capsaicinoids, violaxanthin, ascorbic acid, and beta-carotene. In the nightshade family, their most accepted scientific name is *Capsicum annuum* var. *glabriusculum*.

FENUGREEK

Fenugreek "pea" seeds are caramel colored, hard, and dry. Once they are milled into a powder, they emit a sweet, nutty aroma akin to maple syrup, butterscotch, and bittersweet. This distinctive fragrance is due to the presence of sotolone. The seeds are often toasted before grinding, and can then be used as a flavoring, sweetener, and thickener, giving depth to Egyptian stews, Jordanian *mansafs* and *maqlubas*, Moroccan tagines, and Indian curries and *sambhars*. Its antioxidants include the aromatic pinenes, as well as phenols and flavonoids. In the bean family, it is known by the scientific name *Trigonella foenum-graecum*.

FRANKINCENSE

The hardened droplets of resin from the frankincense tree appear like tears in the wounds of the bark of its scaly, voluptuous trunk. Frankincense tears are not only burnt as an incense for spiritual ceremonies, they have a long history of use in soups and stews. Its primary fragrances are reminiscent of balsam, freshly cut wood, lemon-lime, pine, fir, and desert rain. Its aromatic oils are rich in alpha-pinene, alpha-thuyene, limonene, myrcene, and sabinene. Small quantities of this precious aromatic are often used in baked goods such as cookies and puddings. It is known by the scientific name *Boswellia sacra*.

MAHLAB CHERRY PIT POWDER

Mahlab is ground from the pits of the tart Saint Lucie cherry. It has a pleasant aroma, with hints of cherry, almond, and roses. But then it moves through vanilla and floral flavors before becoming more fruity, rich, and pleasantly bitter. Its fragrances are attributed to its coumarins, tannins, and slight traces of cyanogenic glycosides. It adds a majesty to most sweets and is largely used as a baking spice and thickener in pastries or in a sweet Greek bread made for holidays, *tsoureki*. It is derived from a Middle Eastern stone-fruit tree scientifically known as *Prunus mahaleb*.

SUMAC SEED POWDER

Many kinds of sumac bushes produce maroon berries with tangy, lemony flavor. They are ground into a storable powder that is dusted onto salads such as fattoush and tabbouleh, onto dips such as hummus and baba ghanoush, and mixed into sauces, marinades, grilling rubs, and toppings of all stripes. The elm-leaved sumac (*Rhus coriaria*) of the Middle East is the primary source for the globally commercialized sumac powder. The berries of at least a dozen other nontoxic sumacs can be easily harvested in late fall into early winter. Several terpenes, polyphenols, and essential oils are responsible for the peculiar citrusy flavors and much of the antioxidant activity of sumac. The many edible *Rhus* species belong to the cashew family.

Legumes (Beans)

TEPARY BEANS

The tepary is the most drought- and heat-adapted legume in the world, being able to mature and produce dry beans on as little as two rains per season. White, yellow, and brown varieties all have a nutty flavor and produce thick, savory soups, stews, and cassoulets. Historically, tepary beans were parched over coals and then finely ground as a trail food. For centuries, they have been grown by dozens of Indigenous and immigrant desert cultures. They are rich in prebiotic soluble fiber that lowers blood sugar for diabetics while improving insulin sensitivity. This uniquely American bean is scientifically known as *Phaseolus acutifolius*.

Cereal and Legume Flours

MESQUITE POD FLOUR

One of the most reliably produced staple foods in North American deserts, mesquite pods have been used in breads, pastries, trail foods, probiotic beverages, molasses, and wines for eight millennia. The gluten-free pod flour has an intense but fleeting sweetness to it, with notes of hazelnuts, cinnamon, and molasses. Its galactomannan gums reduce blood sugar and cholesterol levels. In a remarkable revival, mesquite flour tortillas, chips, and beer are now available in restaurants and markets in the US Desert Southwest and adjacent Mexico. Edible mesquites are now in the legume genus *Neltuma* but were once classified as species in the genus *Prosopis*.

WHITE SONORA WHEAT FLOUR

This soft white bread wheat was among the first to be introduced to the New World, reaching the deserts of present-day Mexico and the United States in the 1630s. Descending from the *candeal* wheats of Spain and Morocco, it has a delicate but sweet flavor ideal for both pastries and large wheat tortillas, much like the *saj* flatbreads of the Levant. Thanks to a heritage grain revival in the US and Mexico, this flour is readily available in gourmet grocery stores. It is extremely low in gluten but has good protein, texture, and mineral content.

Sweeteners and Syrups

AGAVE MOLASSES AND NECTARS

Most agave "nectars" are not much different from high-fructose corn syrups. However, dark, thick agave molasses, which is a slow-cooked sugar source derived from agave sweet sap, is far lower on the glycemic index than most other sugar sources, due to its inulin composition. It is now available in some US and Mexican stores. The flavor has been compared to blackstrap sorghum molasses, but it has less of a clawing or bitter aftertaste. It is heavier than other syrups, so only a third should be used for every cup of sugar noted in a standard recipe. It is rich in antioxidants and B vitamins.

POMEGRANATE SOUR MOLASSES

Unlike grenadines and infused waters from sweet fruit, this molasses is made from another set of pomegranate varieties that are sour, with higher acidity suited to longer-term storage. Mix the molasses with lemon or lime juices for salad dressings, beverages, and glazes. Pomegranates are among the highest in antioxidants of any product derived from fruit juices, featuring ellagitannins, punicalagins, and punicic acids in addition to vitamin C.

PRICKLY PEAR CACTUS FRUIT SYRUP
Prickly pear syrup is simply derived from boiling down the pulp of wild or cultivated fruit called *tunas* or cactus pears. It is rich in prebiotic polysaccharide mucilage that can help control thirst and adult-onset diabetes. The syrup can be used in wines or mixed drinks such as margaritas, integrated into pastries such as cheesecakes and pies, or made into ice creams, fruit leathers, and confections. It is typically derived from cultivated varieties of *Opuntia ficus-indica* or its wild kin.

SOUR ORANGE SYRUP
This highly acidic, slightly bitter molasses comes from the bumpy-skinned Seville bitter orange of Seville, Spain. Known in the Latin world as *naranja agria*, it is used just as often as vinegars and lime juice in marinades and salsas that "cook" seafood. It is derived from a cross between the pomelo (*Citrus maxima*) and the mandarin (*Citrus reticulata*), and goes by the scientific name *Citrus × aurantium*.

Better-Known Iconic Ingredients

Herbs and Spices

ALLSPICE
This sweet, warming spice has fragrances akin to cloves and cinnamon. Allspice powder is ground from berries harvested from an evergreen tree native to eastern Mexico and the Caribbean. Originally used with cacao in ceremonial drinks of the Maya, allspice became an ingredient in mulled ciders, marinades, and jerk rubs. The leaves of the allspice tree—sometimes called West Indies bay—are used in rums, and in seasoning fish or meats. The key fragrances in both the leaves and berries come from methyl eugenol. The scientific name for allspice is *Pimienta dioica*, and it is in the myrtle family.

ANISE SEED
The tiny brown seeds of the annual anise plant look like caraway and cumin but have a sweet, dusty, warm flavor akin to licorice and fennel, though are unrelated to these two superpowers. Used in liqueurs such as arak and ouzo from the Middle East to Mexico, they are added to confections, sauces, and pastries throughout the world. The characteristic fragrance in the seed is from anethole, or anise camphor, and from its isomer, methyl chavicol. Anise is in the parsley family, and its scientific name is *Pimpinella anisum*.

CARAWAY

The bittersweet flavors and warming fragrances of caraway pods are familiar to anyone in love with harissa, rye breads, sauerkrauts, semi-dry cheeses, coleslaws, and sweet and savory dishes. Their flavors can be slightly bitter but are memorably akin to anise, coriander, dill, fennel, licorice, mint, and thyme. The seed-like pods are rich with aromatic antioxidants, including norcarvone, limonene, kaempferol, lutein, and zeaxanthin, and most importantly, myrcene, caffeic acid, and quercetin. Caraway is a prebiotic that stimulates a healthy gut biota and is a digestive aid. Caraway is in the parsley family and goes by the scientific name *Carum carvi*.

CARDAMOMS

This name embraces two different spices: the pleasantly warm green (or true) cardamom, and the black cardamom (akin to *malagueta*) that has larger pods often used whole. Both come from pod-bearing shrubs that impart sweet and savory flavors akin to allspice, clove, pepper, and sassafras. Cardamom is recognizable in many gins, chai teas, Arabic coffees, perfumed rice dishes, and curries. The spice carries the essential oils of limonene, 1,8-cineole, and α-terpinyl acetate, with minor notes of α-pinene, β-pinene, terpineol, citronellal, and linalool. Green cardamom is in the ginger family and goes by the scientific name *Elettaria cardamomum*. And don't forget that black cardamom (*Amomum subulatum*) kicks the eggplant dip known as baba ghanoush up two notches!

CLOVE

Like capers, cloves are unopened flower buds. They are picked to be sun dried into flavorful nuggets hard as nails. They are warm, woody, sweet, camphoric, astringent, and savory, and produce a numbing sensation. Their fragrance is akin to allspice, cardamom, cinnamon, nutmeg, and peppercorns. Appearing in dishes such as Easter hams, gingerbread, mincemeat, and pumpkin pie, they are also used in cured meats, salad dressings, spice mixes, desserts, mulled drinks, and punches. They harbor many polyphenols, but eugenol and caryophyllene are the compounds in cloves that position them among the spices highest in antioxidant activity. In the myrtle family, cloves go by the scientific name *Syzygium aromaticum*.

CORIANDER

The tan, seed-like fruits of the cilantro herbs all have a warm, savory, nutty-dominant flavor. But different varieties have distinctive fragrances, some with caraway, floral, lemon, orange, or sage undertones. Sugar-coated coriander seeds are a breath freshener, and in Europe they are used to flavor gin, pickles, sauces, sausages, pastries, cookies, and vegetables. Crushed coriander seeds are also used as a thickener in curries and tagines. Their antioxidant capacities are associated with their many flavonoids, linolenic acid, β-carotene, and phenolic compounds. They are scientifically known as *Coriandrum sativum*.

CUMIN

These small khaki-colored seed-like fruits are bold, warm, earthy, lemony, green, sweaty, and musky. Some have bitter, pungent flavors. Cumin is essential to achiote blends, adobos, baharat, berbere, mole, and ras el hanout spice mixes, and to dishes like tandoori, tagines, and hummus bi tahini. In roasted cumin powder, phenolic acids, flavonoids, coumarins, and cuminaldehyde abound. In the essential oil, cuminaldehyde, cuminal, β-pinene, γ-terpinene, and safranal also generate antioxidant activity. True cumin is scientifically known as *Cuminum cyminum*, but don't forget about black cumin (*Bunium persicum*), with its more complex, resinous flavor.

FENNEL

For the refreshing variation on the sweet, warming fragrances of anise and licorice, fresh fennel seed cannot be beat. Like other spices, the dried "seeds" are tiny, green hard-shelled curved fruit. They are used in all manner of savory and sweet dishes, seasoning seafood, game, sausages, and pork. The aromatic oils of both their seeds and their foliage harbor more than 80 volatile compounds, including antioxidants such as apigenin, chlorogenic acid, quercetin, rosmarinic acid, and fenchone. In the family with carrots and parsley, fennel goes by the scientific name *Foeniculum vulgare*.

MARJORAM

The dried leaves of this cousin of Greek oregano bushes lend their citrusy, peppery, piney, and woody fragrances to the desert world. Available both fresh and dried, marjoram is typically milder and sweeter than other oreganos, and so it blends well with other savory herbs. Its fragrances arise from the carvacrol, sabinene, terpinol, and rotundone in its leaves, all of which generate valuable antioxidant activity when consumed in quantity. It is scientifically known as *Origanum majorana*.

MEXICAN TARRAGON

As marigolds with a distinctive scent of licorice and fennel, the Mexican species carry minor notes of citrus, eucalyptus, and black pepper that distinguish them from the unrelated French tarragon. This arid-adapted set of herbs are used as stand-alones with chicken, condiments, eggs, compound-butter infusions, quail, scallops, and vinegars. They are often rich in vitamins A, C, and B complex, and in rutin, quercetin, naringin, and several coumarins. The most widely used Mexican species is called *Tagetes lucida*.

SAFFRON THREADS

Just a few deeply red threads of floral stigmas of saffron can lend a brilliant yellow-orange color to paellas and curries. One aromatic volatile, safranal, dominates the fragrance of crocus flowers. However, picrocrocin and tumerone add to its unique fragrance mix. The color and odor of saffron make it the most expensive spice in global trade. Two kindred *Crocus* hybridized to bring us this tender spice crop now grown in many parts of the world, but where it cannot be grown, safflower functions as a false saffron. In the iris family, this arid-adapted beauty goes by the name of *Crocus sativus*.

Legumes (Beans)

CHICKPEAS/GARBANZOS

Chickpeas, or garbanzos, are cool-season legumes that are grown as staple crops in many desert regions of the world. They are boiled and eaten whole, mashed, integrated into soups and dips, and offer a flour that is the core ingredient of *farinata*, *fainá*, and *socca* crepes. They are a good food choice for controlling diabetes. They go by the scientific name *Cicer arietinum*.

COWPEAS

There are many common names for this group of warm-season legumes: crowders, black-eyed peas, field peas, and so on. There are also many shapes, colors, and textures of this group. They are ideal for stews, salads, and savory bowls of boiled or baked beans. Some varieties, when immature, are used as green beans that are integrated into goat cheeses and cheese soups. A dryland crop from Africa, they go by the scientific name *Vigna unguiculata*.

LENTILS

Although lentils are among the smallest legume seeds of global importance, they come in many colors, each favored in a different region: red, pink, tan, brown, green, and yellow. They are featured in various dal dishes, and combine well with onions and rice, tomato sauces, and meats, but they do just as well standing alone. They go by the scientific name *Lens culinaris*.

Legume and Cereal Flours

CAROB POD POWDER

This fine, sweet flour from legume pods is the same "locust" eaten by John the Baptist along the River Jordan, hence the nickname St. John's bread. In Biblical times, its molasses-thick syrup—not sugar beets or cane sugar—was the primary source of sugars eaten by Jews, Phoenicians, and Arabs. Like mesquite pods, it is rich in galactomannan gums, which impart an intense but fleeting sweetness, being a complex carbohydrate that is antidiabetic. The syrup is used in beverages, confections, and breads. The talc-like flour is used as a gluten-free substitute for grain flours. Its scientific name is *Ceratonia siliqua*.

MILLET FLOUR

Like the small roundish grain from which it is derived, millet flour is prebiotic, nuttier, and sweeter than wheat or barley, and lighter on the stomach since it is gluten-free. It is arid-adapted, with heads relatively easy to harvest, and grain that is rich in both soluble and insoluble fiber. Its primary antioxidants are catechins and ferulic acid. It is great as a couscous, and is mixed with other flours for breads, pancakes, crackers, and pastries. The primary proso millet in American markets is classified as *Panicum miliaceum*, but there are other millets in the *Setaria* and *Pennisetum* genera of grasses.

Nuts and Oily Seeds

ALMONDS

Almonds of many varieties are used for both their sweet, peach-like pulp and their nuts, sliced or whole. Mamra almonds grown in Iran and Iraq are richer in oil content than most California almonds, and are processed differently. The desert-adapted Texas Mission almond is probably of Moroccan or Canarian origin and has a smaller, darker nut with hard shells. Cultivated almonds are scientifically known as *Prunus dulcis*.

BLACK WALNUTS

The black walnut of North America (*Juglans nigra*) has replaced Carpathian or English walnuts (*Juglans regia*) in North American nut mixes, but the Carpathian group remain the largest source of walnut production in the world.

HAZELNUTS

Two hazelnuts—the European (*Corylus avellana*) and the filbert (*Corylus maxima*)—are in commercial agroforestry production in multiple countries.

PECANS

Related to hickories, pecans were first grafted and cultivated by an enslaved African American named Antoine on the Mississippi River floodplain, but its natural range extends into hotter, drier portions of northeastern Mexico.

PINE NUTS

Commercially available pine nuts, snobas, or pinyons come from a variety of Eurasian species, including the Italian stone pine (*Pinus pinea*), Korean pine (*P. koraiensis*), Siberian pine (*P. sibirica*), and Chilgoza pine (*P. gerardiana*). After Spanish colonization of the desert borderlands of North America, at least two Native American species were also marketed: the single-leaf pine (*P. monophylla*) and the Colorado pine (*P. edulis*).

PISTACHIOS

In the cashew family, pistachio (*Pistacia vera*) is the Mediterranean species most widely eaten as a nut or used as an oil, but its close relative *P. lentiscus* is the source of the mastic gum used in many desert foods.

SESAME

The edible seeds and derivative culinary oil of *Sesamum indicum* enjoy global production and consumption but are originally from India and, later, parts of arid Africa. The seeds are used in confections, salads, and rubs. Their light cooking oil is stable at high temperatures and imparts a subtle toasted flavor to salad dressings and marinades.

Oils

ARGAN OIL

The spiny and sinuously shaped argan tree produces hard nuts that are pressed for oil. It is the most distinctive culinary oil of the Maghreb, from southwestern Morocco eastward into southern Algeria. This oil is fragile under high heat, and so is often added to cooked meals by being drizzled on after the dish is removed from the oven. It is an up-and-comer that has been favorably compared to walnut oil or hazelnut oil, with a nuanced and dreamy aroma of toasted nuts and a creamy texture. It is used like olive oil as a dip for flatbreads, as a dressing drizzled on salads, or in tagines. It is extremely rich in aromatic antioxidant compounds such as caffeic acid, catechol, catechin, oleuropein, resorcinol, tocopherol, tyrosol, vanillic acid, and ferulic acid. Argan trees are ideal for arid-adapted agroforestry and may live up to 200 years. In the tropical sapote family, it bears the scientific name *Sideroxylon spinosa*.

BLACK NIGELLA OIL

The pressed black oil from the seeds of *Nigella sativa* is incredibly rich in the antioxidant thymoquinone, which also has anti-inflammatory and anticancer properties. Commercially sold as black seed oil, it has long been regarded for its medicinal qualities. The oil has a slightly bitter, pungent taste, with a spiciness comparable to cumin, oreganos, or onions. It mixes well in salad dressings and marinades with lemon and lime juice, or honey.

Appendix II
Online Sources of Desert Ingredients

BLUE CORN CUSTOM DESIGN
(602) 679-5801
Blue cornmeal and culinary ashes.

CHERI'S DESERT HARVEST
(800) 743-1141
www.cherisdesertharvest.com
Jellies, syrups, and candies from cactus, mesquite, pomegranate, and citrus.

KALUSTYAN ENTERPRISES
www.kalustyan.com
(800) 441-2133
Enormous range of Middle Eastern and Central Asian herbs and spices.

LOS CHILEROS
www.loschileros.com
(505) 768-1100
Blue corn, dried chiles, epazote and other herbs, and pozole mixes.

MACAR FOODS
www.macarfoods.com
(954) 686-6213
Turkish nuts, tomato and pepper pastes, and spices.

MADE IN NEW MEXICO
www.madeinnewmexico.com
(575) 758-7709
Chile products and prickly pear cactus fruit syrups.

MOUNTAIN ROSE HERBS
www.mountainroseherbs.com
(800) 879-3337
Organic herbs, essential oils, spices, and teas.

MY SPICE SAGE
www.myspicesage.com
(877) 890-5241
Over 500 herbs, seasonings, and spices.

RANCHO GORDO BEANS
www.ranchogordo.com
(800) 599-8323
Heirloom beans and Mexican spices.

NEW MEXICAN CONNECTION
www.newmexicanconnection.com
(505) 269-6077
Beans, chiles, pozoles, sauces, and spices.

RAMONA FARMS
https://ramonafarms.com
(520) 418-0900
Heirloom corns, tepary beans, and wheat products.

RED MESA CUISINE
www.redmesacuisine.com
(505) 466-6306
Anasazi beans, cornmeal, oreganos, chili powder, saffron, and beans.

SADAF (MIDDLE EASTERN AND PERSIAN IMPORTS)
www.sadaf.com
(323) 234-6666
Herbs, seasonings, spices, grains, beans, vinegars, and oils.

SAHADI'S (MIDDLE EASTERN IMPORTS)
www.sahadis.com
(718) 624-4550
Dried fruit leathers, nuts, olives, sauces, spices, and tahini.

THE PERFECT PURÉE OF NAPA VALLEY
www.perfectpuree.com
(707) 261-5100
Purees and concentrates, including prickly pear puree.

FURTHER READING

Batmanglij, Najmieh. 2004. *Silk Road Cooking: A Vegetarian Journey*. Mage Publishers, Washington, DC.

Benkabbou, Nargisse. 2018. *Casablanca: Cocina de Marruecos*. Blume/NatureArt, Lisbon.

Buell, Paul, and Eugene N. Anderson. 2000. *A Soup for the Qan: Chinese Dietary Medicine of the Mongol Era as Seen in Hu Szu-hui's Yin-shan Cheng-yao*. Kegan Paul International. London and New York.

De Herrera, Gabriel Alonso. 2014. *Ancient Agriculture: Roots and Application of Sustainable Farming*. University of New Mexico Press, Albuquerque.

Dooley, Beth. 2021. *The Perennial Kitchen: Simple Recipes for a Healthy Future*. University of Minnesota Press, Minneapolis.

Fitzpatrick, Matthew C., and Robert R. Dunn. 2019. "Contemporary Climate Analogs for 540 North American Urban Areas in the Late 21st Century." *Nature Communications* 10, no. 614.

Fonseca-Chavez, Vanessa. 2020. *Querencia: Reflections on the New Mexico Homeland*. University of New Mexico Press, Albuquerque.

Frank, Lois Ellen, with Walter Whitewater. 2023. *Seed to Plate, Soil to Sky: Modern Plant-Based Recipes Using Native American Ingredients*. Hatchette Books, New York.

Gambrelle, Fabienne. 2008. *The Flavor of Spices*. Flammarion, Paris.

Geha, Joseph. 2023. *Kitchen Arabic*. University of Georgia Press, Athens.

Gray, Patience. 2005. *Honey from a Weed: Fasting and Feasting*. Prospect Books, Devon, UK.

Hansson, Bill S. 2022. *Smelling to Survive: The Amazing World of Our Sense of Smell*. Hero Imprint/Legend Times Group, London.

Hartung, Tammi. 2011. *Homegrown Herbs*. Storey Publishing, North Adams, MA.

Healy, Ernesto Camou, and Alicia Hinojosa. 2002. *Cocina Sonorense*. Instituto Sonorense de Cultura, Hermosillo, MX.

Hill, Tony. 2004. *The Contemporary Encyclopedia of Herbs and Spices*. John Wiley & Sons, Hoboken, NJ.

Jaramillo, Cleofas M. 2008. *New Mexico Tasty Recipes*. Gibbs Smith, Layton, Utah.

Kremezi, Aglaia. 1994. *The Mediterranean Pantry: Creating and Using Condiments and Seasonings*. Artisan Books, New York.

Massaad, Barbara Abdeni. 2020. *Mouneh: Preserving Foods for the Lebanese Pantry*. Interlink, London/New York.

Massaad, Barbara Abdeni. 2014. *Mezze: A Labor of Love*. Alwadi, Beirut.

McGee, Harold. 2020. *Nose Dive: A Field Guide to the World's Smells*. Penguin/Random House, New York.

Nabhan, Gary Paul. 2014. *Cumin, Camels, and Caravans: A Spice Odyssey*. University of California Press, Berkeley.

Nabhan, Gary Paul, Eric Daugherty, and Tammi Hartung. 2022. "Why Does the Desert Smell Like Rain? Desert Bathing in the Diverse Fragrances of Plants and Soil Microbes in Ancient Ironwood/Giant Cactus Forests of the Sonoran Desert." *Desert Plants* magazine, Tucson.

Nabhan, Gary Paul, Eric Daugherty, and Tammi Hartung. 2022. "Health Benefits of the Diverse Volatile Oils in Native Plants of Ancient Ironwood-Giant Cactus Forests of the Sonoran Desert: An Adaptation to Climate Change?" *International Journal of Environmental Research and Public Health*. 19, no. 6: 3250.

Nabhan, Gary Paul, et al. (10 authors). 2020. "An Aridamerican Model for Agriculture in a Hotter, Water-Scarce World." *Plants, People, Planet* 2, no. 3: 627.

Presilla, Maricel. E. 2012. *Gran Cocina Latina: The Food of Latin America*. W. W. Norton, London and New York.

Whelan, Christine Sahadi. 2021. *Flavors of the Sun: The Sahadi's Guide to Understanding, Buying, and Using Middle Eastern Ingredients*. Chronicle Books, San Francisco.

Wolfert, Paula. 1987. *Couscous and Other Good Food from Morocco*. Harper & Row, New York.

Yong, Ed. 2023. *An Immense World: How Animal Senses Reveal the Hidden Realms Around Us*. Random House, New York.

Zaouali, Lilia. 2007. *Medieval Cuisine of the Islamic World: A Concise History with 174 Recipes*. University of California Press, Berkeley.

Zurayk, Rami, Sami Abdul Rahman, and Tanya Traboulsi. 2016. *From 'Akkar to 'Amel: Lebanon's Slow Food Trail*. Slow Food, Beirut.

INDEX

Note: Page references in *italics* indicate photographs.

A

Adaptogens, 9
Agave molasses and nectars, 176
Ajwain (or Bishop's Weed), 173–74
Aleppo pepper, 174
Allspice
    about, 177
    Lebanese Spice Blend, 165
    Moroccan Top of the Shop Spice Blend, 169
Almond(s)
    about, 181
    Canary Islands Pastries, 160, *161*
    Egyptian Dukkah Spice Mix, 165
    Holiday Seed Bread, 148
    Potato Dip, *34,* 41
    Sweet, Salty, Spicy Nuts, Fruit, and Seeds, 54
    White Gazpacho, 125
Anise
    about, 177
    and Pine Nut Wedding Cookies, 159, *159*
Apricot(s)
    Pineapple, and Warm Spices, Goat Tagine with, *82,* 82–83
    Squash, Tomato, and Pepper Sauté, Sun-Dried Desert, 74–75
    Yogurt, and Rose Water, Cold Pistachio-Saffron Soup of, 121, *121*
Arak
    Lebanese Cocktail, 154
Argan oil, 182
Aromatics
    arid-land, 7–10
    aromatic triads, 13–14
    perceiving and using, 11–14
Arugula
    Pomegranate Salad, 130
Asafetida, 174
Avgolemono Sauce, 64
Avocado
    Jicama, and Orange Salad, 139
    Soup, 116, *116*

B

Baharat, Turkish, 164
Bean(s). *See also* Chickpea(s)
    Borderland Ranch-Style, 105
    Brilliant Tomato Harissa Soup with Favas, 117
    Sonoran Tepary Dip, 39
    tepary, about, 175–76
    White, Chili, 118, *119*
Beef Stew, Festive Spicy, 122–23
Black nigella oil, 182
Black pepper
    Kashmiri Spice Blend, 166
    Lebanese Spice Blend, 165
    Moroccan Top of the Shop Spice Blend, 169
    Turkish Baharat, 164
Blue Corn Bread, 146, *147*
Braised New World, 5–6
Breads
    Blue Corn, 146, *147*
    Holiday Seed, 148
    Pocket Flatbreads, 144
    Savory Egg, 149
    Watercress, Tomato, and Toasted Pita Salad with Sumac and Mint, 140, *141*
    Watermelon and Cactus Fruit Gazpacho, 126
    White Gazpacho, 125
    Za'atar Lavash, *142,* 145
Bulgur
    and Lamb, Aromatic, 80
    Parsley, Cilantro, and Mint Salad, *132,* 133
Butter
    Niter Kibbeh, 109

C

Calamari and Okra, Pan-Fried, 68–69
Canary Islands Pastries, 160, *161*
Caper(s)
    -Olive Relish, Pan-Roasted Fish with, 104
    and Tarragon, Roast Chicken with, *92,* 93

Caraway, about, 178
Cardamom
   green and black, about, 178
   Kashmiri Spice Blend, 166
   Moroccan Top of the Shop Spice Blend, 169
Carob pod powder, 180–81
Cauliflower
   Upside-Down Rice, Vegetable, and Chicken Casserole, *88*, 88–89
   Za'atar-Roasted, 135, *135*
Chayote and Melon Salad, 136
Cheese
   Pomegranate Arugula Salad, 130
   Savory Pie of Wild Greens and Feta, 72, *73*
   Sonoran Flat Enchiladas, 56
   Squash Blossom Fritters, 71
   Sun-Dried Desert Squash, Tomato, Pepper, and Apricot Sauté, 74–75
Chermoula, 102
Chicken
   and Okra Stew, 120
   Rice, and Vegetable Casserole, Upside-Down, *88*, 88–89
   Roast, with Tarragon and Capers, *92*, 93
   Sheet Pan, in a Spiced Nut Crust, 81
   Spiced Orange, 90, *91*
   Stew, Tunisian, 114, *115*
   -Stuffed Figs in Tamarind Sauce, *58*, 58–59
   Stuffed Mexican Peppers in Yogurt Walnut Sauce, *76*, 94–95
   Tajín Grilled, 96
Chickpea Flour Crepes, *52*, 60
Chickpea(s)
   about, 180
   Black, Black Sesame, and Black Garlic Dip, 43
   Dip, Aromatic, *37*, 38
   and Lamb Stew, 124
   and lamb stew, origins and variations, 17–19

Chile Pepper(s)
   Aleppo pepper, about, 174
   chiltepin, about, 174
   Mexican Mole Chile Seed Paste, 168
   Paste, North African Aromatic Harissa, 167
Chili, White Bean, 118, *119*
Chiltepin, 174
Chutney, Cilantro, Ginger, and Date, 49
Cilantro
   Ginger, and Date Chutney, 49
   Green Chile Dipping Sauce, 48
   Lamb and Spinach Stew, 127
   Parsley, Mint, and Bulgur Salad, *132*, 133
   -Pistachio Pesto, 45
   Sea Scallops in Tamarind Glaze, 100
   Sonoran Tepary Dip, 39
   Turkey in Pumpkin Seed Sauce, 97
Cinnamon
   Kashmiri Spice Blend, 166
   Lebanese Spice Blend, 165
   Turkish Baharat, 164
Citrus. *See also specific citrus fruits*
   -Marinated White Fish, 57
   Mixed, and Radish Salad, 138
   Salad, Brilliant, 131, *131*
Climate change, 3, 6, 173
Cloves, 178
Cookies, Pine Nut and Anise Wedding, 159, *159*
Coriander
   about, 178–79
   Moroccan Top of the Shop Spice Blend, 169
Corn
   Blue Corn Bread, 146, *147*
   Desert Succotash, *128*, 134
   White Bean Chili, 118, *119*
Cowpeas, 180
Crepes, Chickpea Flour, *52*, 60
Cucumber(s)
   Desert Yogurt Smoothie, *150*, 155

   Fennel, and Garlic Dip, 36, *37*
   -Rosemary Gin and Tonic, 155
   Watercress, Tomato, and Toasted Pita Salad with Sumac and Mint, 140, *141*
   Watermelon and Cactus Fruit Gazpacho, 126
Culinary ashes, 21
Cumin
   about, 179
   Lebanese Za'atar Spice Blend, 170, *171*
   Moroccan Top of the Shop Spice Blend, 169

D

Date(s)
   Cilantro, and Ginger Chutney, 49
   Spiced Orange Chicken, 90, *91*
Desert cooking
   arid-land aromatics, 7–10
   aromatic triads, 13–14
   desert pantry, 20–22, 173–82
   geographic adaptations, 15–19
   making the most of, 4–6
   perceiving and using aromatics, 11–14
Desserts
   Canary Islands Pastries, 160, *161*
   Lebanese Rice Pudding with Rose Water and Mahlab Cherry Powder, 158
   Phyllo Nut Pinwheels, *156*, 156–57
   Pine Nut and Anise Wedding Cookies, 159, *159*
Dips
   Almond Potato, *34*, 41
   Black Chickpea, Black Sesame, and Black Garlic, 43
   Chickpea, Aromatic, *37*, 38
   Cucumber, Fennel, and Garlic, 36, *37*

Fire-Roasted Eggplant, 44
Red Pepper and Walnut, *37,* 42
Tepary, Sonoran, 39
Drinks
Cucumber-Rosemary Gin and Tonic, 155
Desert Yogurt Smoothie, *150,* 155
Lebanese Cocktail, 154
Pineapple Margarita, 152, *153*
Duck, Persian, in Tart Fruit Sauce, 87
Dukkah Spice Mix, Egyptian, 165

E

Eggplant
Fire-Roasted, Dip, 44
Fries with Desert Syrup, 65, *66*
Upside-Down Rice, Vegetable, and Chicken Casserole, *88,* 88–89
Eggs, Poached, in Spicy Tomatoes, 110, *111*
Egyptian Dukkah Spice Mix, 165
Enchiladas, Sonoran Flat, 56

F

Fennel
about, 179
Cucumber, and Garlic Dip, 36, *37*
Fenugreek, 174–75
Fig(s)
Chicken-Stuffed, in Tamarind Sauce, *58,* 58–59
and Pomegranate Jam, 50
Fish
Grilled Fisherman's Catch with Chermoula, 102–3
Pan-Roasted, with Olive-Caper Relish, 104
White, Citrus-Marinated, 57
Flours, 20–21, 176, 180–81
Flower blossoms, 21
Frankincense, 175
Fries
Eggplant, with Desert Syrup, 65, *66*
Sweet Potato, *66,* 67

Fritters, Squash Blossom, 71

G

Garlic
Black, Black Chickpea, and Black Sesame Dip, 43
Chermoula, 102
Cucumber, and Fennel Dip, 36, *37*
Niter Kibbeh, 109
Gazpacho
Watermelon and Cactus Fruit, 126
White, 125
Gin and Tonic, Cucumber-Rosemary, 155
Ginger
Cilantro, and Date Chutney, 49
Niter Kibbeh, 109
Goat Tagine with Apricots, Pineapple, and Warm Spices, *82,* 82–83
Grains, 20–21
Grapefruit
Brilliant Citrus Salad, 131, *131*
Grape Leaves, Stuffed, with Lemon Sauce, 62–64, *64*
Greens. *See also specific greens*
Wild, and Feta, Savory Pie of, *72, 73*
Wild Sea, and Potatoes, Shrimp with, 101

H

Harissa
Chile Pepper Paste, North African Aromatic, 167
Tomato Soup, Brilliant with Favas, 117
Hazelnut(s)
about, 181
Egyptian Dukkah Spice Mix, 165
Phyllo Nut Pinwheels, *156,* 156–57
Sauce, Tiny Lamb Meatballs in, 78–79
Herbs. *See also specific herbs*

dried culinary, 21–22
perceiving and using, 11–14

I

Infusions, 21

J

Jam, Fig and Pomegranate, 50
Jicama, Orange, and Avocado Salad, 139

K

Kashmiri Spice Blend, 166
Kefir
Cucumber, Fennel, and Garlic Dip, 36, *37*
Desert Yogurt Smoothie, *150,* 155

L

Lamb
and Bulgur, Aromatic, 80
and Chickpea Stew, 124
and chickpea stew, origins and variations, 17–19
from desert regions, 8
Kebabs with Moroccan Spices and Pomegranate Molasses Glaze, 86
Meatballs, Tiny, in Hazelnut Sauce, 78–79
Ribs, Sticky, 84, *85*
and Spinach Stew, 127
Stuffed Grape Leaves with Lemon Sauce, 62–64, *64*
Land of Olfactory Delights, 7
Lavash, Za'atar, *142,* 145
Lebanese Cocktail, 154
Lebanese Rice Pudding with Rose Water and Mahlab Cherry Powder, 158
Lebanese Spice Blend, 165
Lebanese Za'atar Spice Blend, 170, *171*
Legumes, 180. *See also* Bean(s)
Spiced Red Lentils, 108
whole dry, 21
Lemon(s)
Avgolemono Sauce, 64

Index ▪ 189

Lemon(s) *(continued)*
   Chermoula, 102
   Preserved, 51, *51*
   Sauce, Stuffed Grape Leaves with, 62–64, *64*
Lentils
   about, 180
   Red, Spiced, 108
Lime
   Avocado Soup, 116, *116*
   Citrus-Marinated White Fish, 57
   Pineapple Margarita, 152, *153*
   Sonoran Tepary Dip, 39

M

Mahlab Cherry Powder
   about, 175
   and Rose Water, Lebanese Rice Pudding with, 158
Margarita, Pineapple, 152, *153*
Marjoram, 179
Masa
   Sonoran Flat Enchiladas, 56
Meatballs, Tiny Lamb, in Hazelnut Sauce, 78–79
Melon
   and Chayote Salad, 136
   Watermelon and Cactus Fruit Gazpacho, 126
Mesquite pod flour, 176
Mexican Mole Chile Seed Paste, 168
Mexican tarragon, 179
Millet flour, 181
Millet Polenta with Blistered Tomatoes, *106,* 107
Mint
   Chayote and Melon Salad, 136
   Desert Yogurt Smoothie, *150,* 155
   Parsley, Cilantro, and Bulgur Salad, *132,* 133
   and Sumac, Watercress, Tomato, and Toasted Pita Salad with, 140, *141*
Mole Chile Seed Paste, Mexican, 168
Moroccan Top of the Shop Spice Blend, 169

N

Niter Kibbeh, 109
Nopalitos. *See* Prickly Pear
North African Aromatic Harissa Chile Pepper Paste, 167
Nut(s), 21. *See also specific nuts*
   Crust, Spiced, Sheet Pan Chicken in a, 81
   Fruit, and Seeds, Sweet, Salty, Spicy, 54
   Pinwheels, Phyllo, *156,* 156–57

O

Oils, 21, 182
Okra
   and Calamari, Pan-Fried, 68–69
   and Chicken Stew, 120
Olive(s)
   Brilliant Citrus Salad, 131, *131*
   -Caper Relish, Pan-Roasted Fish with, 104
   Goat Tagine with Apricots, Pineapple, and Warm Spices, *82,* 82–83
   Spiced Orange Chicken, 90, *91*
   Squash Blossom Fritters, 71
   Stuffed Mexican Peppers in Yogurt Walnut Sauce, *76,* 94–95
   Za'atar-Roasted Cauliflower, *135,* 135
Orange blossom water
   Goat Tagine with Apricots, Pineapple, and Warm Spices, *82,* 82–83
   Mixed Citrus and Radish Salad, 138
Orange(s)
   Brilliant Citrus Salad, 131, *131*
   Chicken, Spiced, 90, *91*
   Citrus-Marinated White Fish, 57
   Jicama, and Avocado Salad, 139
   Mixed Citrus and Radish Salad, 138
   sour, syrup, 177
Osmocosm of arid lands, 7

P

Parsley
   Chermoula, 102
   Mint, Cilantro, and Bulgur Salad, *132,* 133
Pastes, 21
Pastries, Canary Islands, 160, *161*
Pecans
   about, 181
   Phyllo Nut Pinwheels, *156,* 156–57
   Pomegranate Arugula Salad, 130
   Sheet Pan Chicken in a Spiced Nut Crust, 81
Pepper(s). *See also* Chile Pepper(s)
   Blue Corn Bread, 146, *147*
   Green Chile Dipping Sauce, 48
   Lamb Kebabs with Moroccan Spices and Pomegranate Molasses Glaze, 86
   Padrón, Blistered, 55, *55*
   Poached Eggs in Spicy Tomatoes, 110, *111*
   Red, and Walnut Dip, *37,* 42
   Red, Sauce, Aromatic, 47
   Squash, Tomato, and Apricot Sauté, Sun-Dried Desert, 74–75
   Stuffed Mexican, in Yogurt Walnut Sauce, *76,* 94–95
   Watermelon and Cactus Fruit Gazpacho, 126
Persian Duck in Tart Fruit Sauce, 87
Pesto, Cilantro-Pistachio, 45
Phyllo Nut Pinwheels, *156,* 156–57
Pickled leaves, 21

Pickled vegetables, 22
Pie, Savory, of Wild Greens and Feta, 72, *73*
Pineapple
    Apricots, and Warm Spices, Goat Tagine with, *82,* 82–83
    Margarita, 152, *153*
Pine Nut(s)
    about, 181
    and Anise Wedding Cookies, 159, *159*
    Aromatic Lamb and Bulgur, 80
    Stuffed Grape Leaves with Lemon Sauce, 62–64, *64*
Pistachio(s)
    about, 182
    Chayote and Melon Salad, 136
    -Cilantro Pesto, 45
    Lebanese Rice Pudding with Rose Water and Mahlab Cherry Powder, 158
    Phyllo Nut Pinwheels, *156,* 156–57
    -Saffron Soup of Yogurt, Apricots, and Rose Water, Cold, 121, *121*
    Stuffed Mexican Peppers in Yogurt Walnut Sauce, *76,* 94–95
Planet Desert, 5–6
Pocket Flatbreads, 144
Polenta, Millet, with Blistered Tomatoes, *106,* 107
Pomegranate (juice and seeds)
    Arugula Salad, 130
    Brilliant Citrus Salad, 131, *131*
    and Fig Jam, 50
    Persian Duck in Tart Fruit Sauce, 87
Pomegranate Molasses
    about, 176–77
    Fig and Pomegranate Jam, 50
    Glaze and Moroccan Spices, Lamb Kebabs with, 86
    Persian Duck in Tart Fruit Sauce, 87

Pomegranate Arugula Salad, 130
Potato(es)
    Almond Dip, *34,* 41
    Canary Islands Pastries, 160, *161*
    Festive Spicy Beef Stew, 122–23
    Sweet, Fries, *66,* 67
    and Wild Sea Greens, Shrimp with, 101
Preserved Lemons, 51, *51*
Prickly Pear
    Desert Succotash, *128,* 134
    syrup, about, 177
    with Tomatillo Sauce, 46
    Watermelon and Cactus Fruit Gazpacho, 126
Pudding, Lebanese Rice, with Rose Water and Mahlab Cherry Powder, 158
Pulses, 21
Pumpkin Seed(s)
    Mexican Mole Chile Seed Paste, 168
    Sauce, Turkey in, 97
    Sweet, Salty, Spicy Nuts, Fruit, and Seeds, 54
Purslane
    Parsley, Mint, Cilantro, and Bulgur Salad, *132,* 133
    Watercress, Tomato, and Toasted Pita Salad with Sumac and Mint, 140, *141*

Q

Quince with Aromatic Turkey Stuffing, 70

R

Radish and Mixed Citrus Salad, 138
Rainwater, 9–10
Raisins
    Stuffed Grape Leaves with Lemon Sauce, 62–64, *64*
    Stuffed Mexican Peppers in Yogurt Walnut Sauce, *76,* 94–95

Rice
    Pudding, Lebanese, with Rose Water and Mahlab Cherry Powder, 158
    Stuffed Grape Leaves with Lemon Sauce, 62–64, *64*
    Vegetable, and Chicken Casserole, Upside-Down, *88,* 88–89
Roots, aromatic, 22
Rosemary-Cucumber Gin and Tonic, 155
Rose Water
    Desert Yogurt Smoothie, *150,* 155
    and Mahlab Cherry Powder, Lebanese Rice Pudding with, 158
    Yogurt, and Apricots, Cold Pistachio-Saffron Soup of, 121, *121*

S

Saffron
    about, 180
    -Pistachio Soup of Yogurt, Apricots, and Rose Water, Cold, 121, *121*
Salads
    Brilliant Citrus, 131, *131*
    Chayote and Melon, 136
    Jicama, Orange, and Avocado, 139
    Mixed Citrus and Radish, 138
    Parsley, Mint, Cilantro, and Bulgur, *132,* 133
    Pomegranate Arugula, 130
    Spinach with Spices and Yogurt, 137
    Watercress, Tomato, and Toasted Pita, with Sumac and Mint, 140, *141*
Sauces
    Avgolemono, 64
    Chermoula, 102
    Cilantro-Pistachio Pesto, 45
    Green Chile Dipping, 48
    Red Pepper, Aromatic, 47
    Tomatillo with Prickly Pear, 46

Seafood
    Citrus-Marinated White Fish, 57
    Grilled Fisherman's Catch with Chermoula, 102–3
    Pan-Fried Okra and Calamari, 68–69
    Pan-Roasted Fish with Olive-Caper Relish, 104
    Sea Scallops in Tamarind Glaze, 100
    Shrimp with Wild Sea Greens and Potatoes, 101
Sea Greens, Wild, and Potatoes, Shrimp with, 101
Sea Scallops in Tamarind Glaze, 100
Seed(s), 21. *See also* Pumpkin Seed(s); Sesame seeds
    Bread, Holiday, 148
    Nuts, and Fruit, Sweet, Salty, Spicy, 54
    Pocket Flatbreads, 144
Sesame seeds
    about, 182
    Black Chickpea, Black Sesame, and Black Garlic Dip, 43
    Egyptian Dukkah Spice Mix, 165
    Lebanese Za'atar Spice Blend, 170, *171*
    Savory Egg Bread, 149
Shrimp with Wild Sea Greens and Potatoes, 101
Smoothie, Desert Yogurt, *150,* 155
Sonoran Desert, 7
Sonoran Flat Enchiladas, 56
Sonoran Tepary Dip, 39
Sotol
    Pineapple Margarita, 152, *153*
Soups
    Avocado, 116, *116*
    Pistachio-Saffron, of Yogurt, Apricots, and Rose Water, Cold, 121, *121*
    Tomato Harissa, Brilliant with Favas, 117
    Watermelon and Cactus Fruit Gazpacho, 126
    White Gazpacho, 125
Sour juices, 22
Sour orange syrup, 177
Spice Blends
    cooling effects, 29
    Egyptian Dukkah Spice Mix, 165
    health benefits, 27, 29
    Kashmiri, 166
    Lebanese, 165
    Lebanese Za'atar, 170, *171*
    list of, 21
    Mexican Mole Chile Seed Paste, 168
    Moroccan Top of the Shop, 169
    North African Aromatic Harissa Chile Pepper Paste, 167
    sacred nature of, 31
    shelf life, 31
    storing, 31
    Turkish Baharat, 164
    variations in, 29–30
Spices. *See also specific spices*
    dried ground, 22
    perceiving and using, 11–14
    and Yogurt, Spinach with, 137
Spice trade routes, 23–26
Spice traders, 19, 24, 30
Spinach
    Lamb and Chickpea Stew, 124
    and Lamb Stew, 127
    with Spices and Yogurt, 137
Squash
    Blossom Fritters, 71
    Chayote and Melon Salad, 136
    Desert Succotash, *128,* 134
    Lamb Kebabs with Moroccan Spices and Pomegranate Molasses Glaze, 86
    Tomato, Pepper, and Apricot Sauté, Sun-Dried Desert, 74–75
Stews
    Beef, Festive Spicy, 122–23
    Chicken, Tunisian, 114, *115*
    Chicken and Okra, 120
    Goat Tagine with Apricots, Pineapple, and Warm Spices, *82,* 82–83
    Lamb and Chickpea, 124
    lamb and chickpea, origins and variations, 17–19
    Lamb and Spinach, 127
Succotash, Desert, *128,* 134
Sumac
    about, 175
    Lebanese Za'atar Spice Blend, 170, *171*
    and Mint, Watercress, Tomato, and Toasted Pita Salad with, 140, *141*
Sweet Potato(es)
    Canary Islands Pastries, 160, *161*
    Fries, *66,* 67
Syrups
    of flower blossoms, 21
    of pods and fruits, 22
    prickly pear cactus fruit, 177
    sour orange, 177

T

Tacos, Turkey, 98, *99*
Tagine, Goat, with Apricots, Pineapple, and Warm Spices, *82,* 82–83
Tajín Grilled Chicken, 96
Tamarind
    Glaze, Sea Scallops in, 100
    Sauce, Chicken-Stuffed Figs in, *58,* 58–59
Tangerines
    Mixed Citrus and Radish Salad, 138
Tarragon
    and Capers, Roast Chicken with, *92,* 93
    Mexican, about, 179
Thyme
    Lebanese Za'atar Spice Blend, 170, *171*
Tomatillo(s)
    Green Chile Dipping Sauce, 48

with Prickly Pear Sauce, 46
Turkey in Pumpkin Seed
   Sauce, 97
Tomato(es)
   Blistered, Millet Polenta with, *106*, 107
   Chicken and Okra Stew, 120
   Festive Spicy Beef Stew, 122–23
   Harissa Soup, Brilliant with Favas, 117
   Spicy, Poached Eggs in, 110, *111*
   Squash, Pepper, and Apricot Sauté, Sun-Dried Desert, 74–75
   Tunisian Chicken Stew, 114, *115*
   Upside-Down Rice, Vegetable, and Chicken Casserole, *88*, 88–89
   Watercress, and Toasted Pita Salad with Sumac and Mint, 140, *141*
Triads, aromatic, 13–14
Tunisian Chicken Stew, 114, *115*
Turkey
   in Pumpkin Seed Sauce, 97
   Stuffed Mexican Peppers in Yogurt Walnut Sauce, *76*, 94–95
Stuffing, Aromatic, Quince with, 70
Tacos, 98, *99*
Turkish Baharat, 164
Turmeric
   Aromatic Chickpea Dip, *37*, 38
   Lamb and Chickpea Stew, 124
   Lebanese Spice Blend, 165
   Sweet, Salty, Spicy Nuts, Fruit, and Seeds, 54

V

Vegetables. *See also specific vegetables*
   pickled, 22
Vinegars, 22
Volatile oils, 8, 9–10

W

Walnut(s)
   black, about, 181
   Phyllo Nut Pinwheels, *156*, 156–57
   and Red Pepper Dip, *37*, 42
   Yogurt Sauce, Stuffed Mexican Peppers in, *76*, 94–95
Watercress
   Parsley, Mint, Cilantro, and Bulgur Salad, *132*, 133
   Tomato, and Toasted Pita Salad with Sumac and Mint, 140, *141*
Watermelon and Cactus Fruit Gazpacho, 126
White Gazpacho, 125
White Sonora wheat flour, 176
Wild Sea Greens and Potatoes, Shrimp with, 101

Y

Yogurt
   Apricots, and Rose Water, Cold Pistachio-Saffron Soup of, 121, *121*
   Avocado Soup, 116, *116*
   and Spices, Spinach with, 137
   Walnut Sauce, Stuffed Mexican Peppers in, *76*, 94–95

Z

Za'atar
   Lavash, *142*, 145
   -Roasted Cauliflower, 135, *135*
   Spice Blend, Lebanese, 170, *171*
Zucchini
   Lamb Kebabs with Moroccan Spices and Pomegranate Molasses Glaze, 86

ABOUT THE AUTHORS

Beth Dooley is the author or co-author of several award-winning cookbooks, including *The Sioux Chef's Indigenous Kitchen* with Sean Sherman, honored as the Best American Cookbook in 2018 by the James Beard Foundation. Her memoir, *In Winter's Kitchen*, reveals her journey to find her place in the Midwestern food scene. She is regarded as a beloved weekly columnist of food and travel for the Minneapolis-St. Paul *Star Tribune*, and regularly appears on Minnesota Public Radio. She also teaches cooking and food system classes at the University of Minnesota Landscape Arboretum. Her book *The Perennial Kitchen* offers "simple recipes for a healthy future" in the face of climate change. Beth, her husband, and their three sons divide their time between the Twin Cities and Madeline Island in Lake Superior.

Gary Paul Nabhan is an Arab-American ethnobotanist, agrarian activist, and desert ecologist. As a pioneer in the local food movement, seed conservation, and biocultural restoration, he has been called the "lyrical scholar of genetic diversity." He has served as a trainer for collaborative conservation efforts with Indigenous, ranching and refugee farming, and foraging communities in several desert regions around the world. He was a catalyst for the designation of the first UNESCO City of Gastronomy in the United States (in Tucson). Nabhan functioned as founder-facilitator of the Renewing America's Food Traditions initiative of Slow Food USA, Chefs Collaborative, and other nonprofits that initially fleshed out North America's Ark of Taste. He has been honored by the MacArthur Foundation and Takreem Foundation for his innovations in food sustainability and community development. He and his wife divide their time between Patagonia, Arizona, and coastal Sonora, Mexico.